YANNIS RITSOS:
SELECTED POEMS
1938–1988

YANNIS RITSOS: SELECTED POEMS 1938–1988

EDITED AND TRANSLATED

by

KIMON FRIAR AND KOSTAS MYRSIADES

With Additional Translations by:

Athan Anagnostopoulos, Peter Bien, Andonis Decavalles,
N. C. Germanacos, George Giannaris, Karelisa Hartigan,
Edmund Keeley, Thanasis Maskaleris, Gwendolyn MacEwen,
Martin McKinsey, Philip Pastras, George Pilitsis, Minas Savvas,
John Stathatos and Nikos Tsingos

BOA Editions, Ltd. · Brockport, N.Y. · 1989

ISBN: 0–918526–66–3 Cloth
0–918526–67–1 Paper

LC #: 88–71554
First Edition

The publication of this book was made possible
with the assistance of grants from
The Wheatland Foundation,
The Literature Program of the New York State Council on the Arts,
and
The Literature Program of the National Endowment for the Arts.
BOA Editions, Ltd. is a non-profit literary organization.

Cover Painting: Yannis Ritsos
Cover Design: Daphne Poulin
BOA Logo: Mirko

Illustrations:
Xerographic Renderings of
Painted Rocks by Yannis Ritsos.
Photos of Painted Rocks
Greece: Stavros Lagadianos
U.S.: George Platteter.

Typesetting: Sans Serif, Inc.
Manufacturing: McNaughton & Gunn, Lithographers

BOA Editions, Ltd.
A. Poulin, Jr., President
92 Park Avenue
Brockport, NY 14420

YANNIS RITSOS:

SELECTED POEMS 1938–1988

CONTENTS

ᶜᵕᵇ

NOTES AND ESSAYS

ᶜᵕᵇ

PREFATORY NOTE

Kostas Myrsiades

On a May evening in 1974, I stopped by the Elefteroudakis Bookstore in Athens to purchase a copy of *Pablo Neruda: Selected Poems*, edited by Nathaniel Tarn and translated by Tarn and several other poets/translators. What immediately drew my attention to Tarn's anthology was, first, that it contained generous selections from all major phases of Neruda's poetry and, second, that it represented several of Neruda's translators.

Later that same evening, I stopped in at one of Kimon Friar's Friday evening poetry gatherings, which he then regularly hosted in his apartment on Kallidromiou Street. In the course of our discussion, I remarked that an anthology like the one devoted to Neruda was needed for Yannis Ritsos' poetry. Kimon and another translator present, Nikos Germanacos, agreed. The following day I advised Ritsos of our intentions, and with his blessing the project was under way. Fifteen years later, on his 80th birthday, this broad-based collection of Yannis Ritsos' poetry in English translation is complete.

Since the inception of this project, over fifteen book-length translations of Ritsos' poetry have appeared in English, many by translators represented in this volume. Most of those books have followed a similar pattern of usually limiting the number of collections translated to two or three books, presenting the work of only one or two translators, and representing Ritsos' short poems of the sixties and seventies almost exclusively.

Our intention from the beginning was to represent the full range of Yannis Ritsos' poetry, including not only the popular short poems for which he is best known in the United States, but also his epigrammatic poems, his long narratives and chorales and his dramatic monologues. Works selected for inclusion would span Ritsos' entire career in the best translations available and by as many translators as we could bring together to allow the non-Greek reader to experience the full range of Ritsos' poetry. And in that respect, this volume is unique. In *Yannis Ritsos: Selected Poetry 1938-1988*, the reader is offered fifty years of Ritsos' poetry, many poems as yet unpublished in the original Greek, and representing all of Ritsos' poetic styles.

   We present *Yannis Ritsos: Selected Poems 1938-1988* — 444 poems from 43 different books (or collections) and translated by 17 translators — in the belief that the poetry will excite our readers as it did the French poet Louis Aragon:

> This poet knew the secrets of my soul as if he and he alone, you understand, could stir me in such a way. At first I didn't realize that Ritsos was the greatest living poet of our time; I swear I wasn't aware of it. I discovered that in stages, poem by poem, almost secret by secret. For with each poem I experienced an overwhelming sense of revelation — the revelation of a man and of a land, the depths of Man and the depths of Motherland.

May, 1989   (K.M.)

Ἡ μαύρη βάρκα

Ὁ γέρος κάθεται στό κατώφλι. Νύχτα.
Μοναξιά.
Κρατάει στό χέρι του ἕνα μῆλο. Οἱ ἄλλοι
ἄφησαν τή ζωή τῆς στήν ἁρμοδιότητα
τῶν ἄστρων.
Τί νά τῆς πεῖς; Ἡ νύχτα εἶναι νύχτα.
Κι ὅσα πιό ξέρουμε τί ἀκολουθεῖ. Τό φεγγάρι
κάνει πώς διασκεδάζει κάπως
σπιθίζοντας ἀσετζέλωτα στή θάλασσα. Ὡστόσο
μέσα σ'αὐτή τή λαμπρότητα διακρίνεται εὐ-
κριγέσγερα
ἡ μαύρη δίκωπη βάρκα μέ τόν σκοταγνό βαρ-
κάρη πού μαυραίνει.

Αθήνα, 4.V.88

Γιάννης Ρίτσος

YANNIS RITSOS:
SELECTED POEMS
1938–1988

NOTES ON THE MARGINS
OF TIME
(1938–1941)

Translated by Kimon Friar

DOXOLOGY

He was standing at the far end of the street
like a bare and dusty tree
like a tree burned by the sun
glorifying the sun that cannot be burned.

1938–1941   *(K.F.)*

HOUR OF SONG

Beside the jug of wine
beside the baskets of fruit
we forgot to sing.

On the evening of our separation
under the approbation of the evening star
we sang by ourselves.

1938–1941   *(K.F.)*

A SMALL INVITATION

Come to the luminous beaches — he murmured to himself
here where the colors are celebrating — look —
here where the royal family never once passed
with its closed carriages and its official envoys.

Come, it won't do for you to be seen — he used to say —
I am the deserter from the night
I am the breacher of darkness
and my shirt and pockets are crammed with sun.

Come — it's burning my hands and my chest.
Come, let me give it to you.

And I have something to tell you
which not even I must hear.

Athens, 1938   (K.F.)

SUCCESSION

The sun does not consider any of your hesitations —
naked it wants you and naked it takes you,
until night comes to dress you.

After the sun, there is repentance.
After repentance, the sun again.

Athens, September, 1938   (K.F.)

ETESIAN WINDS

Ship after ship after ship . . .
The pushcart peddler gazes down the slope,
The pine trees fling themselves into the sea.
The sea ascends the mountain
and the pushcart peddler mounts
the sun, splattered with white foam.

Poros, July, 1939   (K.F.)

SUMMER IN THE CITY

In this place the light makes us despair. This pitiless month
will not allow you *not* to become two. You are not enough.
The monotonous clang, the street cars turning round corners,
the marble cutters hewing stones in the blazing noon.

Above the wall can be seen the same old memorial columns,
marble flowers, marble ribbons,
the bust of a banker,
the face of a child shadowed by an angel's wing.

On these professional sculptures the Attic sun stamps its seal,
the shadows add their unbelievable extensions —
and so it was not strange at all that yesterday afternoon
as you were returning home from the office
holding a shopping net of bread and tomatoes —
it was not strange at all that yesterday as the sun was setting
in the copse you met the marble youth
strolling languidly as he smiled.

You sat on a park bench, by the pond, casting your bread to the
    goldfish,
and all that night, even though you had not eaten,
you were not at all hungry.

Athens, August, 1939   (K.F.)

ASSISTANCE

The wind converses before the windows
like those who are about to separate.
The furniture becomes like the impoverished girls who gather
fallen olives. Beneath the olive trees, the evening walks
all alone, and the field with the harvested wheat
is a denial. The cicada's shed husk
seems like a small, fallen bell-tower in the dry grass.

The drizzle comes later — it pursues the sparrows,
slowly the moon lies down beneath the cypresses
like the abandoned plow. The ploughman
sleeps beneath the soil —
his wife alone with the dog and the thin ox.

The hands of silence are frozen
as she ties her black kerchief beneath her chin.
But the trace of his hand stays more strongly than his hand on the
    wood of the plow
and the back of the chair keeps the warmth of his broad shoulder
    blades.

About these insignificant things — I don't know —
I want to write a small song that will show I don't know

anything about any of them—only that they are as they are, alone, completely alone, and neither do they ask for any mediation between themselves and someone else.

1938—1941 (K.F.)

THE CONQUEROR

He unlocked his dark room with hesitation
to try out once more what sound his footsteps would make
on the pure-white stone pavements of day.

All were waiting for him to exit from the sun's door.

He put on a golden denture of light
and tried to learn a few green leaves by heart
but felt his mouth looked even more empty
and so he neither spoke nor smiled.

The others kept listening to their cheers.
They never noticed that he remained silent.
Then he stooped down, picked up a stone and chased
the last faithful dog that had followed him.

Men hoisted him on their shoulders in the sun.
And thus, raised high above their heads,
no one saw him weeping.

Athens, July, 1941 (K.F.)

THE HILL

Someone had a great many dead.
He dug the ground and buried them himself.
Stone by stone, earth on earth,
he built a hill.
On the hill's summit
he built his sunwashed hut.

Afterwards he opened up pathways,
planted trees
carefully, geometrically, thoughtfully.
His eyes were always smiling.
His hands hardly trembled.
The hill.

Now on Sunday afternoons
mothers climb up there pushing their baby carriages,
and workers from the neighborhood with washed shirts
come to sun themselves and breathe in a little air.
There in the twilight loving couples stroll
and learn to read the stars.
Under the trees a child plays the harmonica.
A peddler shouts his soft drinks for sale.
On that hill all know
they have come closer to the sky.

But no one knows how the hill was made,
no one knows how many sleep in the hill's bowels.

Athens, September, 1941   *(K.F.)*

ﻼ

ROMIOSINI
(1945–1947)

Translated by Kimon Friar

I

These trees are not at ease with lesser air,
these stones are not at ease under the tread of strangers,
these faces are not at ease unless they feel the sun,
these hearts are not at ease unless they live with justice.

This landscape is as harsh as silence,
it hugs to its breast the scorching stones,
clasps in the light its orphaned olive trees and vineyards,
clenches its teeth. There is no water. Light only.
Roads vanish in light and the shadow of the sheepfold is made of
    iron.

Trees, rivers, and voices have turned to stone in the sun's quicklime.
Roots trip on marble. Dust-laden lentisk shrubs.
Mules and rocks. All panting. There is no water.
All are parched. For years now. All chew a morsel of sky to choke
    down their bitterness.

Their eyes are bloodshot for lack of sleep,
a deep furrow is wedged between their eyebrows
like a cypress tree between two mountains at sunset.

Their hands are glued to their rifles
their rifles are extensions of their hands
their hands are extensions of their souls—
anger lies upon their lips
and anguish deep within their eyes
like a star in a salt pit.

When they clasp hands, the sun becomes certain of the world,
when they smile, a small swallow flies out of their savage beards,
when they sleep, twelve stars fall out of their empty pockets,
when they are killed, life sweeps uphill with kettledrums and flags
     flying.

For so many years all have starved, all have thirsted, all were
     slaughtered,
besieged by land and sea;
drought has consumed their fields and brine has drenched their
     houses,
the wind has knocked down their doors and the few lilac shrubs in the
     village square,
death comes and goes through the holes in their overcoats,
their tongues have become as acrid as cypress cones,
their dogs have perished wrapped up in their own shadows,
the rain beats down on their bones.

Transfixed on their outposts, they smoke cow-dung and the night,
scanning the frenzied sea where the broken
mast of the moon has sunk.

They have run out of bread, exhausted their ammunition,
now they load their cannons only with their hearts.

So many years besieged by land and sea,
they are all hungry, they are all killed, yet no one has perished—
there on their outposts their eyes glow,
a huge flag, a great crimson conflagration,
and every dawn a thousand doves soar out of their hands
toward the four gates of the horizon.

II

When night begins to fall, and the thyme is already scorched on the
     rock's breast,

10

there is a drop of water that for a long time has been carving silence
   down to its marrow,
there is a bell hung from the ancient plane tree that calls out the
   years.

Sparks sleep lightly in the embers of the desert
and rooftops meditate on the golden down on the upper lip of the
   Harvester Month
—a yellow down like the corn's tassel smoked by the anguish of the
   West.
Virgin Mary lies down among the myrtles with her wide skirt stained
   by grapes.
A child cries in the road and is answered in the field
by the ewe that has lost her children.

Shadows at the fountain. The barrel, frozen.
The blacksmith's daughter with her feet wet.
Bread and olives on the table,
the lamp of the Evening Star in the vine bower,
and high above, turning on its spit, the Galaxy is fragrant
with burnt fat, garlic, and pepper.

Ah, how many silken threads of stars won't the pine needles not need
   to embroider,
on the scorched stone wall of summer, "And this too shall pass";
how many times will a mother not wring her hair over her seven slain
   sons
until light can find its way along the upward slope of her spirit.

This bone that emerges from the earth
measures the earth span by span, and the chords of the lute,
and the lute with the violin from evening to daybreak
speak of their anguish and pain to the rosemary and the pines;
the rigging on the caïques tinkle like lyres
and a sailor drinks bitter sea from the winecup of Odysseus.

Ah, who will barricade the passes, what sword will cleave through
   courage,

and what key will lock up the heart that with its door-leaves open
gazes on God's star-strewn gardens?

An hour as huge as the Saturday evenings of May in a sailor's tavern,
a night as huge as the baker's tray hung on the wall,
a song as huge as the bread of the sponge-diver's dinner.

See how the Cretan moon rolls through its pulleys,
creak, crack, with twenty rows of cleats on its bootsoles,
and look at those ascending the steps of Náfplion,
filling their pipes with the coarse leaves of darkness,
their mustaches like the star-splattered thyme of Roúmeli
and their teeth like pineroots in Aegean rock and salt.

They have been thrust in iron and fire, they have conversed with
     stones,
they have treated death to wine in their grandfathers' skulls,
they have met Dhighenís on those same threshing floors and have
     dined there,
cutting their sufferings in two, just as they cut their loaves of barley
     bread over their knees.

Come, lady, with your salty eyelashes, with your hand bronzed
by the cares of the poor and many, many years—
love awaits you among the mastic shrubs,
the seagull hangs your black icon in its cave,
and the embittered sea-urchin kisses your toenail.

In each dark grape of the vineyard, the crimson must boils,
the shoot of holly boils in the burnt ilex,
under the earth the root of the dead man seeks for water that it may
     toss a pine tree in the air,
and the mother grips a knife firmly under her wrinkles.

Come, lady, brooding on the golden eggs of the thunderbolt—
when will you cast off your headscarf on a seablue day and take up
     arms again
that a hailstorm in May may beat upon your brow
that the sun may burst like a pomegranate in your homespun apron

12

that you may share it alone seed by seed among your twelve orphans
that the seashore may glitter everywhere as glitters a sword's blade or
    an April's snow
and that the crab may climb up the shingle to run itself and cross its
    claws.

III

Here the sky never for a moment lessens the oil of our eyes —
here the sun takes upon itself half the weight of the stone we carry on
    our backs;
the rooftiles break without a single ah under the knee of noon,
men stride in front of their shadows like dolphins in front of the
    caïques of Skiathos
and their shadow afterwards becomes an eagle that paints its feathers
    in the sunset
and still later roosts on their heads and contemplates the stars
when they lie down on the sun-terrace with its black raisins.

Here every door has a name chiseled for some three thousand years or
    more,
every stone has been painted with a saint with wild eyes and ropy
    hair,
every man has had his left hand etched needlepoint by point with a
    red mermaid,
every girl has a fistful of salted light under her skirt
and children wear five or six golden crosses above their hearts
like traces from the feet of seagulls on the beaches of an afternoon.

It's not necessary for you to remember. We know it.
All the footpaths lead to the High Threshing Floors. The air is sharp
    up there.

When the Minoan mural of the West scales away in the distance
and the conflagration fades away on the haystacks of the seashore,

the old women climb up here on steps carved in the rocks,
they sit on the Great Stone, spinning the sea with their eyes,
they sit and count the stars as though they were counting their
    ancestral silver knives and forks
then slowly descend to feed their grandsons with gunpowder from
    Misolóngi.

Yes, truly, the Prince of Chains has two hands filled with sorrow in
    their shackles,
and yet his eyebrows sway like a rock that seems on the point of
    breaking away
above his bitter eye.
From the sea-depths a wave rises that doesn't know how to beg,
from the heights of the sky a wind surges with resinated vein and
    sage-brush lung.

Ah, may it blow once to obliterate the orange trees of memory,
ah, may it blow twice that the iron stone may cast sparks like a
    percussion cap,
ah, may it blow thrice to drive the pine forests of Liákoura crazy,
may it strike once with its fist to toss tyranny into the air
and pull at the nose-ring of bearish night that it might dance a
    tsamiko for us in the village square
while the tambourine moon resounds until all island balconies
are filled with half-awakened children and Souliót mothers.

A messenger arrives from the Great Valley every morning,
the sweating sun glitters on his face,
under his armpit he holds on tightly to Romiosíni*
as the worker grips his cap in church.
"The hour has come," he says. "Be prepared.
Every hour is an hour that belongs to us."

---

*For a discussion of the concept of "Romiosíni," see "The Long Poems of Yannis
Ritsos," pp. 449–450.

IV

They pushed on straight into dawn with the disdain of hungry men,
a star had thickened in their motionless eyes,
they carried the stricken summer on their shoulders.

The armies passed through here with banners clinging to their
    bodies,
with stubborness clenched between their teeth like an acrid pear,
with the moon's sand in their heavy army boots,
with the coaldust of night sticking in their ears and their nostrils.

Tree by tree, stone by stone, they passed through the world,
passed through sleep with thorns for pillow.
They brought life like a river cupped in their parched hands.

At every step they won a league of sky—to give it away.
At their outposts they turned to stone like scorched trees,
and when they danced in the village squares the ceilings in the houses
    shook
and the glassware clattered on the shelves.

Ah, what songs shook the mountain summits!
They held the earthen platter of the moon between their knees and
    ate,
and squashed an Ah in the depths of their hearts
as they would squash a louse between their hard thumbnails.

Who will now bring you a warm loaf of bread in the night that you
    may feed your dreams?
Who will stand in the shade of an olive tree to keep the cicada
    company lest the cicada fall silent,
now that the whitewash of noon paints all around the low stone wall
    of the horizon,
obliterating their great and virile names?

This earth that smelled so fragrantly at daybreak,
the earth that was theirs and ours—their blood—how fragrant that
    earth—
and now how is it that our vineyards have locked their doors,
how has the light thinned out on roofs and trees,
who would have said that now half would be found under the earth
and the other half in chains?

Though the sun waves you good morning with so many leaves
and the sky glitters with so many banners,
these are in chains and those lie under the ground.

Be silent, the bells will ring out at any moment.
This earth is theirs, and this earth is ours.
Under the earth, in their crossed hands
they hold the bell rope, waiting for the hour, they don't sleep, they
    never die,
waiting to ring in the resurrection. This earth
is theirs and ours—no one can take it from us.

V

They sat under the olive trees in the early afternoon
sifting the ashy light through their coarse fingers,
they unbuckled their cartridge belts, estimating how much toil could
    be crammed into the path of night,
how much bitterness in the knots of the wild mallow,
how much courage in the eyes of the barefoot boy who holds the flag
    aloft.

In the field the last swallow had lingered late,
balancing in the air like a black ribbon on the sleeve of autumn.
Nothing else remained. Only the burned houses smouldering still.

The others left us some time ago to lie under the stones,
with their torn shirts and their vows scratched on the fallen door.

No one wept. We had no time. Only the silence grew deeper still,
and the light down by the beach was as tidy as the housekeeping of
     the murdered woman.

What will happen to them now when the rain seeps into the earth
     with its rotted plane tree leaves?
What will happen to them when the sun dries out in the woolen
     bedsheets of the clouds
like a squashed bedbug on a peasant's bed,
when the stork of snows stands embalmed on the chimney stack of
     the previous night?

Old mothers scatter salt into the fire, scatter earth over their hair,
they have uprooted the vines of Monovasía lest even one black grape
     sweeten the mouth of a foe;
they have put the bones of their grandfathers in a sack together with
     their knives and forks
and wander outside the walls of their homeland searching for a place
     in which to take root in the night.

It would be hard for us to find a language
less powerful, less stony, than that of the cherry tree —
those hands that were left in the fields
or up on the mountains or down under the sea
do not forget, they never forget —
it will be hard for us to forget their hands,
it will be hard for hands that grew calloused on a trigger to question a
     daisy,
to say thank you on their knees or on a book
or in the bosom of the starlight.

It will take time. And we must speak up.
Until they find their bread and their rights.

Two oars nailed in the sand in the dawn and the storm. Where is the
     fishing boat?
A plough thrust into earth and the wind blowing.
The earth scorched. Where is the ploughman?

Ashes—the olive tree, the vineyard, and the house.
Niggardly night with its stars in a peasant's sock.
Dry bayleaves and oregano in the middle cupboard on the wall. The
    fire has not touched them.
Blackened kettle in the hearth—and the water boiling
by itself in the bolted house. They hadn't time to eat.

On the burned leaves of their door, the veins of the forest—blood
    runs in the veins.
And the footsteps familiar. Who is it?
Familiar footsteps with cleats on the slope.
The root creeping in the stone. Someone is coming.
The password, the response. A brother. Good evening.

Old Lady West sells spices and thread in her wooden hovel.
No one buys. They've gone off to the mountains.
It's difficult now for them to descend to a lower level.
It's difficult for them to tell what their height is.
On the threshing floor where one night the gallant young men took
    their supper
the olive pits and the moon's dried blood remain
with the folk meter of their weapons.
The cypress trees and laurel groves remain.

Next day the sparrows ate the crumbs of their army bread,
children fashioned toys out of the matches
they had lit their cigarettes with and the thorns of the stars.

And the stone where they sat under the olive trees in early afternoon
    by the sea
will be turned into whitewash in the kiln tomorrow,
on the day after tomorrow we shall whitewash our houses and the
    low stone wall of St. Savior,
and the day after that we shall sow seed where they slept and a
    pomegranate bud
shall burst like a baby's first laughter at the sunlight's breast.

Afterwards we shall sit on the ground to read all their hearts
as though we were reading the history of the world for the first time.

VI

Thus with the sun breasting the sea that whitewashes the opposite
     shore of day,
the latching and pangs of thirst are reckoned twice and three times
     over,
the old wound is reckoned from the beginning,
and the heart is roasted dry by the heat like Cytherian onions left by
     the door.

As time passes, their hands begin to resemble the earth more,
as time goes by, their eyes resemble the sky more and more.

The oil jar has emptied. A few lees on the bottom. And the dead
     mouse.
The mother's courage has emptied together with the clay pitcher and
     the cistern.
The gums of the wilderness are acrid with gunpowder.

Where can oil be found now for St. Barbara's oil-wick,
where is there mint now to incense the golden icon of the twilight,
where is there a bit of bread for the night-beggar to play her
     star-couplets for you on her lyre?

In the upper fortress of the island the barbery figs and the asphodels
     have grown rank.
The earth is ploughed up by cannon fire and graves.
The bombed-out Headquarters gapes, patched by sky. There is not
     the slightest room
for more dead. There is no room for sorrow to stand in and braid her
     hair.

Burnt houses that with eyes gouged out scan the enmarbled sea
and bullets wedged in the walls
like knives in the ribcage of the saint tied to a cypress tree.

All day long the dead bask on their backs in the sun,
and only when night falls do soldiers drag themselves on their bellies
    over smoked stones,
and with their nostrils search for the air beyond death,
search for the shoes of the moon as they chew a piece of bootleather,
strike at a rock with their fists in hopes a knot of water will flow,
but the wall is hollow on the other side
and once again they hear the shell twisting and turning as it strikes
    and falls into the sea
and once again they hear the screams of the wounded before the
    gate.

Where can one go now? Your brother is calling you.
The night is built everywhere with the shadows of alien ships.
The streets are barricaded with rafters.
There are ways open only for the high mountains.
And they curse the ships and bite their tongues
to hear their pain that as yet has not turned to bone.

On the parapets the slain captains stand guard at the fortress;
their flesh is melting away under their clothing. Eh, brother, haven't
    you tired?
The bullet in your heart has budded,
five hyacinths have poked out their heads in the armpit of the dry
    rock
breath by breath the musk-fragrance tells you the legend — don't you
    remember?
tooth by tooth the wound speaks to you of life,
the cammomile planted in the filth of your large toe
speaks to you of the beauty of the world.

You take hold of the hand. It is yours. Damp with brine.
Yours is the sea. When you uproot a hair from the head of silence
the fig tree drips with bitter milk. Wherever you may be, the sun sees
    you.

The Evening Star twists your soul in its fingers like a cigarette,
as it is, you smoke your soul lying on your back,
wetting your left hand in the starlight,

your gun glued to your right hand like your betrothed
to remember that the sun has never forgotten you
when you take out your old letter from your inner pocket
as you unfold the moon with your burned fingers you will read of
    gallantry and glory.

Then you will climb to the highest outpost of your island
and using the star as a percussion cap, you will fire in the air
above the walls and the masts
above the mountains that stoop like wounded infantrymen
only that you may boo at ghosts until they scurry under the blanket's
    shadow.

You will fire a shot into the bosom of the sky to find the azure mark
somewhat as though you were trying to find the ripple of a woman
somewhere on her blouse, and who tomorrow will suckle your child,
somehow as though you were finding, after many years, the knob on
    the outer door of your ancestral home.

VII

The house, the street, the barbery fig tree, the peel of the sun in the
    yard where all these are pecked at by chickens.
We know them, they know us. Down here among the briars,
the tree snake has abandoned its yellow shirt.

Down here is the ant's hut and the wasp's tower with its many
    battlements,
on the same olive tree the husk of last year's cicada and the voice of
    this year's cicada,
the shadow on the mastic tree that follows you from behind like a
    much tortured silent dog,
a faithful dog—at noon he sits beside your earthen sleep sniffing at
    the oleanders,
at night he coils up at your feet, looking at a star.

There is a silence of pears that grows larger between the thighs of
    summer
a drowsiness of water that is always gaping amid the roots of the carob
    tree;
summer has seven orphans sleeping in her lap,
a half-dead eagle in her eyes,
and there on high, behind the pine forest,
the chapel of St. John the Eremite
like a sparrow's white dropping drying out in the sun on a wide
    mulberry leaf.

This shepherd wrapped up in his sheepskin
has a dry river on every hair of his body
has a forest of oak trees in every hole of his flute
and his staff has the same knots
as that of the oak that first dipped in the blue of the Hellespont.

It's not necessary to remember. The leaf of the plane tree
shares your blood, together with the island asphodel and the caper.

The unspeaking well raises up from its depths on the drop of noon
a round voice made of black glass and white wind,
a round sound like that of old jars — the same primordial sound,
and the sky washes the stones and our eyes with blueing.

Every night in the fields the moon turns the magnificent dead over
    on their backs,
searching their faces with savage, frozen fingers to find her son
by the cut of his chin and his stony eyebrows,
searching their pockets. She will always find something. There is
    always something to find.
A locket with a splinter of the Cross. A stubbed-out cigarette.
A key, a letter, a watch stopped at seven.
We wind up the watch again. The hours plod on.

When tomorrow their clothing rots away
and leaves them naked amid their army buttons
like pieces of sky between summer stars,
like a river between laurel shrubs,

like a footpath meandering between lemon trees in early spring,
we may then perhaps find their names and we may shout: I love.

Then, But again, these things are perhaps a little too early,
perhaps a little too close, as when you clasp a hand in the darkness
    and say good-evening
with the bitter civility of the exile who returns to his ancestral home
and not even his own kinsfolk recognize him
because he has known death,
because he has known the life that comes before life and beyond
    death,
but he recognizes them. He is not embittered. Tomorrow, he says.
    And he is certain
that the longest road is the shortest road into the heart of God.

And now the hour has come when the moon kisses him below the ear
    with some distress;
the seaweed, the flowerpot, the footstool, and the stone ladder bid
    him good evening,
and the mountains and the seas and the cities and the sky bid him
    good evening,
and then at last, flicking his cigarette ash between the balcony
    railings,
he may weep in his assurance,
he may weep in the assurance of the trees and the stars and his
    brothers.

Athens, 1945–1947

(K.F.)

23

from

PARENTHESES I
(1946–1947)

Translated by Kimon Friar, Edmund Keeley,
and by Thanasis Maskaleris

THE MEANING OF SIMPLICITY

I hide behind simple things that you may find me;
if you don't find me, you'll find the things,
you'll touch what my hand touches,
the imprints of our hands will merge.

The August moon glitters in the kitchen
like a pewter pot (it becomes like this because of what I tell you)
it lights up the empty house and the kneeling silence of the house —
always the silence remains kneeling.

Every word is a way out
for an encounter often canceled,
and it's then a word is true, when it insists on the encounter.

(K.F.)

MAYBE, SOMEDAY

I want to show you these rose clouds in the night.
But you don't see. It's night — what can one see?

Now, I have no choice but to see with your eyes, he said,
so I'm not alone, so you're not alone. And really,
there's nothing over there where I pointed.

Only the stars crowded together in the night, tired,
like those people coming back in a truck from a picnic,
disappointed, hungry, nobody singing,
with wilted wildflowers in their sweaty palms.

But I'm going to insist on seeing and showing you, he said,
because if you too don't see, it will be as if I hadn't—
I'll insist at least on not seeing with your eyes—
and maybe someday, from a different direction, we'll meet.

(E.K.)

FINAL AGREEMENT

When the rain struck the windowpane with one of its fingers,
the window opened toward the inside. Deep within,
an unknown face, a sound—was it your voice?
Your voice distrusted your own ear. The other day,
the sun plunged down the fields, like a descent
of farmers with scythes and pitchforks. You went out into the road,
shouting, not knowing what you were shouting,
pausing for a moment with a smile under your voice
as though under the pink, radiant umbrella of a woman
sauntering along the railing of a park.
There you recognized abruptly that this was your true voice
in agreement with all the unsuspecting voices that filled the air.

(K.F.)

REFORMATION

This which you call serenity or discipline, kindness or apathy,
this which you call a closed mouth with clenched teeth,
showing the sweet silence of the mouth, hiding the clenched teeth,
is only the metal's endurance under the useful hammer,
under the dreadful hammer — it is what you know:
that from the formless you pass toward form.

                                                    (K.F.)

SUDDENLY

Silent night. Silent. And you had stopped
waiting. It was almost quiet.
Then suddenly on your face the so intense
touch of him who is absent. He will come. It was then
you heard window shutters clanging by themselves.
A breeze had sprung up. And a little further down, the sea
was drowning in its own voice.

                                                    (K.F.)

AFTERNOON

The afternoon is full of fallen plaster, black stones, dry thorns,
The afternoon has a difficult color made of old footsteps that stopped
    halfway,
of old clay jars buried in the courtyard, weariness and grass above
    them.

Two persons killed, five killed, twelve—one after the other.
Every hour has its slain. Behind the windows
stand those who are missing, and the pitcher with water they never
    drank.

And this star that fell at the edge of night
is like the amputated ear that does not hear the crickets,
that does not hear our excuses—it disdains
to hear our songs—alone, alone,
alone, cut off from others, indifferent to condemnation or
    justification.

(K.F.)

UNDERSTANDING

Sunday. Buttons glitter on every coat
like small laughter. The bus has gone.
A few cheerful voices—it's strange
how you can hear and reply. Under the pine trees
a worker is learning to play the harmonica. A woman
says good morning to someone—such a simple and natural good
    morning
that you too would like to learn how to play a harmonica under the
    pine trees.

Neither division nor subtraction. To be able to gaze
outside yourself—warmth and quiet. Not to be
"only yourself," but "you too." A small addition,
a small act of practical arithmetic, easily understood,
in which even a child can succeed, playing with his fingers in the
    light
or playing this harmonica for the woman to hear.

(K.F.)

MINIATURE

The woman stood before the table. Her sad hands
cut thin slices of lemon for tea
like yellow wheels for a very small carriage
in a child's fairy tale. The young officer across from her
is sunk deep in the old armchair. He does not look at her.
He lights his cigarette. His hand holding the match trembles,
lighting up his tender chin and the teacup's handle. The clock
for a moment holds its heartbeat. Something has been postponed.
The moment has gone. It is now too late. Let's drink our tea.
Well then, is it possible for death to come in such a carriage?
To pass by and disappear? Until only this carriage
remains with its little yellow wheels of lemon
halted for so many years on a side street with darkened lamps,
and then a small song, a bit of mist, and then nothing?

(K.F.)

WOMEN

Women are very distant. Their bedsheets smell of good-night.
They leave bread on the table so we won't feel they've gone.
Then we understand we were to blame. We get up from the chair and
     say:
"You've overtired yourself today," or "Don't bother, I'll light the
     lamp myself."

When we strike a match, she turns slowly and goes
toward the kitchen with an inexplicable concentration. Her back
is a sad, small mountain laden with many dead —
the family dead, her dead, and your own death.

You hear the old floorboards creaking under her footsteps,
you hear the dishes weeping in the dishracks, and then that train
is heard taking soldiers to the front.

(K.F.)

THE SAME STAR

Drenched, the roofs glisten in the moon's light. The women
wrap themselves in their shawls. They rush to hide in their houses.
If they hover a little longer on the threshold, the moon will catch
   them crying.

That man suspects that in every mirror
there's another, transparent woman, locked in her nakedness
—much as you may want to wake her, she won't wake up.
She fell asleep smelling a star.

And he lies awake smelling that same star.

(E.K.)

WE ARE WAITING

Night falls in the borough. We can't sleep.
We wait for dawn. We are waiting
for the sun to strike the tin roofs of the sheds like a powerful
   hammer
to strike our foreheads, our hearts,
to become sound, sound to be heard—a different sound,
because the silence is filled with gun shots from unknown points.

1946–1947   (T.M.)

from

DISPLACEMENTS
(1942–1949)

Translated by Martin McKinsey

---

from

THE WAVERING SCALES

INSUFFICIENCY

The noise will startle the dolphins
the fisherman's tracks stop dead in the sand
mothers will fear for their children.

In a corner of the room the harpoon will not bend—
certitude and misery in its rigor.

Its narrow shadow is bent. Many fish have felt its point,
we have eaten and been nourished, and had some left to sell. It never
    speared the sea.
A woman wrapped herself in nets. She couldn't hide her nakedness.

The moon reeks of tar. You don't know what you're after tonight
and if you know, don't say. There's a strange glow coming from the
    horizon
wet ropes glistening in the moonlight
the oars' flat palms slapping the face of the stillness.

Someone took the boat out alone. He never came back.
He was seen rising into the moon's open hand. Nothing

Octopuses stiffen on the wall like tiny crucifixes.
The sea thickens to salt. The salt is stored in jars.
It can never become sea again.

Beyond the whitewashed sheepfolds, the ocean calls on its secret
    conches
and sometimes the moon is a spider devouring blue flies

sometimes a jellyfish of glass drifting above the city's slumber
sometimes a helmet of gold for those who go unarmed
and sometimes it is a comb for the blue woman reclining naked at the
    edge of the sea and sky.

When the chowderbowls have been taken up from the table
and all trace of roundness is gone from the bread
leaving the meal with the sorrow of the fragmented circle
then at last the signal will be given,
and the corsair with its crimson sail will proudly round the cape.

Don't squander still another hour
with forecasts and remorse, with self-reproach
as your fingertips roll another fat cigarette.

The ship's boy is waiting at the secret meeting-place
with the points of the wind on his arm
and the night's secret coal in his armpit.
Cap askew. And the smoke rising crooked from his mouth like some
    enigma of the deep
like smoke from a ship borne away from you on the winds.

It is enough for you to change your weather
to draw an X in the ledger of your expenses
to watch the searchlights crisscross in the infinite
unknitting their fingers to snatch away your youth.

(M.M.)

THE INEXHAUSTIBLE

This whitewashed house that stood waiting for the sailors lost at sea
has been saturated with shadows gradually
its beams have rotted, its stairs creak
the sea beats against the windows then runs
and the chimney breathes an old storm.

The shoes you bought two years ago are still new under the bed
your untouched clothes dream of a cloudless Sunday
with boys diving naked from the ancient breakwater.

The silence here is ambiguous, full of postponements and
    repentences
the lamp's flame wavers in the dark
like the tongue in a mouth that can't decide whether to kiss or to
    speak.

What's the point your starting over now? No one's used up the sea.
An endless, already repented journey. And the mouse-trap carefully
    placed
under the stairs. Precaution is required at all times.
The tumult lessens passing from memory,
the groan of the masts, the boat rolling to one side
the massive wave carrying off baggage and men.

Now you can point to these splintered planks, these splintered
    oars—
revenge for those who've gone to sea.

One night, out in the great woods, before they cut it down,
before it became a ship—there in the woods, with the stars overhead
as the hunters were setting out for home with their dogs
—remember?—they called out her name,
and it hung there in the night as if dumbfounded
waiting to be divided among the trees and stars and silence
forgotten by men, who search one more time then leave.

But now that the winds are lashing, nobody hears it,
we only pace our rooms to hear the sound of our own steps.
Every so often we knock on the wall to test the silence of the stone.
No one hears. When we light the lamp on the table
we look at the shadows our hands cast on the door
we make a few playful shapes
an anchor, a seagull, a boat with three masts
but we never forget that it's only the shadow of our hands
that behind the door lie the winds
and beyond the winds the ocean, that will never be fooled by our
    shadows, that takes into account
neither fear nor remorse, neither our cowardice nor our pride.

January, 1943   (M.M.)

from

PETRIFIED TIME
(1949)

Translated by Athan Anagnostopoulos and by Martin McKinsey

RECOGNITION

A stone sun traveled beside us
burning the wind and the thorns of the wilderness.
The afternoon stood at the selvedge of the sea
like a yellow lightbulb in a big forest of memory.

We had no time for such things—but in any case,
sometimes we cast a glance—and on our blankets,
along with the oil stains, the dirt, the olive pits,
there were some leaves left from the willows, some pine needles.

They had their weight too—not very much—
the shadow of a pitchfork on the stone wall, late at sunset,
the passing of the horse at midnight,
a rose color dying on the water
leaving silence behind, even lonelier,
the moon's leaves fallen amid the reeds and wild ducks.

We don't have time—we don't,
when the doors become like folded hands
when the road becomes like the man who says, "I know nothing."

Yet we knew that far off at the big crossroads
there's a city with thousands of multicolored lights,
men greet each other there with only a movement of the forehead—
we know them from the position of their hands,
from the way they cut the bread,
from their shadow on the dinner table,
the hour when all the voices turn drowsy in their eyes
and a big lone star marks their pillows with a cross.

We know them from the struggle's furrow between their eyebrows
and above all — in the nights, when the sky grows larger above
    them —
we recognize them from that considered conspiratorial movement
as they throw their hearts like an illegal proclamation
under the closed door of the world.

August-September, 1949   *(A.A.)*

READY

Tents climb the hillside one step at a time
straight up into the sky;
tents hammered to rock,
staked to stubborness,
with the sun's harpoon through their heart.

The days come and go. The rock never changes.
Sometimes a ship sails past, or a cloud —
leaving behind it a scrap of shade,
a tiny window opening onto the memory of trees.
Nothing ever changes.
Neither heart nor rock changes.

The bed we sleep in is of stone,
stone the bread that sharpens our teeth,
stone the hand that cups the chin of night.
The wind can't take them.

Evening folds up its red banner.
Once again we will sleep with a stone between our teeth,
with the sea's breathing at the back of our ears.

Comrades, whatever comes now
will find us with our bundles slung over shoulders,
and in those bundles, all of our hearts
turning our commitment to the pledge of Democracy over in our
    minds

the way we twist our finger in the button-hole of a friend's jacket
not because we have nothing to say
but because of all the love we feel for him—and so it is:
when we love we cannot speak,
we toy with a branch of wild olive,
scratch a name in the dirt,
and it's always the same, and we'll always be ready,
and it's always the name of Freedom.

August–September, 1949   (M.M.)

THE ROOTS OF THE WORLD

Some parched boxwood shrubs in the summer's armpit,
some sage, thyme, fern.

We were very thirsty.
We were very hungry.
We suffered a lot.

We would never have believed
that men would be so cruel.
We would never have believed
that our hearts had such fortitude.

Unshaven—with a piece of death in our pockets.
Where is there a stalk of wheat to bend its knee to the sky?

It grows dark late. The shadow doesn't hide the stone's hardness.

The dead man's canteen buried in the sand.
The moon moored at another beach
while the stillness rolls it along with its little finger—
on which sea? Which stillness?

We were very thirsty,
working the stone all day long.
Beneath our thirst
are the roots of the world.

August-September, 1949   *(A.A)*

OUR OLD MEN

Sometimes new ships arrive, with their cargo
of old men from the Moreá or Róumeli
or from farther north, from Trikala and Macedonia.
Lean, thick-boned men with white moustaches and sheepskin
     cloaks,
they reek of pastures and of cowdung,
the flocks of evening bleat in their eyes,
the leafy shadows of plane trees dangle from their hair;
they speak little or not at all.
Yet often you can tell they're related to the fir trees
as when they lift their eyes a moment from the ground and gaze off
     over our shoulders.

When evening colors the tents a shade of blue
and the wind's moustache gets tangled in the thyme,
when the sky climbs down the rocks vaulting over memory on the
     cleats of the stars
and Death paces silently to and fro on the other side of the barbed
     wire,
you'll see them assembling into groups of three or four,
as once long ago in the powderhouse of Mesolóngi.

And then you're no longer sure—when you see them gathered like
     that in the confines of evening, unshaven, unspeaking,
you're no longer sure when they strike a match
whether it's only to light a cigarette
or to light the dynamite's fuse.

They don't say a word.
Their sons have all taken to the hills.
They've sunken their hearts in the mountain
like a keg full of gunpowder.

They keep a sapling of kindness close to their eyes
between their brows a falcon of strength
and a mule of anger in their hearts
that won't be slave to injustice.

And now they sit on Makrónisos,
under the raised tent-flap, staring seaward
like lions of stone at the gateway of night
digging their claws into stone. They do not speak.

They are gazing toward the warm glow of Athens,
they are gazing toward the Galaxy's River Jordan,
clutching a rock in their hands of clay,
holding the gun-shot of the stars in their eyes,
and in the depths of their hearts gripping a potent silence,
the silence that falls before the first stroke of thunder.

August–September, 1949   (M.M.)

ولى

from

EXILE'S JOURNALS
(1948–1950)

Translated by Kostas Myrsiades and by Minas Savvas

---

from

EXILE'S JOURNALS, I

6 November 1948

Night. The little bell of the mess hall.
Voices of the boys playing soccer.
Was it yesterday? — I don't remember — that fantastic sunset
full of purple, gold, and rose colors.
We were standing. Staring at the distance. Talked
to ourselves, alone, our voices cast to the wind
to bind things together, to loosen our hearts.

A letter came in the front yard:
Panousis' son was killed.
Words perched from wall to wall.
By evening, nothing.

Night had no hours. The knot untied.
Panousis' aluminum plate was frozen on the table.
We lay down. Covered ourselves. We loved each other
around that untouched plate which no longer steamed.

Around midnight the black cat came through the window
and ate some of Panousis' food.
Then the moon entered
standing silently over the plate.
Panousis' hand over the coarse blanket
was a severed plane tree.

Is that it then? — must we grieve
in order to love each other?

12 November 1948

In the afternoon we carried rocks. Fast work
from hand to hand. The winter sun,
the barbed-wire, the water jugs, the guard's whistle.
Here the day ends. The chill comes at night.
We should shut ourselves in early. To eat our bread.
Good job, comrades, easy work
from hand to hand. All is not so easy;
other things do not move from hand to hand. You notice it,
though the face does not change much. You notice it
from a slit within the brows
from the mouth which opened but did not speak
from the silence before dinner and even
from the two fingers which pull the wick of the lamp.

When we're through eating, the dishes remain unwashed,
the rats climb the table,
the moon places its chin on the rail.

Everything stops like the watch of the murdered man.
The hand which attempts to grip something falls limp on the knee.
The scissors cutting the toenails will not move—
the nail is hard. And neither can you become angry.
Warmth is postponed. Postponed are speech and silence.
Only the lighting of the cigarette around midnight
places an untimely period to all that remained undone.

17 November 1948

We lit a fire with some dry twigs,
we heated water, we bathed, naked
out in the open air. The wind was blowing. We were cold. We were
    laughing.
Perhaps it wasn't because of the cold. Later
a bitterness remained. Certainly my cats,
outside the locked house, will be climbing to the windows,
will be scratching the shutters. And not to be able
to say two words to them, to explain,
not to think that you've forgotten them. Not to be able.

42

21 November 1948

Sunday is a large closet with winter clothing.
Sunday smells of mothballs and sage;
it has the shape of a closed umbrella on the hallway paved with tiles.

People speak louder on Sunday afternoon
walk faster on Sunday afternoon
laugh louder on Sunday night
maybe so as not to understand that they have nothing to say,
so that they will not hear they are not walking
so that they will not know that they have nothing to laugh about.

But old Psomas has a lot to say;
he can construct swings and boats from fallen trees
he can read fortunes in dried beans
he can speak about the braids of corn, about birds and the years
even about the shadow of the calf at sunset
or even about his shoes which he hangs over his shoulder
as if he is about to make a long journey.

Then I realize that I know nothing
and that it's not proper to indiscriminately scribble away verses
since I have not learned to build a straight road
so that old Psomas can walk on it
without fear of ruining his shoes.

Makrónisos, 1948   *(M.S.)*

from
EXILE'S JOURNALS, II

24 November 1948

A day of stone, words of stone.
Caterpillars saunter up the wall.
A snail lugs its house,
it stands on its doorsill,
it may stay, it may leave.

All things are as they are.
Nothing.
Nothingness is not soft.
It is stone.

*

All were forgotten before they were spoken.
And silence is not refuge.

*

The stool has its patience.
The rain arrives
cleans the birds' rooftops
and takes upon itself the burden of a mute.
The toothbrush is sad
like all things.

We pretend not to see.
We light the lamp.

26 November 1948

This cold puts us in a quandary.
The water is frozen, the food is frozen.
The white sun is stuck to the windowpanes,
a sun of snow and used stamps.
Only the water jugs retain
a bit of home and memory.

*

A hand walking in the air
with needle and thread,
an episode without continuity.
On the wall, the motionless shadow
of a voice that said nothing.

*

44

Intercourse with a broken hand
a broken phonograph record
a moon in frozen water
the evening chill.

Sleep is slow.
Turn off the lamp, then.
I can't have light
and be sightless.

27 November 1948

An order on the kitchen's wooden door.
We had decided to be frugal.
Saturday expired
with a rusted zinc moon.

A dog cloud chews our sleep.

*

On Sunday we always have a headache.
Smoke rises from within.
The cigarette is a pretext.

*

We eat, sweep, and sleep.
The sleepless blind man
searches the air with his hands.

30 November 1948

When the snow melts
we might hear our voices.
Might we?

1 December 1948

Old newspapers
caught on dried cotton bolls.
A dog tears the wind
with its snout.
A week's garbage
bones, snow, poems
under the bed.

7 December 1948

The cook left his pots
to feed a sparrow.

But the song doesn't last long,
the dead take it beneath the earth.

*

On cigarette packs
we jot down hurried numbers
that pertain to nothing.

Addition, subtraction, addition, subtraction.

Nevertheless, calculating, calculating
in the end you manage not to cry.

23 January 1949

Finally
the mirror reflects
your severed hands
while you lack hands to applaud
your victory.

26 January 1949

I want to compare a cloud
to a deer,
But I can't.
Good lies
diminish in time.

30 January 1949

Night arrives
speechless
with her hands under her armpits
immersed in our fear's dimness.
All suspicions are realized.
Darkness hides nothing.
A bat came through the window.
This has no meaning.

Lemnos Concentration Camp,
1948–1949   *(K.M.)*

from

EXILE'S JOURNALS, III

1 May 1950

The soldier stepped on his cigarette.
How easily everything is stepped on . . .
Lávrion is across the sea.
Who was it that said: the women-reapers
with the sickles of the swallows?

Cover your ears with your palms.
Shame. Shame.

6 May 1950

One vessel leaves, another comes
a man comes another leaves —
once and for all, where does death end?

The ashes cover the fire,
the flag covers the dead.
The one who won the one who was defeated
under the flag or without the flag
dead.
You'll never learn if he repented.

7 May 1950

Black, black island.
Above the black rock with the lanterns lit.
Huge rats enter the lavatories.
They pause to listen to the megaphones
stare us in the eyes
and then leave quietly.

Flayed rams hang
above our sleep.

19 May 1950

The insane and the invalids increase —
exactly now
now that the great ordeals have gone to rest.
During the nights from the roof can be heard
the howl of the madman,
magnifying over the sea.
The eyes expand
dark, dark
like two blacksmith shops at the edge of the town.

In them two half-naked blacksmiths
strike the iron.

These blows
prevent you from writing a letter
and, even more, from writing a poem.

Here everything has been written in blood.

24 May 1950

We've written our wills so beautifully.
They haven't been opened
they haven't read them
because we haven't died.

We said things
that one has to say one day
we gave things
that one has to give one day.

Big words
so simple
like the spoons in the knapsacks
of the murdered.

We saw eternity
reflected erect
on the glasses of the myopic man
who was killed two months ago.

And, just think,
you no longer can say
"We"
without lowering your eyes
without blushing.

30 May 1950

The soldiers, unshaven,
on the stone wall
have a sadness yawning in their eyes

they listen to the loud-speakers, the sea,
they hear nothing —
perhaps they wanted to forget.

At dusk
they go slowly to the ravine for their physical needs.
When they button their trousers
their eyes catch a glimpse of the new moon.

The world could have been beautiful.

Makrónisos, 1950   (M.S.)

VIGILANCE
(1938–1953)

Translated by Kimon Friar

PEACE

To Kostas Varnalis

The dreams of a child are peace.
The dreams of a mother are peace.
The words of love under the trees
are peace.

The father who returns at dusk with a wide smile in his eyes
with a basket in his hands full of fruit
and the drops of sweat on his brow
are like drops on a jug as it cools its water on the windowsill,
are peace.

When wounds heal on the world's face
and in the pits dug by shellfire we have planted trees
and in hearts scorched by conflagration hope sprouts its first buds
and the dead can turn over on their side and sleep without
    complaining
knowing their blood was not spilled in vain,
this is peace.

Peace is the odor of food at evening,
when an automobile stopping in the street does not mean fear,
when a knock on the door means a friend,
and the opening of a window every hour means sky
feasting our eyes with the distant bells of its colors,
this is peace.

Peace is a glass of warm milk and a book before the awakening child.
When wheatstalks lean toward one another saying: the light, the
    light,

and the horizon's wreath overbrims with light,
this is peace.

When jails have been made over into libraries,
when a song ascends from threshold to threshold in the night
when the spring moon emerges from a cloud
like the worker who comes out of the neighborhood barber shop
    freshly shaven on a weekend,
this is peace,

When a day gone by is not a day lost
but a root that raises the leaves of joy in the night
and is a day won and a just sleep,
when you feel again the sun hurriedly tying its reins
to pursue and chase sorrow out of the corners of time,
this is peace.

Peace is the stacks of sunrays on the fields of summer,
it is the alphabet book of kindness on the knees of dawn.
When you say: my brother — when we say: tomorrow we shall build,
when we build and sing,
this is peace.

When death takes up but little room in the heart
and chimneys point with firm fingers at happiness,
when the large carnation of sunset
can be smelled equally by poet and proletariat,
this is peace.

Peace is the clenched fists of men,
it is warm bread on the world's table,
it is a mother's smile.
Only this.
Peace is nothing else.
And the ploughs that cut deep furrows in all earth
write one name only:
Peace. Nothing else. Peace.

On the backbone of my verses
the train advancing toward the future
laden with wheat and roses
is peace.

My brothers,
all the world with all its dreams
breathes deeply in peace.
Give us your hands, brothers,
this is peace.

January, 1953   (K.F.)

ﭼﻮ

from

TRAIN WHISTLES
(1939–1954)

Translated by Athan Anagnostopoulos

MIDNIGHT

A great starry night showing its bare claws,
foreign footsteps stealing your sleep,
what is this shadow climbing on the ceiling
cutting the room in half?

Footsteps, a motorcycle, the trigger's sound —
the lantern at the windowpanes,
the cockroaches in the soldiers' shoes and helmets.

What's the use of the moon's compassion now?
Some have hidden in the trunks of the night,
some have climbed into coffins and travel,
some have taken the cashier's keys and surrendered their earth,
and this dog that forgot us barks at the moon again,
awakens the sentries at the distant watchtowers,
the first explosion blows up the bridge,
then the doors creak, the squadron stands at the corner,
the street lamps fall face down and the train's whistling is heard
when all five roads are closed by the bayonets.

Athens, October, 1941   *(A.A.)*

POSTPONED DECISION

Old winds have replaced us on the bare plains.
Everything is so old — and this lamp lighting a faded seascape
and the bed's shadow falling obliquely on the floor

and the clothes thrown on the chair
—the dead man abandoned them here.

And you, what are you seeking so persistently,
extending your hands as if pulling the ropes of a ship gliding into the
     unknown?

The wind encircles the lights of the city, torments the trees,
uproots the little grass around the telegraph poles—
large shadows pace on the cobblestones,
each man has a piece of ice in his heart,
the soliders wrap themselves up in their jackets,
the guards' feet freeze at the watchtowers.

Well, you know it. Yet what's the use of knowing?
The matches get wet too—you can't light your cigarette. Now the
     smoke
stands voiceless over the kiss that burned
like the smoke staying on the horizon above the ship that vanished.

What signal flickers over the spread-out map
in the wooden barracks? Outside, the rain
lashes at the desolate camp,
smothers that bugle which had called the names one by one,
moistens the benches in the gardens. The children have no place to
     sit.

A bloodstained shoe in the street.
A foot stuck in the shoe.
Someone leaps out of the window. What cold.
Yet if you'd brought your hand to your forehead—he said—
you'd have found the last window easily. And opposite you is the
     mirror
with the thick sky over the smoking lamp.
You'd easily have made a hole in the night.

But perhaps dawn will reveal a new face
as the shutters noisily open,

perhaps the dawn. The shining square on the floor.
The bed's railings gilded. An ironed shirt.
And outside in the street a child crying out the first Greek grapes.

Athens, March, 1942   (A.A)

MOONLIGHT SONATA
(1956)

Translated by Kimon Friar

(*A spring night. A large room of an old house. A middle-aged woman, dressed in black, is speaking to a young man. They have not put on any lights. Through the two windows a merciless light enters. I've neglected to say that the Woman in Black has published two or three interesting collections of poetry of a religious nature. Well, the Woman in Black is speaking to the Young Man*):

Let me come with you. What a moon tonight!
The moon is good to me—you can't tell
my hair has turned white. The moon
will make my hair golden again. You won't be able to tell the
    difference.
Let me come with you.

When there's a moon, the shadows in the house grow larger,
invisible hands draw the curtains,
a ghostly finger writes forgotten words in the dust
on the piano—I don't want to hear them. Be still.

Let me come with you
a little ways down, as far as the brick factory's low wall,
there where the road turns and you can see
the cement yet airy city, whitewashed with moonlight,
so indifferent and immaterial,
so positive, like metaphysics,
that at last you can believe you exist and do not exist,
that you have never existed, that neither time nor its ravaging ever
    existed.
Let me come with you.

We shall sit for a while on the low wall, there on that height,
and as the spring wind blows about us
we may even imagine we shall fly

because many times, even now, I hear my dress rustling
like the flapping of two strong wings beating the air;
and when you enclose yourself within that sound of flying
you feel that your throat, your ribs, your flesh have grown firm;
and thus tightly wedged within the muscles of blue air,
within the vigorous nerves of those heights,
it doesn't matter whether you go or come back,
nor does it matter that my hair has turned white,
(this is not my sorrow—my sorrow is
that my heart, also, has not turned white).
Let me come with you.

I know that every human being goes his way alone toward love,
alone toward glory and toward death.
I know this. I've tried it. It doesn't help.
Let me come with you.

This house has become haunted, it repels me—
I mean to say, it's grown very old, its nails are falling out,
its picture frames tumble down as easily as though plunging
     through a void,
its plaster falls as noiselessly
as the hat of a dead man from its peg in a dark corridor,
as the worn woolen glove from the knees of silence
or a strip of moonlight on the old, gutted armchair.

Even it was new once—no, not the photographs you're looking at
     so incredulously—
I'm speaking of the armchair, very restful, where you could sit for
     hours on end
and with closed eyes dream of any random thing
—of smooth, sandy beaches, wet, polished by the moon,
even more highly polished than the old patent leather shoes I send
     every month to the corner shoestand,
or the sail of a fishing boat that vanishes in the distance, rocked
     by its own breathing,
a triangular sail like a handkerchief folded diagonally only in two
as though it had nothing to cover up or to hold,
or to flutter wide open in farewell. I was always crazy about
     handkerchiefs—
not to keep anything tied within them,

like flower seed or camomile plucked in the fields at sunset,
nor to knot in each of their four corners like those worn by the
    workers of the half-built house opposite,
or to wipe my eyes with—I've taken good care of my eyes,
and I've never worn glasses. A mere whim, those handkerchiefs.

Now I fold them in four, in eight, in sixteen
simply to keep my fingers busy. And now I remember
that's how I kept beat to the music when I was attending the
    Conservatory
in a blue smock with a white collar, with two blond braids
—8, 16, 32, 64—
clinging to the hand of a small peach tree friend of mine, all light
    and rose-colored flowers,
(forgive these works of mine—it's a bad habit)—32, 64—and my
    folks cherished
great hopes for my musical talent. Well, I was telling you about
    the armchair—
—disemboweled—its rusty springs are showing, the stuffing—
I was thinking of taking it to the furniture man next door,
but where's the time or the money or the mood—what's one to fix
    first?—
I thought of throwing a sheet over it—but I was afraid
of a white sheet in such moonlight. Here sat
those who dreamt great dreams, even like you or me,
and now they're resting under the earth where neither rain nor
    moon can trouble them.
Let me come with you.

We shall pause for awhile on the top of the marble staircase of St.
    Nikólaos
and then you shall walk down and I shall turn back,
retaining on my left side the warmth of your coat as it touches me
    by chance,
and even some square-shaked lights from small windows in the
    poorer neighborhoods,
and this pure white mist from the moon like a long retinue of
    silver swans—
I'm not afraid of using such an expression because
on many a spring night, formerly, I have conversed with God
    when He appeared to me

robed in the haze and glory of such a moonlight;
and many a young man, even more handsome than you, have I
    sacrificed to Him
as thus, white and unapproachable, I turned to mist in my white
    flame, in the moon's whiteness,
inflamed by the voracious eyes of men, by the hesitant ecstasy of
    youths,
besieged by splendid, sunburnt bodies,
vigorous limbs exercised in swimming, rowing, track, and soccer
    (though I pretended not to notice),
brows, lips, and throat, knees, fingers, and eyes,
chests and arms and thighs (as in truth I didn't notice)
—you know, at times, in admiring, you forget what you're
    admiring, your admiration is enough—
Dear God, what starry eyes, and I was lifted high to an apotheosis
    of stars denied
because, thus besieged from within and without,
no other road was left me but to go upward or downward. —No,
    it's not enough.
Let me come with you.

I know it's very late now. Let me come,
because for so many years, days and nights and crimson noons, I've
    remained alone,
unyielding, alone and immaculate,
even on my marriage bed, alone and immaculate,
writing glorious verses on the knees of God,
verses which shall survive, I assure you, as though carved on
    faultless marble
beyond your life or mine, much beyond. It's not enough.
Let me come with you.

I can't bear this house much longer.
I can't bear to keep carrying it on my back.
You must always be careful, very careful
to support the wall with the large buffet
to support the buffet with the carved antique table
to support the table with the chairs
to support the chairs with your hands
to place your shoulder under the dangling beams.
And the piano like a closed black coffin. You don't dare open it.

You must always be careful, very careful, for fear they'll fall, for
    fear you'll fall. I can't bear it.
Let me come with you.

This house, despite all its dead, does not intend to die.
It insists on living with its dead
on living off its dead
on living on the certainty of its own death
and even on accommodating its dead on dilapidated beds and
    shelves.
Let me come with you.

Here no matter how softly I walk in the evening's haze,
either in my slippers or my bare feet,
something or other will creak—a windowpane cracks, or a mirror,
certain footsteps are heard—they're not mine.
Outside in the street it's possible these steps cannot be heard—
repentance, they say, wears wooden clogs—
and if you try to look into this or that mirror,
behind the dust and the cracks,
you'll discern your face even more dim and more fragmented,
your face, though you wanted nothing more from life than to keep
    it clear and indivisible.

The rim of the water glass glitters in the moonlight
like a circular razor—how can I bring it to my lips?
no matter how thirsty I get, how can I bring it? Do you see?
I'm still in the mood for metaphor—this is still left me,
this assures me that I'm still here.
Let me come with you.

At times, as night is falling, I have the feeling
that outside the window the bear trainer is passing by with his old
    lumbering she-bear,
her fur covered with thorns and thistles,
raising a cloud of dust in the neighboring street,
a desolate cloud of dust that rises like incense in the twilight;
and the children have gone home for supper and are not allowed
    to go out again,
though behind their walls they guess at the plodding steps of the
    old bear,

and the bear proceeds wearily in the wisdom of her loneliness, not
    knowing where or why —
for she has grown heavy, she can't dance on her hind legs any
    more,
she can't wear her lace bonnet to amuse the children, the idlers, or
    those who make demands on her,
for she wants only to lie down on the earth,
letting them tread on her belly, thus playing her last game,
her disobediance to the interests of others, to the rings in her
    snout, to the needs of her teeth,
her disobediance to pain and to life
with an assured alliance with death — even though with a slow
    death —
her supreme disobediance to death with the continuity and
    knowledge of life
that ascends with knowledge and action above her slavery.

But who can play this game to its end?
And the bear once more rises and plods on,
obedient to her leash, to her rings, to her teeth,
smiling with her torn lips at the nickels and dimes thrown her by
    the beautiful and unsuspecting children
(beautiful precisely because they are unsuspecting)
and saying: Thank you. Because the only thing
that bears grown old have learned to say is: Thank you, thank
    you.
Let me come with you.

This house stifles me. The kitchen in particular
is like the bottom of the sea. The hanging kettles glitter
like the large, round eyes of improbable fish,
the plates move sluggishly like jelly-fish,
shells and seaweed catch in my hair — I can't pull them out
    afterwards,
I can't rise to the surface again,
the tray falls noiselessly from my fingers — I collapse
and watch the bubbles from my breath rising and rising
and I try to divert myself by watching them,
and ask myself what would someone from above say if he saw
    these bubbles —

that somebody was drowning, perhaps, or that a diver was
  searching the sea's depths?

And in truth there in the depths of drowning I've discovered, and
  not a few times only,
corals and pearls and treasures of shipwrecked vessels,
unexpected encounters, things of today and yesterday and of the
  future,
a verification, almost, of eternity,
a certain breathing spell, a certain smile of immortality, as they
  say,
a happiness, an intoxication—an enthusiasm even,
corals and pearls and sapphires—
only, I don't know how to give them—and yet I do give them—
only, I don't know if they are capable of receiving them—
  nevertheless, I do give them.
Let me come with you.

One moment till I get my jacket.
In this unsettled weather, however, we should take care of
  ourselves.
The evenings are damp, and the moon—
honestly, don't you think it intensifies the chill?
Let me button your shirt—how strong your chest is!—
what a strong moon . . . the armchair, I say . . . and when I lift
  the cup from the table
a hole of silence is left under it, and immediately I cover it with
  my hand
that I may not gaze inside—I place the cup in its place again,
and the moon is a hole in the world's skull—don't look inside,
there's a magnetic power that attracts you—don't look, don't let
  anyone look,
listen to what I'm saying—you'll all fall inside. This dizziness
is beautiful and weightless—you'll fall—
the moon is a marble well,
shadows and silent wings are moving, mysterious voices—don't you
  hear them?
Deep, deep is the falling,
deep, deep is the rising,
the airy statue is firmly knit amid its outspread wings,
deep, deep is the implacable beneficence of silence,

tremulous illuminations on the other bank as you sway in your
   own wave,
the breathing of the ocean. This vertigo
is beautiful and weightless—be careful, you'll fall. Don't look at
   me,
for my role is to waver—the exquisite vertigo. Thus every day
   toward evening
I have a slight headache, a few dizzy spells.

Often I run to the drugstore across the street for an aspirin,
then at times I can't be bothered going, and remain with my
   headache
and listen to the hollow noise made by the waterpipes in the
   walls,
or I brew some coffee and, absent-minded as always,
forget and make enough for two—who will drink the other cup?
It's really amusing; I let it get cold on the windowsill,
or sometimes I drink the second cup too, gazing from my window
   at the green electric light of the drugstore,
like the green light of a noiseless train coming to carry me off
with my handkerchiefs, my lopsided shoes, my black bag, my
   poems,
and with no luggage at all—of what use would it be?
Let me come with you.

Ah, you're going? Good night. No, I'm not coming. Good night.
I'll go out myself in a little while. Thank you. Because, really, I
   must
get out of this exhausted house.
I must see a bit of the city—no, no, not the moon—
the city with its calloused hands, the city of the wage-earner,
the city that swears on its bread and its fist,
the city that can bear us all on its back
with our trivialities, our vices, our hates,
with our ambitions, our ignorance, our old age,
to hear the large strides of the city
that I may no longer hear your own footsteps
nor the footsteps of God, not even my own footsteps. Good
   night.

(The room grows dark. It seems that a cloud must have hidden the moon. Suddenly, as though someone had turned up the radio in the neighboring bar, an extremely familiar phrase is heard. I understand then that this entire scene has been accompanied softly by "The Moonlight Sonata," by the first part only. The Young Man now must be descending the slope with an ironical and perhaps compassionate smile on his beautifully chiseled lips, and with a feeling of being freed at last. Just as he reaches St. Nikólaos — before he descends the marble stairs — he will laugh, a loud uncontrollable laugh. His laughter will not sound at all discordant under the moon. Perhaps the only discordant thing about it may be that it is not at all discordant. In a little while the Young Man will fall silent, he will turn sober and say: "The decadence of an age." Thus, thoroughly calm once more, he will unbutton his shirt again and continue on his way. As for the Woman in Black, I don't know whether or not she finally went out of the house. The moonlight glitters once more. And in the corners of the room the shadows stiffen and grow tense out of an unbearable repentance, out of rage almost, not so much against life as against a confession that was quite futile. Do you hear? The radio continues):

Athens, June, 1956

(K.F.)

THE BRIDGE

An Uncalled-for Apology
(1959)

Translated by George Giannaris

(*Eight men are sitting around a long table. They have written and signed some kind of declaration—perhaps about human rights, or about the everlasting yet timely subject of peace—one of those declarations which are so customary and standardized that even its authors have already forgotten why it should be needed or useful. All of them seem to be important, yet displaced agents in politics, sciences, and Letters. A ninth chair, at the same table, is empty. They are waiting for someone whose authority and name must certainly be of importance. The Ninth man enters right on time. He greets the others cordially, sits in his chair and starts talking in a somewhat odd and elevated manner, as though he were guilty, while the others wait for him to sign. They all know one another well, are almost friends— perhaps they pursued their careers together or were persecuted and sent to the same detention camps. Their respect for the speaker, however, is not displaced by their friendship and their common remembrances. They listen to him therefore with great attention, so great that unintentionally they betray their anxiety and absorption. The central chandelier multiplies and enlarges on the table the shadows of the controlled gestures of the speaker. Occasionally, the shadow of his hand passes over the paper on which the declaration has been written, as though he were writing one signature after the other, so that the others feel that the meeting is over and that they may now leave. The Ninth man starts speaking*):

Every now and then I return to you and it's a great joy for me to
    know
that I have a place to return to, an eye
that says "Yes" and welcomes me; that a straw mattress
on which I may lie down is always ready in the hall—and take
a deep, filling, and companionable sleep, without anyone lying in
    wait
for the creaking of the lock, the creaking of the door
as I entered cautiously, without anyone asking me,

pretending indifference, for the time, or whether the last train
has gone by; the only tick heard
would be from the big clock in the marketplace, over the sleeping
    drivers,
over the trucks, the crates, and the empty baskets;
simply one tick — one only —
and not that suspicious half of $1^1/_2$, $2^1/_2$, $3^1/_2$
that slips away into the vagueness of the night,
confuses the reflections of the streetlights with the clandestine light
    of daybreak,
leaves allusions of guilt, orgies, adventures,
taverns and fights, knives stained with blood,
wooden stairs of police stations, an electric globe
casting the shade of a railing on the street
and the street fenced on all sides by effective repressions
at the moment when a piece of pop music leaks out of a basement
    window
like a dead cat accompanied by the cursing of a young voice.

The halves of an hour are strange, indeed, especially for those who
    are sleeping
and have lost count of time; more so for those
who are awake and keep counting. The half hours
maintain that indefinite half which seeks a supplement
and are conscious of being halves; and conscious
of the indefinite other half in the previous or the after, always in
    the beyond and the outside;
strange, indeed, are the half hours — they are
a suspended, sonorous "perhaps" —
$1^1/_2$, $2^1/_2$, $3^1/_2$. Perhaps — a "perhaps"
that sounds like a slash in the wholeness of time —
a sensitive, metallic beat; a vibration
like that of the thin blade of a stiletto thrust in the middle of a
    bull's forehead
like that of a sharp knife which, whizzing
through a dark void, was nailed in a shut door.
And it's a great joy for me to be returning amongst you.
Those halves cannot be heard here; and even if they are,
they are only a whole beat. The whizzing

of the knife in the void cannot be heard. I feel
the time I was not with you and its remorse more deeply only
when I say I am returning amongst you. I know
the last train has gone by, although you have not asked me,
a train almost empty except for the drowsy railway men
who let their arms dangle between their knees.
The baggage car bounces silently and its own jolting
is echoed in its hollowness
although its air is filled by the floating and still vivid
odors from the large baskets of roving fishermen,
the cool odors from starched rolls of calico,
chintz, and cotton fabrics,
or from the multi-colored carpets and rugs of gypsy peddlers.

The lighting in the hollow carriages has an expression
of a meditating weariness which does not even care
to be designated so that it can relax, and it is already
completely tranquil — while the trampled cigarette stubs remain
    between
the wooden floor slots like useless stars made out of paper. And
    then,
on their behalf, I try to elucidate them,
to find out their meaning in a neutral utility; to match
the lighting of the carriages with the silence of the switchmen,
the electric globes of the Stations with the rails,
the noise of iron on iron with what is unheard,
the separation with an unrealized meeting; and all these
only because a dog was crossing with his shadow through the
    yellow field,
and a woman was leaning against the Station's lamppost while the
    moon
had noiselessly replaced the electric globe
high up, behind the glass of the lantern, without her noticing it.
    Was it necessary
for her to have noticed it?
What for? It's for this I seek your forgiveness. Even now I can't
explain my remorse and my guilt.

It's a wonderful rambling, almost an escape —
I don't know from where to where — a secret escape which gives
a kind of secrecy to each of our movements, to our shadow on the
    wall,
to the unlikely relations of our fingers,
to the sounds of our steps — a superb feeling
of illegality towards everything,
like that of the adulterer, the thief, the murderer, the pederast or
    the stowaway,
and the feeling of such illegality imposes on you
a vigilant watchfulness to avoid being arrested,
while such watchfulness grasps
the meaning of an initial guilt,
grasps the most imperceptible expression of silence; but then
    again
you feel that in this way you violate a big, strange, dark cashbox
    with a passkey
after having gone up many stairs and long, tiled corridors
which make your joints echo endlessly,
and a suspicious moon enters through iron-barred attic-windows —
a big, yellow, treacherous moon, bringing you face to face
with your own enormous shadow which holds
the elongated shadows of the keys you hold, as though they already
    were
the iron bars of the prison which will lock you up for life; until
    finally
you find out that this cashbox
is your own, completely your own,
and that you can open it freely
and can give away as much as you want to your friends
and can scatter as much as you want in the wind
with that joy which is offered by what is inexhaustible
with that gesture of a purposeless bravery and dissipation
which is, perhaps, your only true intention.

But then suddenly you yourself feel how suspicious this movement
    appears
in the darkness nailed by stars, with the metalic sound of keys

like the clashing of swords high in the air, of invisible gladiators or
    horsemen
with this dark, enormous mouth of the cashbox
that gapes open in the night while piles of coins
from strange times and places shine at its bottom,
bars of gold like huge nails for a crucifixion; stacks of paper
    money
like secret playing cards of Fate. And all those,
who for a moment accepted your offer, will test your coins on
    stone
as soon as you turn your head, but they make no sound,
they try to decipher the numbers and seals
on the paper money, but they cannot be distinguished
in the astonishing darkness,
and so they throw them again at your feet and leave.
And you are left alone with all your trampled wealth,
alone before the magnetic gaping mouth of the now empty cashbox,
alone before the uncovered hole of chaos
with one or your hands half-raised
in a half-completed pose of theatrical generosity
like the statue of a hero whose heroism
was proven fraudulent after his death—or like an endless effort
to become a statue so as not to collapse on the ground—a statue
which in vain holds out, like a cluster of grapes, the unacceptable
    keys of a paradise.

I don't even know what wealth I'm talking to you about.
And yet I believe it's the one that sustains us
when we lose everything. Nor
do I know anything about that statue,
about its rocky solitude, or its half-finished
and somewhat comic pose. What keys, I wonder?
What cashbox? I don't know. Sometimes I feel I hear
the persistant ringing of a telephone in a quiet room next door,
and no one picks up the receiver because the tenant has died
and lies frozen on his bed with open eyes. His eyes,
tranquil and glazed, do not follow the whirling ring of the
    telephone. Alone, staring all alone,

they follow an unfamiliar perpendicular that comes out of the
     ceiling
expressing a certain proud vengeance and causeless malice,
something from the secret happiness of a certain knowledge: that
     these eyes
remain untouched forever by the anxiety of the caller,
free from any mournful or cheerful message.

I, too, can hear this insistant ringing in the other room;
I know that he who was to receive the call is dead,
I know the meaning of this call which, although it does not
     concern me,
seems as though meant for me. However,
I don't have the right to accept this most important message
which could have clarified many things, could have straightened
     out much, could have solved much; besides,
I don't possess the necessary strength to break down
the door of the dead man. I only visualize
the telephone receiver beautifully curved
on the smooth desolation of the table
next to the half-filled glass of water and the ashtray
in the tranquil, glassy room of the dead man —
the receiver like a small impassable bridge
of an improbable time in the early days of an unknown autumn,
and this relieves me somewhat; indeed, it gives me the attitude
of one who has received the call but does not want to say so.

It's especially for this attitude of mine that I want to apologize,
and about which you — not out of ignorance,
but out of the politeness of your simplicity — have neither paid any
     attention to,
nor questioned me about, and indeed you once even
acknowledged that it suited me, as though it were similar to
a grave and splendid message I was bringing — what message?

A silent turn takes place inside us that changes

death into life, desolation into companionship, humiliation
into pride—and this is the other side of the coin—
this very same coin, unique and whole and changeless. I
    remember
a woman who was weeding up the flower-beds in her garden
with slow, gentle, thoughtful movements
in order to facilitate the rhythm of her dream.
She was fastening the tall carnations,
tying the stalks with thin strings as though plaiting
the infantile hair of the garden. A smile
stirred on her face like a pale bird
in an empty, strange nest—just a smile. Nevertheless,
the tall trees were lurking for her,
holding their nets wide open in the air,
and, over her stooped back, claiming her silence,
converting her tenderness almost into agony
as she had herself converted her agony into gratitude a while
    earlier—
so much so that the woman slowly left her weeder on the ground,
turned, looked around, and discerned someone under the trees,
half of whose shadow passed over the flowers. No one.
Only a big afternoon star was strolling tiptoe on the glittering
    leaves,
rendering her smile into another tongue,
an unknown tongue, which, however, assured her with exactness
that she was alone and incommunicable,
that absence always remains unalterable—just absence.

And again in the evening she was possessed
by that luminous frankness of her sorrow like something restful,
something truly her own, hers only—she herself
submissive yet closed, whole yet completely alone.

She then gathered the rest of the strings in a paper box,
picked up her weeder with care,
with that inevitable moderation and attention to order
and turned on the electric globe in the garden, knowing what
    consequences would follow a change of lighting,

calm, retired; acceptable to herself. In a little while
she felt an exceptional joy in her grief,
she felt that her grief was her attachment
to what had been, to what is, to what will be,
to everything around and above and below,
to everything within and without—a silent attachment,
a touch of immortality, a remote and balanced light of eternity
that abolishes the difference, abolishes the distance
between the here and the beyond,
among foreign languages, nor is any translation necessary
from her smile to the star, from the star
to the garden's electric globe, from silence to confession,
from the carnations to the weeder and to her own hand,
from one hour to the next. She turned on the faucet then
and with the rubber hose started watering the flowers and trees
    near and far
under the intimate light of the stars and the globe. Yet this
    insignificant move of hers
brought her back again from her dream to life. She sensed around
    her
the echoes of her own movements, her presence, her participation,
and felt herself to be commingling with the cool sound of the
    water,
with the thirst of the sun-scorched soil,
with the sugary fragrance of the carnations,
with the light of the electric globe and the stars, with the shades
    of the trees. She also felt
that her own consciousness and movement
were the expression and act of all these. She smiled again.
She rose upright and stood there. She crossed her arms,
listening to the splashing and rushing water,
erect, beautiful, modest and proud
like a perpendicular bridge between earth and the sky, or the
    reverse.

This is what I wanted to talk about—about this consciousness and
    movement,
this expression and act, about this modest intervention,
which assures our friendship. It's this we sometimes forget,

and this is my remorse.
You understand. It's always happening that when we reach the
    edge of silence, that impasse
of the narrow or the immense, there
where at once every word and every movement is rendered useless,
it's a woman's simple and intimate gesture again
that fixes a man's tie before a huge glass door
whose pane barely separates the darkness of the doorman's desk
from the darkness of the street—exactly at the moment of
    departure. A beautiful gesture
that ascends from the roots of the world. Her arm
traverses all solitude, venerable but also determined
as though holding a man above a precipice,
as though strangling him in order to keep him. And perhaps the
    tie
tightens like a slip knot for a moment,
like a noose that holds him over the abyss. And truly,
see, he has not fallen. He is standing on his feet
gazing around himself, bewildered
by the horror of chaos, even to the tips of his feet,
with the feeling of a dreadful wavering
and a new equilibrium again.

The woman smiles—a child's smile
beyond bitterness and experience. The man smiles too. And the
    tie
is an unexpected bridge in spring
at that most difficult passage of the river, at that most difficult
    silence, that most difficult night.

How beautiful and strange, indeed, is life. Don't you often feel
her fingers fixing your tie? That bridge—
ah, yes, also that other one of the woman who waters the garden
late in the evening—and the healthy pulse of the water—what
    bridge?—
and that other, that silent one of the telephone receiver above
    death—.

Again I forget and become absent-minded. As though I am trying
to justify myself for my long delay
and my infidelity—yes—by mobilizing again
the most unjustifiable matters; perhaps in this way
I might show you how defenseless I am,
how unjustified; and perhaps in this manner
I might obtain your forgiveness, even your sympathy,
and perhaps (above all) I might show you
that which I cannot prove—this sublime dimension of the
    dazzlement
that wipes out my mistakes and yours as well,
that exists and neither can be shown nor proven,
that doesn't even ask for sympathy and forgiveness,
and, by remaining always unjustified, justifies our struggles and
    our entire life.

How beautiful and strange life really is. That short gesture,
that watered garden with the electric globe and the fragrance of
    the soil—
again I keep forgetting—and I must ask again: I wonder
how many men have felt those admirable fingers on their tie?—
but even if they were once touched by them, they neither felt
nor were aware of it—having neither the time nor the mood—and
    how many
don't have a tie even for a Sunday, and know nothing
of these useless and cunning bridges and these complex
    pretenses—
because when there is no bread on the table
—what richness of the stars? No, no,
I don't want to stay with what can't be proven. I don't want to.

Often, our beautiful independence is nothing
but a fear of action,—a fear
of exercising our freedom in this world—as for that dazzlement of
    which I told you,
it's a good covering for self-deception, for deceit, for escape
—it doesn't annoy the enemy, doesn't insult the friend,
and thus we secure the approval of both,

—or at least their tolerance. Perhaps I'm already
wronging myself, but I prefer this
rather than continuing to wrong you as I already have

How beautiful and strange, indeed, is life—is it not?—
as I return among you with another gratefulness
to ask you for a piece of your daily bread,
a hard portion of your responsibility,
a straw mattress, even outside in the corridor
like the one we shared in our detention camps,
when each sharing was an augmentation,
when "we divided our cigarettes into two
and our hearts into the four points of the horizon."* There I go
    again,
reciting from my old verses. Do you see? Consequently,
the need for a piece of bread, a kiss, friendship, the air, does not
    humiliate us—
a window facing eastward that we may breathe when evening
    falls,
justifiably letting our arm rest for a while,
calm and idle, on the shoulder of silence—this hand
that will labor and be rewarded and will have lost
the crooked shape of theft, of supplication, of beggary, of charity,
and will be extended, honest and positive and straight,
into life's palm with the solemn dignity of the knowledge
that it digs, writes, gives, and deserves to take,
while the light, lawful and useful,
will always curve spherically in the eager hollow of its palm
like a fresh, transparent, tepid egg of an eternal birth.

Our small needs do not humiliate us;
on the contrary, they save us: they give us
ground again to walk on, to stand erect, to work,
and their knowledge and their approval is our new brotherhood,
is the beginning of our profound freedom,
is that sacred frankness,

---

*From a poem by Yiannis Ritsos, "Unsubdued City."

man's first and last, so much so that you sometimes
weep out of tenderness
for this confession of yours, this humiliation,
for this pride with which you were born and will die,
for this work caused by these needs of yours
in order to be offered to the needs of others,
to the eternal needs of man—an eternal work.

I always return among you—and it's a great joy for me
to know you await me, to know of your beautiful patience
and your deep trust. Let me then repeat
the articles of our faith with the simple sanctity of a novice,
with that sweet enthusiasm of the young proselyte who recites by
      heart
the articles of life written in large red letters
on the facade of history and the horizon:
    I believe that the first act of justice is the correct distribution
        of bread,
    I believe that the first step to progress is the increase of the
        production of bread for all,
    I believe that our first duty is peace,
    I believe that our first freedom is not our loneliness
    but our comradeship; as for the rest
    there will always be time even for them, but only from there
        on.
It was about this bridge I wanted to speak to you—

(*He took a pen out of his pocket, with a movement as though he were
drawing a sword out of its sheath, and signed the declaration—an
arrogant yet modest movement, as when you finally decide to beg for
forgiveness or sign a petition for an apology. The others looked at
each other astonished, unable to understand why he was asking for
forgiveness, what they should do and say, dizzied as they were by his
groundless eloquence and yet dazzled by the superb representation of
a vagueness that forced them to guess at its meaning and at the
gravity of their own movements, of their cuffs sticking out of their
coats and outlined on the dark table, of the voice that moved the
chair, hearing its creaking along the floor, seeing now the whole chair
emerging from the shadows of their bodies and the table, and feeling*

with a startling clarity that they had risen, had put the chair aside, had finished something and were beginning something, sensing, especially in their touch, the secret contact of the chair's back, the time they took and their delay. A feeling like that which a novice gets when reading about the special composition of matter and anti-matter, about the splitting of the atom, or about the fourth dimension — a confused feeling of admiration and fatigue, or omnipotence and insignificance, of explicit vagueness and immortality. Finally, a feeling of the inexplicable uniqueness of man — of his needs and his potentialities. In one word, we would say: something apocalyptic, if such words did not scare us. They said good-night then, clasping one another's hand firmly, as if they were leaving for a battle, or as if they were renewing — with a clear consciousness now — the oath they had taken instinctually on other occasions under a momentarily social and incidentally individual need. And around the paper with the first nine signatures, shining white on the table, they could already see cyclical waves of air — white, sparkling white — widening endlessly, opening the four walls, bursting out, engraving the night and enlightening with repeated luminous circles the sleep of the big, trustworthy city and the world).

Athens, June, 1959   *(G.G.)*

cb

EXERCISES
(1950–1960)

Translated by Kimon Friar, Thanasis Maskaleris, Minas Savvas, John Stathatos, and by Gwendolyn MacEwen and Nikos Tsingos

---

THE STATUES

He turned the key in the door
to enter his house, to lie down.
Suddenly he remembered that he'd forgotten something.
It was late, he couldn't go back.

So, alone in the night,
with his hand on the key,
away from the street, away from his door,
the whole man, facing his fate,
turned into marble like the statues.

Yet the statues smile indifferently.

1953–1954   *(M.S.)*

DEADLY VICTORY

Alone at night, she rose noiselessly,
fearing her own footsteps.
She descended to the cellar to check on those noises
— from rats, from a spider, from time, from her brain? —
so that at last she could get some sleep.

As she descended, the wind blew out the lamp
and on both her cheeks she felt the upraised hairs of silence.

Next morning they found her in a heap under the stairs. She was
  smiling.
She had not confirmed anything. She had conquered.

1955–1956   (M.S.)

COURAGE OR IGNORANCE

He said: "The birds go against the wind
not because of anger or a spirit of struggle or excessive vitality.
No. Only out of vanity — in order not to ruffle their feathers."
                  The others were startled and silent
as if feeling guilty for not having thought of it,
uncomfortable because it might be true
guilty in their ability to believe it.
They bent their heads and, imperceptively, ruffled their hair.
Fortunately it had grown dark and no one saw the other's gesture,
not even the one who had spoken and who stood there
dignified, immaculately combed. At that moment
the moon stuck its ear on the windowpane.
The silence was now becoming perceptible. And they separated.

1950–1960   (T.M.)

AFTER THE FIRE

When it dawned, the silence was heavy amidst the smoking ruins.
Those who had wrestled with the fire all night
were now sleeping, weary and tranquil within their sweet
  submission,
others with the smile of a vague and aimless triumph.

Only he was awake. He was, in fact, avoiding sleep,
without knowing if he was the victor or the defeated,
guessing only vaguely that perhaps — perhaps
the only victory was this: his decision to learn which.

1955–1956   (M.S.)

THE UNJUST

Night. Only one look. A noiseless bullet.
The metallic shield of loneliness is pierced.
That roundness shattered.
And pride on its knees.

Beloved night. My beloved wound — he said.
The road, the sky, the stars — exist
in order to sink again. Only one look.

Outside of loneliness lurks the great danger
of loneliness — beloved danger:
to rival that other person and with justice on your side,
while the whole injustice of it is that justice also belongs to that
    other.

1955–1956   (M.S.)

A PROLETARIAN SPEAKER

He tried to speak; he faltered.
He repeated the same things; he stopped.
"That's all," he declared and placed his hand on the table.

His hand, steady, with a clear outline,
was a wide spatula. We could trust
in the words he had not said, and in his hands.

Outside the room, the light descended in a roar.

1955–1956   (M.S.)

INTERCHANGES

They took the plough to the field,
they brought the field into the house —
an endless interchange shaped
the meaning of things.

The woman changed places with the swallow,
she sat in the swallow's nest on the roof and warbled.
The swallow sat at the woman's loom and wove
stars, birds, flowers, fishing boats, and fish.

If only you knew how beautiful your mouth is
you would kiss me on the eyes that I might not see you.

July, 1955   (K.F.)

BEAUTY

Naked — she took her red handkerchief
and covered her eyes so as not to be seen,
in case fear would force them not to look. Silent and overbearing —
    maybe even afraid.
Within the darkness of her bound eyes
she may have even touched or even mixed the light; then she did not
    wake.

Under the garden wicker chair, her shoes remained
with the bare form of her feet. On the tree branch,
her white dress streamed, unfastening all her nudity.

She had hoped for this after death. The light of the garden
fluttered — I don't know how — like mockery, like applause.

1955–1956   (M.S.)

EPISODE

The rider remained on the plain, half-hidden in the grass.
At night the horse returned alone. It did not whinny.
It bowed its head before the wall of the house and wept with large
    tears.
At that moment lamps were brought into the dining room.

They all understood that a yellow, frozen moon was expiring in the
    garden
and expected a horrible shriek on the horizon. Nothing was heard.
Disappointed, they resumed with their eating, their cigarettes, their
    newspapers.
The rider was buried with a lot of formality the next day
and within a week the horse died.

1955–1956   (M.S.)

TO AN UNKNOWN DIRECTION

When he sensed her hand on his shoulder,
everything returned to its place in the sun,
silently, orderly, almost prearranged.

Well, his coat would have to go to the tailor;
he would remake his cape into a political overcoat,

he would be able to work more than eight hours
here and there, at Customs, in the Bank, in an Office.

At night he carved a cross on the table of the coffeehouse with his
    jackknife,
as if he had already died, as if his old expatriation
was his house, his door, his garden.

Her tranquil arm, lying on his neck, weighed
indispensable, accommodating, unguided
like his last day; because every death — he said —
is invisible and useless. He pulled off his cap
and saluted her shamelessly like a stranger; indeed, he even saluted
as if he were saluting his own death. Since then
we learned nothing about him — if he embarked again or if he
    drowned.

1955–1956   (M.S.)

NECESSARY EXPLANATION

There are certain stanzas — sometimes entire poems —
whose meaning not even I know. It's what I do not know
that holds me still. You were right to ask me. But don't ask me.
I don't know, I tell you.
                        The parallel lights
from the same center. The sound of water
falling in winter from an overbrimming drain pipe,
or the sound of a waterdrop as it falls
from a rose in a watered garden
slowly, slowly on a spring evening
like a bird's sobbing. I don't know
what this sound means; even so, I acknowledge it.
I've explained to you whatever else I know. I've not been neglectful.
But even these add to our lives. I would notice,
as she slept, how her knees formed an angle on the bedsheet —
It was not only a matter of love. This corner

was a ridge of tenderness, and the fragrance
of the bedsheet, of cleanliness, and of spring supplemented
that inexplicable thing I sought — in vain again — to explain to you.

1956–1957   (K.F.)

MATURITY

We knew him when he was dressed, austere, collected,
athletic and handsome, in a way. We all greeted him
quite naturally, possibly with a certain distrust
of the unbearable feeling weighing itself
in his half-closed eyes. Until, during a red sunset
in mid-August — a blazing, terrible summer —
he cast off all his clothes and stood there
stark naked, red all over, dyed with that
deep red of solitude and endlessness,
utterly skinned
like a magnificent ram hanging from the hook in the middle of the
    marketplace
with his diaphanous, exposed veins
showing the circulation of blood and God. Some man couldn't take
    it;
he threw a sackcloth over him and ran away. The old people spat on
    him.
The men took out their pistols and fired at him. The kids
stoned him. Only the women and the youths
hid their faces in their hands and knelt.

1956–1957   (G.M. & N.T.)

89

A MYOPIC CHILD

The other kids romped around the playground; their voices
rose up to the roofs of the quarter, also the "splock" of their ball
like a globular world, all joy and impertinence.

But he was reading the whole time, there in the spring window,
within a rectangle of bitter silence,
until he finally fell asleep on the window sill in the afternoon,
oblivious to the voices of those his own age
and to premature fears of his own superiority.

The glasses on his nose looked like
a little bike left leaning against a tree,
off in a far-flung, light-flooded countryside,
a bike of some child who had died.

1956–1957   (G.M. & N.T.)

A LIFE

Rigid, uncompromising throughout his entire life.
Towards the end he grew to fear this rigidity,
seeing it not as a virtue but a pose,
a punishing of others and, of course, himself.

Then he lay down in silence, slack and rigid
like a repentant line. A long coffin
lying across two common chairs
became a narrow bridge over his fears and suspicions.

1956–1957   (J.S.)

FULFILLMENT

That which we waited for as a justification of our lives
has now come. No trace of desire, memory or terror
is left in the center of our cells.
We are two hollow bodies thrown on the shore of night.
Later, as you were putting on your stockings, I noticed
that the bed had become a prehistoric animal petrified
in a position of copulation
stepping with its four dead feet on nothingness.

1950–1960   (T.M.)

A LONE MAN'S NIGHT

How sad the furniture in a lone man's room.
The table is an animal frozen stiff with cold,
the chair a child lost in a snowfilled forest,
the sofa a naked tree felled by the wind.

And yet in a little while a round, translucent silence
will be formed within there as in the glass-bottom bucket of a fishing
      boat,
and you, bent entirely over that hollow,
gaze through the glass at the diaphanous,
luminous sea-depths with their crystalline, deep-green crevices,
with their exotic sea vegetation, gaze
so long at the rose-colored, indifferent, enormous fishes
with their wide, noble movements, that you don't know
whether they are lying in ambush, taking shelter, or dreaming,
because their eyes are opened so wide they seem tightly closed.

But this is of no significance. Isn't it perhaps enough
that their movement is like beauty and like immobility?

March, 1957   (K.F.)

COUNTRY WOMAN

When she sensed that her hour had come, she called her two sons and
    made her will;
justly she divided the olive trees, the vineyard, the melon field, the
    cow, the donkey,
and then she invited her pregnant daughter-in law to make the
    candles for her burial.

From her straw mattress, the matriarch's eye supervised,
corrected this or that, watched her work, specified the shape and
    size,
gave her good advice, so they would know—she said—about the
    christenings also.

When that was finished, too, she closed her eyes, but since she
    couldn't die yet,
ordered them to light the candles. In their gentle glow
she saw her thin, dry hands, as powerful as those of the saints,
like dry trees that have yielded much fruit—rough hands
hewn by housekeeping and the field. At that moment
she loved her hands. She smiled remotely
and fell asleep like a girl of twenty. Her two daughters-in-law
folded their hands over their bellies
and remained staring at her with their young eyes wide-open and
    tearless.

Later they set the table, went to the doorway, and called their
    husbands for dinner.
The four candles lighted the large loaf of bread.
Now they would know, of course, about the christenings, too.

1957–1958   (K.F.)

92

ALWAYS SO

Every night, all things are shattered in the dark,
but the clamor from their collapse survives. This clamor
seems to reconstruct all things anew.
                                    And, in fact,
the next day, with the freshness of sunrise, amidst
the newly-built houses, within the lights
that reflect the large white and yellow public squares, life stands
before unshaven time as a woman stands before a man,
waiting silently to be kissed and to be sung
and then to give birth and to sing alone.

January–February, 1958   (M.S.)

CONTRADICTIONS

One night when he seemed a little drunk he said in a funny tone of
        voice:
"I often hold the stars in my palm by the end of their rays
like the strings of thousands of kites,
feeling in all my nerves the counter-thrust of their every motion,
their inclinations, the tension of their distances
and that cold calm found on the highest plane of night,
and sharp tang of oxygen and the throbs of their fringed tails."

With that he stopped, as though holding back the most important
        point.
Then, honestly, we examined on his naked upper arm, the stigmata
        of stars,
strange marks made by the mad vibrations of a burning needle,
things like triremes, numbers, mermaids,
and we understood that he'd been imprisoned for years
and perhaps still was.

But oh no,
you can't say we were the metal bars of his prison,
nor that we foresaw the nature of his freedom.

January–February, 1958   *(G.M. & N.T.)*

HARVEST OF THE VOID

Tall plane trees, muscular torsos of coolness.
The shade is not intended to hide anything. Daring light, daring
    shade—
useless daring—to confront what?—
simplicity breathes in the air.

People sit under the trees,
they dine on small wooden tables, they talk,
they do not suspect the magnitude covering them, the magnitude
that regulates their innocent gestures. Toward evening
someone sang (drunk perhaps). The plane trees
moved in a silent procession toward the horizon.
The area emptied. And the waiter, with his white apron,
appeared for a moment at a distance, in the crimson sunset,
holding in a priestly fashion the tray with empty glasses.

August–September, 1958   *(M.S.)*

NOON

A white horse dissected in two by the blue shadow of a cypress tree.
Someone shouted further up. (Who was it?)
I don't know—he was shouting—I don't know, life is powerful like a
    fist in the stomach.

A naked man with a golden knife between his teeth passed by.

Behind the horns of the bulls, a fire, like a rosebush, smoked.

August–September, 1958   (M.S.)

WONDER

Before going to bed, he placed his watch under his pillow.
Then he went to sleep. The wind outside was blowing. You
who know the wondrous succession of the slightest movements,
you will understand. A man, his watch, the wind. Nothing more.

Samos, August–September, 1958   (M.S.)

GREEK CART-DRIVERS

Late, about midday, after they've sold their produce
at the market—vegetables, grapes, pears—
they return with their carts along the seaside road
toward their small, distant fields—
sweat-drenched, they and their horses,
with their paper money tied in their handkerchiefs
and the coins jingling in their pockets,
foolish, exhausted, almost wild
with anger at an unknown delay and injustice,
with the clumps of their coarse hair, all dust and sweat,
matted beneath their caps.

But when they turn off the public road, when they reach
the first deserted sandy beach, they unharness their horses,
undress hurriedly, throw their clothes onto the rocks
and go into the sea to wash their horses.

And then, drenched, all naked and all golden, men and horses
glistened in the sun with a lofty nobility,
energetic and all-powerful, as though they had stepped out
of very ancient myths. The youngest cart-driver,
just eighteen, gleaming all over in the midday, naked, riding his
    horse, galloped off in the sea
while a white cloud marked his shadow in the blue.

And at the seashore, the carts, all golden, too,
shone in the circular reflections of their wheels
like glorious chariots in ancient Greek races
that stopped here, and from here will begin again.

Samos, August-September, 1958   (K.F.)

QUESTION

A man fades at the distant end of the street
slowly, silently. What does he seek
in the neighborhood up there when twilight vanishes,
when the round mirrors of the parked bicycles
throw their reflections on the empty public-square?
A woman contemplates by a darkened window.
An older woman fetches water from a well.
A tiny spider sits on her water-pitcher. Explain to me:
what do they all want? Who will drink the dark water? As night
falls, they bend silently over the well. . . . How did
a wrinkled face get into the well,
the wet rope, the tiny spider
on the pitcher and the shadow of the pitcher
and the woman by the window and the man who walks
for years and years? Explain to me. Shortly
the lights will be turned on. Besieged houses. Tell me.

The moon will pull its knife over the well.
No one saw us. Explain to me. This hanged man
sways beautifully in the air, like an infant in its cradle—
is it the same swaying then? The rope creaks and asks. Tell me.

August–September, 1958   (M.S.)

ABSTRACTED PAINTER

A painter one afternoon drew a train.
The last carriage cut away from the paper
and returned to the carbarn all by itself.

Precisely in that carriage sat the artist.

June, 1959   (K.F.)

RETURN OF A DESERTER

He'd felt uneasy these last days, as though he were a sentry who'd
        deserted,
leaving the town unguarded. For a long time
he feared they would discover his defection,
that the town might have fallen by his fault. A deserter,
hiding among the bushes, he could not see the walls,
only imagine frightful consequences for the unguarded citizens
and above all for himself. Later, he learned
that the town had not fallen, that no one had noticed his absence.
They did not even search for him. His name was not included
in the lists of survivors, lost or missing.
A great stillness spread uselessly around him. And now,
it was precisely that which tortured him—the stillness
he had dreamt of. At dusk, he sensed around the house
thousands of shadows sliding like stray cats
among the thorns in the deserted playing field; and in the wardrobe

he sensed his hanging, flabby suits like the cast-off clothing of
    corpses. Then
he tightened the cartridge belts crosswise over his chest
as though securing a bundle of his most precious possessions
and turned up at the sentry post exactly on time.

May–June, 1959   (J.S.)

MOMENT

A downtrodden sailor's quarter. The light globes sleepy.
Shabby beer pubs strung out in a row like poverty-stricken women
waiting patiently in front of the County Hospital.
The street is dark. Everyone planned to sleep early. But suddenly
the beer pubs lit up to their very last chairs
from the pure white laughter of a young man. And immediately
    afterwards
was heard the endless, uniform, unconquerable sea.

May, 1960   (K.F.)

THERAPY

A historic weariness had spread over the afternoon
like the hide of an animal spread out in the invalid's room.
The invalid always remained in bed. His fever had fallen.
A smell of a sweat-drenched undershirt and alcohol. This hide
was taken from an animal skinned alive (that is what he claimed).
The fur, obedient, neutral, dead; but from the other, the bare side,
the dehydrated pain still remained, flattened out. He insisted on
    this:
the animal had been alive when it was skinned. And when at last
he placed his naked feet there, its hair stood on end,
the hide curved up and shaped a back, and the invalid

tore through the corridor astride the animal's back, whizzed
through the kitchen, dashed out into the yard, into the road,
and the pots boomed behind him like metal drums

May, 1960   (K.F.)

HUNTERS

An autumn strewn with broken, chesnut-coloured branches
and the yellow down of shot birds. The hunters
left the forest years behind them,
emptied their haversacks upon the kitchen table and were gone.
That evening, they did not come back to eat. Why, then,
so many preparations — cartridges, powder, shot,
the tiresome cleaning of guns, the early morning start,
and in such damp? By midnight they were back.
No one expected them, everyone was asleep.
The whole house, even the bedroom, smelt unbearably
of some fine meal they had not tasted.
As they undressed, a tiny golden feather
drifted out silently from the hair on their chest.

May, 1960   (J.S.)

COINCIDENTALLY

Exchanges and repayments. We cheated no one.
Nor were we cheated — no. In a bird's flight
we saw our history writ clear.

Later, of course, we felt the need as always
for bread and salt, a quiet woman's smile,

to finish our night's sleep
in an improvised house, with three strange dogs
which barked all night guarding the house, not us.

July–August, 1960   (J.S.)

THE USEFULNESS OF ART

It was not only those that came of themselves,
those that were, the inevitable, but also the others,
those he himself added, those he wanted or the others wanted,
those he chose, and the manner in which they multiplied or were
    added.

And perhaps these last were particularly his,
that continued as arrested or diffused things,
presenting a story or a face to the immobile, like a transparent
    windowpane
that suddenly thickens when darkness comes and turns into a mirror,
presenting noble performances out of unsuspecting events,
presenting their forms and their phantoms, presenting
the interior of nocturnal rooms illuminated by lamps or by a bouquet
    of flowers,
or by anger or privation or poverty. Presenting
things known and unknown, known in another way,
in a sequence, even though constrained in a value at least
    interchangeable.

1956–1957   (K.F.)

PARENTHESES II
(1950–1961)

Translated by Edmund Keeley

HANDS

Often hands are like faces
or like whole bodies. These hands
remain listless in the premature spring,
they sneeze, cough, complain, grow silent,
like two old men on their stools, unbuttoned,
with their genitals withered in the sun.

Opposite, a woman suckles her infant.
Her hands, though motionless, are
two naked runners in a large marble arena.

(E.K.)

NOCTURNAL

Night undresses you. Her hands tremble.
All naked, your body shines in the shadows.

That wise zero that squeezed our necks
is suddenly cut in two
like a boiled egg sliced by a knife.

(E.K.)

INCENSE

He gazed at the morning through the windowpanes. He felt with
    precision
that the blue rolls along the bird's skin or the cloud's.
He suspected that the same sense of touch was at the tree's disposal
    also.
The smoke emerged from the chimneys as though confessing the
    secret
of heat in the rooms that were still closed.

In this way, every morning, all the houses smoke.
And the men, emerging early for work,
light up their cigarettes while still on the threshold, as though
    remembering
some unknown, unapproachable deity entirely their own.

(E.K.)

A WREATH

Your face was hidden in the leaves.
I cut the leaves one by one to get near you.
When I cut the last leaf, you were gone. Then
out of the cut leaves I wove a wreath. I didn't have
anyone to give it to. I hung it on my forehead.

(E.K.)

MESSAGE

The plumber in his blue overalls on the ladder.
The soles of his feet broad. The pipes of the heating stove
shine on the floor like the trunks of trees
from a silver forest. Up there, against the wall,
he lit his cigarette. His hammer strikes
among small red sparks. What business did we have
putting in a heating stove at this point? Any day now
summer will be here. And the chickens have already begun to lay
some sturdy blue eggs beside the wine barrel and the plough.

1950–1961

(E.K.)

THE PRISON TREE AND THE WOMEN

(1962)

Translated by Kimon Friar

(Evening has fallen. The bell for silence has rung some time ago. The women, gathered in the hall, in the dark, are not yet asleep. The beds of boards with their sheets glimmer indistinctly. Before going to bed, the women sit in a semicircle on the ground, as though around an invisible well, and converse softly, almost inaudibly. Though they remain there motionless, they seem to be moving rhythmically as in the chorus of an ancient tragedy. Helen does not speak. She lets her long black hair down over her shoulders and stands before the window with its iron grille.)

ALL THE
    WOMEN:
A walled-in yard, a tree, a bit of sun in the morn-
    ing hours on the wall—
this tree is our diary, our friend, our postman, our
    child,

FIRST
    WOMAN:
at times, indeed, our husband—but often

SECOND:
often, very often—our husband; with it we take
    part in time,

THIRD:
we take part in duration and in memory,

FOURTH:
and also in what we call alteration and renewal.
    This tree
in the middle of a closed and empty space
insists on existing, insists
on noticing, distinguishing, responding;

FIFTH:
bound down, it insists on rising upwards;

FOURTH:
severed into four seasons, on uniting the seasons
    and the landscapes;

FIRST:
sometimes it looks in our stead beyond the wall,

THIRD:
sucks up the voice of the child selling matches,

SECOND:	the voice of the roving iceman,
FOURTH:	the silence of a woman who bought five roses from the corner flower stall,
FIFTH:	the footsteps of a man reading his newspaper on the sidewalk;

ALL:	distinct are the colors of so many different hours, many are their colors, of course, throughout the length of the day,
FIRST:	and the stars throughout the length of the night — strange stars, toothed wheels, pentagrams, wagons, peaceful animals, and the two ox-carts of the clouds come to a halt at the castle gate of the moon —

THIRD:	there was no one sitting in the moon;
SECOND:	perhaps he was sleeping, perhaps he was pretending to be asleep;
FIRST:	the keys were heard in the great corridor,
FIFTH:	a white thrust of a knife in the darkness,

FOURTH:	and to be or not to be was so simple, almost painless, almost insignificant. This simplicity was taught us by this tree — this is our knowledge,

ALL:	this is our quiet courage; to be away, to wait, or not to wait — the silent delight of offering ourselves even when others forget it or do not even know of it —

FIRST:	simple, humble, noble understanding,
SECOND:	like a stone in the wall of a house,
THIRD:	like a log in the fire,
FIFTH:	like a piece of glass in the window frame; this modest glass, without pride, itself unseen, helps others to see,

THIRD:	makes things clear, protects from the wind,
SECOND:	protects from the cold, allows the light to penetrate and the heat also—

FOURTH:	a delicate, diaphanous loneliness that protects from
	    loneliness,
	a small silence between two bitter words—
	you have time to reflect—the second bitter word
	    was never uttered;

ALL:	the air clears, the eye clears, it clears— a silent understanding, a distant and close understanding—
FOURTH:	this is our most modest grandeur, and we find no difficulty in uttering this word, though we fall silent here, stopped, locked, and withdrawn from events,
FIRST:	barred from things outside. But the tree observes and looks toward the outside in our stead, and afterwards
ALL:	the tree is transplanted within us—
FIFTH:	Many times, at the hour of sleep, lying down, we remain upright, in the position of this tree—perhaps this tree will not let us rest,
FIRST:	will not let us forget,
FOURTH:	will not let us die.
FIFTH:	This tree keeps vigil without effort or ostentation.
FIRST:	Its most delicate branches become entwined with our fingers;
SECOND:	sometimes, when we are eating, a yellow leaf chances to fall beside the bread from Maria's hands—and none of us is surprised;
FIFTH:	at other times again a little green branch happens to flutter down from the black kerchief of Aunt Kóstena

SECOND:	or a white blossom falls from Ismíni's eyes
	into the communal pot — and we are not surprised,
ALL:	we push aside that flower with our spoons
	and go on with our meal in silence,
FOURTH:	but now we know with certainty
	that spring is on its way, that there are many stars,
	many trees,
FIFTH:	many people, much grief, much courage beyond
	the walls,
THIRD:	many walls behind the walls,
FIRST:	and much sky above the walls,
THIRD:	and hope? and hope?
ALL:	Do not speak — be silent, keep still.
THIRD:	Fear is the single tap of an invisible finger on the
	wall,
	a spider beneath a heap of leaves,
	a thud — they are nailing up the door — they are
	nailing us —
FIRST:	yes, the thud — they are hammering a nail outside
	the door, to hang . . .
THIRD:	Death is hammering a nail on the door — it is wait-
	ing, there —
	the nail grows rusty from the dampness — it is
	waiting
FIRST:	for them to hang up garlands of flowers on the First
	of May — for May is approaching;
THIRD:	the flowers conceal the nail, but it is under the
	flowers —
SECOND:	And how else can they hang the garlands? Be
	quiet.
THIRD:	And underneath the garlands, the rusted nail — the
	blackened blood —
ALL:	This is not our May; the May we know
	has long strides, drums and smoke and flags,

THIRD: and blood blackened in the shadows cast by the
             flags—

FOURTH: living veins branching out on the flags—a huge
             body
             above the shadow of Death—it is prow-shaped

FIFTH: as it cuts through the air—an extremely tall mast—

FIRST: and the rope ladder hanging from the sun—

SECOND: a sea smell—brine and musk geraniums—can't you
             feel
             the tingling about your nostrils—two small semicir-
             cles of salt?

ALL: It is the world's odor—the great circle, the incalcu-
             lable one—

FOURTH: the tingling, yes, around your nostrils as though
             you were about to sneeze, looking straight into the
             sun—don't you feel it?

FIRST: It's the flags—they flap in the air as though large
             door-shutters were opening wide—

THIRD: as we sit here, behind the walls, without flags,

ALL: we with our duties, behind the walls,
             transforming the motionless tree into thousands of
             fluttering leaves,
             transforming the separate movements into an indi-
             visible simplicity,
             almost into an eternity.

FIRST: Look, Helen
             is sitting at the window, looking far away,
             looking at the blue haze that rises from the garden
             stones,
             beating her finger lightly on the window grilles—
             a deep, a silent sound—a small rhythm, our own—

ALL: this is the knocking you hear—listen, listen;

FIRST: the sound penetrates the irons, the stones,

SECOND: a springtime pulse in a vein of iron, in a vein of
             stone,

FIFTH: a small wireless set, hidden away, gives the signal—

THIRD: and we, entangled amid the boughs of darkness,
                  glued with our elbows
              to the sides of silence, in the dampness of night,
              waiting for the answer—what answer?—waiting—

ALL: And the answer comes

SECOND: at times from the last bird of twilight,
FIFTH: at times from a cricket that saws the night,
FIRST: at times from a star that repeats, "I am coming, I
                  am coming, I am coming,"

THIRD: at times from a torn love letter which a wind sud-
                  denly tosses in the street—

FOURTH: and we hear within and without—this is another
                  year together with the year,
              with doors and windows multiplied,

THIRD: and with walls multiplied,

FOURTH: yes, and with walls—why not?—with many
                  windows,
FIRST: and suddenly the doorknob shines like a large drop
                  of water,
SECOND: and a curved landscape shines in the waterdrop,
THIRD: and the naked jawbone of a horse shines inside it
                  there.

ALL: Be quiet, keep still. Look, Helen's back,
              turned towards us is a hillock with small cypress
                  trees,

FIFTH:	there a flock of white sheep ascends — the night is growing white,
FIRST.	it's because the stars are appearing,
SECOND:	it's because we are waiting,
THIRD:	it's because spring is coming again — why is it coming? When day breaks we stand in line again, one by one, before the illuminated square of the wall,
FOURTH:	patiently, silently, in an orderly fashion,
THIRD:	one by one, each in her turn — each one alone,
FOURTH:	one by one, and all together, scooping up a little sunshine
ALL:	one by one, submissively, although the shadows of us all penetrate, one into the other, and crisscross on the ground in lozenges of light and dark, until they merge into an only well. Opposite the well, the tree still stands, erect again, in our stead.
FIRST:	And we fall silent and listen leaf by leaf, to the far distance, and further still,
SECOND:	and in Marie's hair, green leaves poke out — until we are afraid of being betrayed, of the keys jangling at the waist of the prison guard, of a water glass falling from on high and smashing on the tiles,
ALL:	of words being heard which we repressed — perhaps this is why the sparrows walk so awkwardly when, at times, they come down to earth.

(The women have gone to bed. Beyond the walls and in the ward there are many stars, indescribably many stars, like toothed wheels, like pentagrams, like wagons, like quiet animals, like birds, like wide leaves — and they all shine so that Helen is unable to sleep. She covers her face then with her long black hair, while opposite, flashing with all its leaves, in the middle of the world, that solitary tree and its shadow mounts up the wall of the jail like an enormous staircase. Anyone can climb it. And of course it was spring.)

Prague, September, 1962   *(K.F.)*

∾

TESTIMONIES I
(1957–1963)

Translated by Kimon Friar

DANGER OUTSTRIPPED

Every so often a star or a voice
falls to such a great depth that he holds himself
by the balcony railing or by a hand
(if a hand can be found) for fear of sinking into himself.

His most trusted hand is his other hand,
but his hands thus enclose him within a circle.
He can't endure this, and so stretches out his hands
as though to embrace someone, or to balance himself.

And thus, like a tightrope walker, looking straight before him,
he holds himself upright above his own depth.

Athens, September, 1956   *(K.F.)*

NEW VICTORY

So many battles, so many wounds, so many honorable defeats and
     victories,
so many medals — they filled his chest, weighed upon him heavily,
hurt his eyes with their glitter. He became terrified
lest this would be the only light that might illuminate
the wooden stairs at night when he returned home. He undressed,
put away his uniform in the closet, the medals in their cases,

and went to enlist as a volunteer—as a simple soldier.
No one recognized him. Perhaps that new smile of his
might bring him to the age level of the other volunteers.

1957–1963   (K.F.)

REMEMBRANCE

A warm odor remained in the armpits of her coat,
her coat in the hall rack, like a drawn curtain.
Whatever was happening now was of another time. The light
      changed faces,
all of them unfamiliar. And if anyone tried to enter the house,
that empty coat slowly and bitterfully raised its arms
and silently closed the door again.

Athens, December, 1958   (K.F.)

BUILDERS

Have you seen those who build out of instinct
and those who build professionally
and the third who build to avenge themselves against death
and those who build consciously, with resolution?

Both these and others stop from time to time,
wipe their plastered hands on their blue jeans,
wipe away their sweat, and weep.
They do not wipe their eyes.

In this way, moreover, the mortar knits better.
And this proceeds much beyond their purpose.

114

Because of this, all builders dream at night
of that unknown, that invisible "beyond,"
and every morning they build the "here" a bit better,

Athens, 1958   (K.F.)

THE AUDIBLE AND THE INAUDIBLE

An abrupt, unexpected movement; his hand
clutched his wound, to stanch the blood,
though we had not heard a single shot
nor a bullet whistling. After a while
he dropped his hand and smiled;
but again he placed his palm slowly
on the same place. Then he took out his wallet,
paid the waiter politely, and left.
It was then the coffee cup cracked by itself.
This at least we heard quite clearly.

Athens, May, 1960   (K.F.)

HONEST CONFRONTATION

All night long they talked, raged, wrangled,
strove with passion and sincerity to find a compromise
or some separation; humbled and were humbled; regretted
the time lost—the fools; at last they cast off their clothes
and stood there, beautiful, naked, humiliated, defenseless. Dawn
    was breaking.
From the roof opposite, a flock of birds took wing
as though some gambler had finally cast into the air a marked pack of
    cards.

Thus, without arguments, justifications, or assurances,
day ascended from the hills with the cruel pride of action.

Athens, May, 1960   (K.F.)

CONFORMITY

This bronze statue had its place in the midst of winter;
this heroic stride of the horse as though it were leaping over
powerful, contrary winds; even the somewhat pompous
and haughty air of the horseman matched well enough
with the downpours, the bolting clouds, and the storms
when lightning flashes changed the reins into two steadfast,
      narrow flames
until you couldn't tell whether the howling rose out of the wind
      along the desolate avenues
or out of the statue's open mouth. But now
with this spring, relaxed, facilitated acquiescent,
with this forgetful, this good-tempered light (perhaps out of timidity
      already
or exhausted from the heat) that with improvised sunrays
links up one leaf with another,
one tree with another or with houses,
one glance with another or with mouths — the attitude
of this statue had now become unbearable, provocative, almost
      unseemly,
so much so that the bronze horseman himself dismounted,
called three unemployed who were waiting in the park with
      pickaxes,
and began, perspiring and satisfied, to tear down his statue.

Athens, May, 1960   (K.F.)

FOR GREATER ACCURACY

He would always return to the same themes. One and one — he kept
  repeating
simply, in order to convince himself — make two. Two and two: four.
  But then,
before he could make this addition, the slightest interval
would intervene, a slight breath, and then he felt the need
to add even this, for greater accuracy — a breath,
and behind its vapor the same number could be discerned
as though written on a door or on the sides of a ship,
or like a star behind a light veil of mist at that quivering hour,
so very beautiful, between dusk and night.

Athens, May, 1960   (K.F.)

PERSPECTIVE

Our houses are built on other, straightlined houses, made of marble,
and these on other houses. Their foundations
are supported on the heads of upright armless statues.
And so, no matter how much lower our huts roost in the fields under
  the olive trees,
small, grimy with smoke, with only a water pitcher by the door,
you imagine you are living high up, that all about you the air shines,
or at times you imagine you are outside the houses, that you have
no house at all, that you are walking naked,
alone, under a sky startlingly azure or white,
and a statue, now and then, leans his hand lightly on your shoulder.

Athens, January 1962   (K.F.)

117

THE IDIOT

The wagon had stopped, facing from the sea,
loaded with six iron barrels, red,
and another one in an astonishing green. The horse
browsed in the meadow. The wagon driver
was drinking in the tavern. The island's idiot
stood by the breakwater and shouted:
"With this green I'll conquer you!"
And he pointed to the seventh barrel, without knowing
what it contained or to whom it belonged.

Samos, January, 1962   (K.F.)

SILENT AGREEMENT

Two of them were looking at the large wall map.
The third was looking out of the window.
Afterwards the two took the window
and fitted it over the map.
The third remained by the empty window.

When the two happened to turn toward the third,
he was now a map hanging
in the sky. The wind blew on him
and now and again the paper crackled at the edges.

Then the three agreed without any discussion
on the significance of music and metamorphosis.

Samos, January, 1962   (K.F.)

THE END OF A DAY

Above the closed day only this star remained,
like the knot on a string tied around a sack
deep, soft, of uncertain bulk. What could there possibly be
in that sack? What selection could you make? You'd have to cut
the knot with your teeth or fingernails. Your ten fingers
become silver, almost gold. Is it this, then, that was in the sack?

Athens, February, 1962   (K.F.)

KNOWLEDGE OF THE AMBIGUOUS

When the clock struck at a goodly distance from his window,
he knew that night had fallen—not from the number of times it
    struck—
he didn't even count them—but from the quality of the sound. He
    knew,
from the somewhat moist fragrance of the bedsheets, that it was
    spring.
He even knew, from the manner in which a woman took off her
    shoes
under the table with its five glasses, that she was weary.
This he knew particularly from the bearing of the fifth glass,
from its tempered glow—so much weariness, wonderful, proud,
    deathless.

Athens, February, 1962   (K.F.)

THE THIEF

A thief—truly a thief, insignificant, a marked man; he ambushes
men and women, old people and children, leaves, windows, lamps,
old guitars, sewing machines, dry branches, himself. He was always
    stealing
some posture of theirs, some expression, the cigarette butts they
    throw in the street,
their clothes when they undress to make love, their thoughts,
their unknown shapes, what belongs to them, to him, and he would
    make
large, strange bouquets of flowers or plant them in pots. Now,
in the neighborhood florist shop, behind the windows, we would see
    him
spraying the large roses, the dahlias, the carnations,
without selling them or even giving them away—an eccentric thief,
a decadent prince in his greenhouse. Only his face,
pale, could be singled out among the towering lilies,
like a dead man in his glass coffin. Even so,
in the cold of winter this flowershop with its unsold flowers
always gave us the impression of an eternal spring; even though we
    learned later
that all these flowers were made of paper, smeared
with red and yellow paint—mostly red—in various hues.

(1957–1963)   *(K.F.)*

UNDER OBLIVION

The only tangible thing of his that remained was his coat.
They hung it there, in the large closet. It was forgotten,
cramped far back by our own summer or winter clothing,

new ones every year for our new needs. Until,
one day, it caught our eye — perhaps because of its strange color,
perhaps because of its old-fashioned cut. On its buttons
three round, similar landscapes remained.
the firing wall with four bullet holes, and our remorse everywhere.

Athens, February, 1962   (K.F.)

MISCONSTRUCTIONS

The first drops of rain struck the sea. Being young, they didn't
    mind.
Though their hair and clothes were drenched, they laughed. At last
they opened their umbrellas — a whole forest of umbrellas,
blue, yellow, violet, but above all black,
the sea for background, and a boat in the distance
lightly leaping from umbrella to umbrella. He liked that much
    better,
as though the umbrellas were not made for the rain
but the rain for the umbrellas. Many years ago — how many? —
and how could he simply be an onlooker and yet be young,
always an onlooker, observing himself, and always young —
without an umbrella, in the rain, a few feet away,
changing his distance under the necessity for perspective,
his physical distance, alone in this distant happiness of his?

Athens, March, 1962   (K.F.)

KNOCKING

Water, salt, and the sun devour houses bit by bit.
One day, where men and windows once stood, only drenched stones
    remain
and a statue face down on the earth. The doors, alone,
voyage on the sea, stiff, unpracticed, clumsy. At times toward
    sunset,
you can see them glittering on the waters, flat, shut forever. The
    fishermen
do not look at them. From an early hour they sit in their houses
    before the lamp,
hearing the fishes gliding in the cracks of their bodies,
hearing the sea knocking on them with a thousand hands (all
    unknown),
and then they fall asleep with shells entangled in their hair.
Suddenly they hear knocking on these doors, and awaken.

Samos, 1962   *(K.F.)*

ANCIENT AMPHITHEATER

When toward noon a Greek youth stood in the center
of an ancient amphitheater, unsuspecting, and yet as handsome
    as they had been,
he let out a shout (not of admiration, for he felt
no admiration at all, and even if he had,
would certainly not have shown it), a simple shout,
perhaps from the untamed joy of his youth
or simply to try out the acoustics of the place. Opposite,
high above the precipitous mountain, the echo answered —
the Greek echo, which does not imitate or repeat
but simply continues to a height immeasurable,
the eternal cry of the dithyramb.

Delphi, March, 1962   *(K.F.)*

UNTIL DAYBREAK

She was running in the field with the tall nettles,
Behind her, large clocks and bells were shouting.
Then a kettledrum, then a second one—she ran on;
many kettledrums at midnight; her blood
flowed out of her hands and feet; she panted;
stumbled somewhere and fell; her onrush stopped,
and her fear also; only the tranquil wonder:
what could have been the obstacle? . . . curiosity almost.

Thus fallen to earth, she groped with all her limbs
then lifted up the amputated head of a statue.
She wiped its eyes; the clocks stopped;
the bells and drums stopped. Day was breaking.
This thing she held like an infant in her hands
was her own face. From its lips flowed
a thread of milk dully glowing in the dawn.

Delphi, March, 1962   (K.F.)

A TREE

This tree had taken root in the far side of the garden,
tall, slender, solitary—perhaps its height
betrayed a secret idea of intrusion. It never produced
either fruit or flower, only a long shadow that split the garden in
    two,
and a measurement not applicable to the stooped, laden trees.
Every evening, when the glorious sunset was fading,
a strange, orange bird roosted silently in its foliage
like its only fruit—a small golden bell
in a green, enormous belfry. When the tree was cut down,
this bird flew above it with small, savage cries,
describing circles in the air, describing in the sunset

the inexhaustible shape of the tree, and this small bell
rang invisibly on high, and even higher than the tree's original
     height.

Samos, June, 1963   (K.F.)

PROCESS

Day by day he disarmed himself. First he stripped off his clothing,
a little later his underwear, then later his skin,
and finally his flesh and bones until in the end
only this simple, warm, limpid essence remained
which indiscernably and without hands he shaped
into small jars, poems and men.
And most likely he was one of these things.

1957–1963   (K.F.)

ASCENT

He sat for days in a stranger's field, always planning
to climb up the fig tree secretly one day and gaze
at the world from high up, with a leaf's sensation
or that of a bird's, but always someone would pass by,
and so he always kept putting it off.
                              One twilight
he looked carefully about him — not a soul — and clambered up
to the highest branch. It was then
voices were heard among the bushes: "What are you doing up
     there?"

Loud voices, and he answered: "A fig,
there was a last fig here." The branch broke.
They raised him up. His right hand was tightly clenched
When they forced his fingers open, they found nothing.

Samos, August 1963   (K.F.)

STONES

Days come and go without haste, without surprises.
Stones become drenched with light and memory.
Someone sets a stone for a pillow.
Another, before swimming, leaves his clothes under a stone
so that the wind won't take them. Another uses a stone for a stool
or as a boundary mark on his farm, the cemetery, the sheepfold, the
        forest.

Late, after sunset, when you've returned home,
whatever stone from the seashore you place on your table
becomes a statuette—a small Nike or the hound of Artemis,
and this stone, on which a young man at noon leaned his feet,
is a Patroclos, with shadowed, closed eyelashes.

Samos, August 1963   (K.F.)

PRIVATE PLACE

The fisherman took his gear and left.
The woman stood by the door.
She gazed at the misty dawn.
A bit of rose on the horizon is painful.
Behind her back she heard the breathing
of the dark house with its washtub and broom.

She heard the small wheels of the plates
rolling on the air. She turned back inside,
took the large scissors from the table
and began cutting her fingernails with care.
Then she gathered her nails into a little hillock
and looked for some place to hide them, but couldn't find one.
And if her husband or children should come across them one day?

Samos, August, 1963   *(K.F.)*

REMORSE

At noon they spread their lunch on cool vineleaves —
olives, bread, tomatoes, salt — hungry,
they didn't hear or see anything, they chewed. Only the stranger
was not hungry and did not eat, but gazed
at the field steaming in the sun, embittered
because he was not hungry. Then he took his jacknife, which had
        never cut bread,
and on the bark of a fig tree carved a large hand.

Perhaps this empty hand would later be able to hold
the entire vineyard with its vintagers and their straw hats.

Samos, August, 1963   *(K.F.)*

PLASTER MODEL

When he closed his eyes he could remember nothing of that
        summer,
only a golden haze and his ring warm on his finger,
but still more the naked, broad, sunburnt shoulders of a young
        farmer
whom he managed partly to see behind the willows — at two in the
        afternoon —

as he was returning from the sea—an odor of burnt grass everywhere.
At that very moment the crickets shrilled, and a ship's siren shrilled.
Statues, of course, are made much later.

Samos, August, 1963   (K.F.)

MOMENT OF CONTRITION

They sieved the beach sand and loaded the wagons,
dripping with sweat in the burning heat. Past noon,
they undressed, mounted their horses, and plunged into the sea,
blackened by the hair on their bodies, gold in the searing sun. A
    handsome youth
uttered a cry and dropped his hand on his groin. The others
sped to him, lifted him on their arms, laid him on the sand,
and looked at him silently, with awe, until one of them
reverently took the hand away from the groin,
and then all in a circle around him made the sign of the cross.
The horses, drenched, all-golden, sniffed at the far horizon.

Samos, August, 1963   (K.F.)

MORNING

She opened the window shutters, spread the bedsheets on the
    windowsill, saw the day.
A bird stared her in the eyes. "I am alone," she whispered.
"I am alive." She went back into the room. The mirror too is a
    window.
If I leap from here, I shall fall into my hands.

Samos, August, 1963   (K.F.)

SUMMER

He strolled from one end of the beach to the other, his entire body
    glowing
in the glory of the sun and his youth. Now and then he would plunge
    into the sea
until his skin was burnished to brick-red and gold. Admiring
    whispers followed him everywhere
from men and women both. A few feet behind him a small girl from
    the village followed, carrying his clothes devoutly,
but always at a distance — she wouldn't raise her eyes to look at
    him — a bit angry,
yet happy in her devotion. Once, they had quarelled,
and then he had forbidden her to carry his clothes. She had
thrown them on the sand and, keeping only his sandals,
had tucked them under both armpits, run away and vanished,
leaving in the blazing sun the small awkward cloud from her bare
    feet.

Samos, August, 1963   *(K.F.)*

SCRUTINY

An old blind woman was sitting on her doorstep by the street.
    Afternoon.
At her right, the other woman, much younger, sitting in a chair a
    little further off,
felt free; she could gaze on the passers-by with immunity,
boys and girls returning half naked from the seaside,
and she could rivet her glance on any part of their bodies she pleased.
    Suddenly
she felt a hole in her left shoulder
from which everything within her was being watched. Wasn't
the old woman blind after all?

Samos, August, 1963   *(K.F.)*

ALMOST A CONJUROR

From a distance, he dims the lamp, moves chairs
without touching them. Tired, he takes off his hat and fans himself.
Then, with a gliding movement, he produces three playing cards
from the side of his ear. He dissolves a green, painkilling star
in a glass of water, stirring it with a silver teaspoon.
He drinks the water, and the spoon becomes transparent.
A goldfish can be seen swimming in his chest.
Then, exhausted, he lies down on the couch and closes his eyes.
"I have a bird in my head," he says. "I can't make it come out."
The shadows of two vast wings fill the room.

Samos, August 1963   *(K.F.)*

NEED OF PROOF

He hung up his coat on the clothes rack in the corridor.
The house was agreeable, tidied up, well heated,
as though it had been transported into another time. The silent
    objects,
chairs, sofas, picture frames, tea cups,
obliquely observed the ease of his movement, but so intently
that he himself became aware of it. Then,
under the cancelled accounts in his expense book,
he tried to sketch the glass saltshaker,
attempting to catch a representation of its transparency—a proof,
at least in a sketch, of the usefulness of his freedom.

1957–1963   *(K.F.)*

ﭼ

TWELVE POEMS FOR CAVAFIS
(1963)

Translated by Kimon Friar

I. THE POET'S SPACE

The black carved desk, the two silver candlesticks,
his red pipe. He sits, almost invisible, in his armchair,
keeping the window always at his back. Behind his glasses,
enormous and circumspect, he scrutinizes whatever young man he's
    talking with
and whom he's bathed in light, while he himself remains hidden
    behind his words,
behind history, behind persons of his own creation, distant and
    invulnerable,
ensnaring the attention of others with the delicate reflections
of the sapphire he wears on his finger and, thoroughly prepared,
savors the expressions of the foolish adolescents the moment
they moisten their lips with their tongues admiringly. And he,
cunning, voracious, carnal, the great innocent,
wavers with his whole being between the yes and the no, desire and
    repentance,
like a scale in the hand of God,
while the light from the window behind him
sets on his head a crown of forgiveness and saintliness.
"If poetry cannot absolve us"—he whispers to himself—
then let's not expect mercy from anywhere."

II. HIS LAMP

The lamp is calm and convenient; he prefers it
to other forms of illumination. Its light can be adjusted

according to the needs of the moment, according
to eternal, unconfessed desire. And always
the odor of kerosene, a subtle presence
very discreet at night when he returns alone
with such weariness in his limbs, such futility
in the weave of his jacket, the seams of his pockets,
that every moment seems superfluous and unbearable—
the lamp something to occupy him once more—the wick,
the match, the endangered flame (with its shadows
on the bed, the desk, the walls), and above all
the glass itself—its fragile translucence
which from the beginning, in a simple and human gesture,
compels you to protect yourself or to protect others.

III. HIS LAMP TOWARD DAYBREAK

Well, good evening; the two of them again, face to face,
he and his lamp—he loves it, even though he seems
indifferent and self-complacent; and not solely
because it serves him, but even more so, particularly,
because it deserves his care—the fragile survival
of ancient Greek lamps, it gathers about it
memories and sensitive insects of the night, smooths over
the wrinkles of old men, broadens foreheads,
magnifies the shadows of adolescent bodies, covers
with a gentle glow the whiteness of blank pages
or the hidden purple of poems; and when
toward daybreak its light grows pale and merges
with the rose of day, with the first noises
of the shops' iron shutters, the pushcarts, the fruit-peddlers,
it becomes a tangible image of his own vigil, and even
a glass bridge that crosses from his eyeglasses to the lamp's glass,
and from there to the window panes, and then out further, and still
    further—
a glass bridge that holds him above the city, within the city,
in his Alexandria, uniting, with his own will now, the night and the
    day.

IV. PUTTING OUT THE LAMP

There comes a time of great lassitude. A dazzling morning,
treacherous   it marks the end of another of his nights, outdoes
the sleek remorse of the mirror, vindictively digging
the lines around his lips and eyes. Now,
neither the lamp's affability nor the drawn curtains can help;
a rigid awareness of the end lies on the bedsheets where the hot
breath of a summer's night grows chill, and only a few ringlets
    remain—
fallen from youthful curls—a severed chain—
that very same chain—who wrought it? No,
neither remembrance nor even poetry help. Nevertheless,
at the final moment, before falling asleep, bending over the lamp's
    glass
to blow out its flame, that it too might finally be extinguished, he
    realizes
he's blowing directly into the glass ear of eternity,
a deathless word entirely his own, his very breath—the sigh of
    substance.
How beautifully the smoke from his lamp perfumes his room at
    dawn.

V. HIS GLASSES

Always between his eyes and objects stood
his impenetrable glasses, cautious, abstracted,
scrutinizing and eclectic—an impersonal stronghold of glass,
both barrier and lookout tower—two water-filled moats
around his secret, his denuding gaze, or rather
two trays of a balance that stands—how strange—not vertically
but horizontally. And thus, finally, what could a horizontal balance
hold other than the void, other than
the knowledge of the void, naked, crystalline, glittering,
as on its polished surface a procession is reflected
of his inner and outer visions in a balanced unity
so material, so incorruptible, that it refutes the entire void.

VI. PLACES OF REFUGE

"Expression," he says, "does not mean to say something,
but simply to speak; and to speak
means to reveal yourself—so how should you speak?"
And then his silence became so transparent
that he hid himself completely behind the curtain,
pretending to be looking out of the window.
But as he felt our gaze on his back,
he turned and poked his head out of the curtain
as though he were wearing a long, white chiton,
somewhat ridiculous, somewhat out of keeping with the times;
and this is what he wanted (or preferred), believing perhaps
that in this manner, somehow, he was diverting
our suspicion, our hostility or our pity,
or that he was providing us with some kind of an excuse
(as he had foreseen) for our future admiration.

VII. ON FORM

He said: "Form cannot be contrived nor imposed;
it is contained in its material and is sometimes revealed
in its movements outwards." Platitudes, we said,
vague words—what revelations now? He said nothing more,
but cupped his chin between his two hands like a word
between quotation marks. His cigarette remained hesitant
between his closed lips—a white, glowing dash
in place of the ellipses he always left out on purpose
(or perhaps unconsciously?), eliding thus his silence.

In this position, it vaguely seemed to us, he stayed awake all night
in a small railroad station, under the overhang
where on a winter's night lonely travellers
meet for a moment, with that taste of coal
from the impossibility of the journey and from the mutual
    endlessness
of their secret, age-old friendship. The train's smoke

hung placidly above the two horizontal cones
of the headlights, solid and sculptural, between
two separations. He stubbed out his cigarette and left,

VIII. MISUNDERSTANDINGS

These ambiguities of his, intolerable; they try us;
and he himself is also tried; his vagueness is obviously
betrayed, his hesitations, his ignorance, his timidity,
and his lack of firm principles. Surely he's trying to involve us
in his own complexities. And he kept gazing somewhere beyond us,
as though he had been generous, somehow, and tolerant (like those
    who need to be tolerated),
wearing a pure-white shirt, an impeccable slate-grey suit,
with a crysanthemum in his buttonhole. Nevertheless,
when he left, we detected on the floor, in the place where he had
    stood,
a small, extremely red lake, beautifully shaped,
roughly like a map of Greece, like a miniature globe of the world
with many omissions and great inaccuracies of frontiers,
with frontiers almost blurred in the uniformity of their coloring —
a globe in a tightly shut, white school, in the month of July,
when all the pupils have left for a dazzling countryside by the sea.

IX. TWILIGHT

You know that moment of twilight in summer
inside the closed room; a slight rosy reflection
slanting on the ceiling planks; and the poem
half finished on the table — two verses all in all,
the broken promise of a splendid voyage,
of a certain freedom, a certain self-sufficiency,
of a certain (relative, of course) immortality.

Outside on the street, the invocation already of the night,
the weightless shadows of the gods, of people, of bicycles,
when work on the construction sites has stopped and the young
    workers
with their tools, their wet, vigorous hair,
with a few splashes of whitewash on their worn clothing,
vanish in the apotheosis of the evening mists.

Eight sharp strokes of the grandfather clock on the top of the stairs
heard down the whole length of the corridor—the implacable
    strokes
of an imperative hammer hidden behind the shaded
crystal; and at the same time the age-old noise
of those keys about which he could never tell
whether they were for locking or unlocking.

X. FINAL HOUR

A fragrance lingered in his room, perhaps
a memory only, perhaps even from the window
half opened in the spring night. He sorted out
the things he would take with him. He covered
the large mirror with a bedsheet. And still
on his fingers that feel of beautifully proportioned bodies,
and the solitary feel of his pen—no contradiction;
the supreme union of poetry. He never wanted
to delude anyone. The end was drawing near. He asked
one more time: "Gratitude, perhaps, or only the desire
to be grateful?" From under his bed his old
worn-out slippers stuck out. He had no wish
to cover them (oh, at another time, of course). Only
after he had put the small key in his vest pocket
did he sit on his suitcase, in the middle of the room,
all alone, and began to weep, knowing
his innocence for the first time with such certainty.

XI. AFTER DEATH

Many claimed him, squabbled over him,
perhaps because of his apparel — a strange outfit,
formal, imposing, yet not without a certain charm,
with a certain air to it, like those fantastic outfits the gods wore
when they consorted with mortals — in disguise —
but as they talked about common matters in plain language
    suddenly
a fold of their garments would billow out from the breath
of the infinite or what's beyond — or so they say.

Well then, they squabbled. What could he do? They ripped
his clothes and his underwear; they even broke his belt. He became
nothing more than a common, naked mortal standing in shame.
    Everyone
forsook him. And there precisely he turned to marble. Years later,
in that same place they discovered a magnificent statue,
naked, proud, tall, of Pentelic marble,
the Eternal Youth of Self-Punishment — this is what they called it,
covered it with a long, linen cloth, and prepared
an unprecedented ceremony for the public unveiling.

XII. EVALUATION

He who died was, in truth, remarkable,
unique; he left us an excellent standard by which
to measure ourselves and, above all, to measure
our neighbor — no one higher than that,
very short; another skinny; a third
as tall as a man on stilts; not one
of any value, of any value at all.
Only we can make proper use
of this standard — but what standard do you mean? —

of this Nemesis, of this Archangel's sword
which we've already sharpened, and can now
set them all up in a row and cut off their heads.

Athens, February 1963, revised, 1974   *(K.F.)*

ىﻟ

from
SUMMER PREPARATORY SCHOOL
(1953–1964)

Translated by Athan Anagnostopoulos and by Kimon Friar

SUMMER AT DHIMINIO

A ship leaves at nightfall. The light glows.
Everything is utterly transparent, almost nonexistent.
Someone is sitting on a chair by the seashore —
how does his chair support itself on silence?

In the streets trucks loaded with melons and watermelons pass by.
In the small pine grove a girl is undressing.
Her clothes on the ground are a small mound of light.

Verses no longer know what to do in the dry mouth.

Dhiminió, August, 1953   *(K.F.)*

BODIES

Bodies, sunburned, youthful — redblack earth —
sometimes in their thick hair or even in their pores
the cubes of salt glitter, so much so that you tremble
lest the poets remain voiceless.

Athens, Dhiminió, Sámos, 1953–1957   *(A.A.)*

SUNFLOWERS

Large blinding sunflowers in deserted gardens.
The thousand eyes of midday are yellow.
Yellow glow, yellow emptiness of summer,
burning stones, cornfields, bodies. Poetry
blinded by this luster, seeks some shade,
creates a shade, becomes more luminous.

Athens, Dhiminió, Sámos, 1953–1957   (A.A)

SUMMER NOON AT KARLOVASI

Melted iron, noon, stone shadows.
Cicadas and cicadas. Hammer blows at the blacksmith's.
Veins of water lurking under the stones.
The cupola of the closed church glitters.
Insufficient fullness—he said. And there is no one to speak,
there is no one to hear. The passing of a seagull:
a sudden burst of semen. And immediately after,
that unaccountable, inexplicable repentence. Under the mulberry tree
a very significant thud was heard as the donkey
flipped one of its ears to chase away a fly.

Athens, Dhiminió, Sámos, 1953–1957   (K.F.)

ABSENCE

The setting sun is a red lion.
Smell of sun and burned horsehair.
A rose girl at the door.
A yellow girl under the trees.

A blue girl on the mountain. Nothing.
Broad, inexplicable, immaculate absence.
The sky lifts high the girls, the houses, the statues

Athens, Dhiminió, Sámos, 1953–1957   *(A.A.)*

NOCTURNE

As he was walking alone in the deserted street,
he felt behind his back a star's knife
piercing into the warm darkness of his body. He did not turn.
The point had already penetrated his left breast.
He saw it glittering through his open chest, seized it
with two fingers, drew it out, and lit his cigarette.

Athens, Dhiminió, Karlóvasi,
Platanákia, St. Constantine, 1953–1964   *(K.F.)*

SUMMER SORROW

Handsome is the peasant sprawling under the shadow of the plane
    tree.
Around him the golden heat of the sun buzzed, gasping.
His chest naked. His bare feet stuck out
of his rolled trouser legs. Wide soles
with wellshaped toes, like a statue's.
And that dark-skinned air of indifferent masculinity.

His wife came, skinny, sallow, with an infant at her breast,
and two small children tugging at her faded dress.
He got up, stuck a bundle of wood under his arm,
took one of the children by the hand and walked away
into the depths of the golden noon. A few steps behind him
followed his skinny wife.

Infinite sorrow:
No one will tell him he is handsome. He will never know it.

Athens, Dhiminió, Karlóvasi,
Platanákia, St. Constantine, 1953–1964   (K.F.)

THE CENTER

The sea, the sun, the tree. And again:
the tree, the sun, the sea.
                              Notice
that in this inverted repetition
the sun is once again found in the middle
like sensual delight in the center of the body.

Athens, Dhiminió, Karlóvasi,
Platanákia, St. Constantine, 1953–1964   (K.F.)

FARMER

He left his pickaxe by the wall and said:
"The field breaks your back. Every day
you struggle with thousands of tons of earth. Afterwards,
even two spans of earth are too much for you. And not even
one sheep bleating behind you."
                              The sunset
was fading away in deep crimson. And Poetry
hid speechless behind the trees,
staring at her luminous and useless hands.

Athens, Dhiminió, Karlóvasi,
Platanákia, St. Constantine, 1953–1964   (K.F.)

HELEN'S HOUSE

The trees hide the view from the window
Broad leaves, delicate, curled, elongated.
A white plate with fruit on the table.
The child's bicycle, the wooden pony
all confused with the cries of the cicadas.
                              What secret
sequence has raised up this insignificant scene
into that region of incorruptibility, barely held
above chaos by a green branch, as by the finger
of a handsome young god?

Athens, Dhiminió, Karlóvasi,
Platanákia, St. Constantine, 1953–1964   (K.F.)

PROBABILITIES

The caïque all white, and behind it red boats.
He counted them, counted them again: six. He wondered
what meaning the number and the counting might have. In a while
both the number and the counting faded in the dusk,
along with the question. Well then, it's possible
that what we call "beauty" may exist; it may also be
the silent, inexplicable certainty of a postponed happiness.

Athens, Dhiminió, Karlóvasi,
Platanákia, St. Constantine, 1953–1964   (A.A.)

STRIPPED NAKED

With his eyes closed, in the sun: naked. Seaweed and salt
about him and within him. Not a soul. Dark light to the edge of the
    world.
He sank into his body. Quietness. Outside his body

143

the mule-drivers shouted, the ships, the cicadas, history.
In the world of water, only one fish leapt.

Athens, Dhiminió, Karlóvasi,
Platanákia, St. Constantine, 1953–1964   (K.F.)

ADOLESCENT

He stood behind the rock to undress. He couldn't be seen.
Only his black hair, gleaming, vigorous,
stood out against the sky. In a little while he put
his clothes on the rock, and swam.
The sun gathered at his white shirt.
The shirt shone like a small marble wing
on the shoulder blades of the golden noon.

Athens, Dhiminió, Karlóvasi,
Platanákia, St. Constantine, 1953–1964   (A.A.)

ACCENTED COLORS

The mountain is red. The sea is green.
The sky is yellow. The earth blue.

Between a bird and a leaf sits death.

Athens, Dhiminió, Karlóvasi,
Platanákia, St. Constantine,
1953–1964   (A.A)

ᴄᴧ

from

SMALL DEDICATION
(1960–1965)

Translated by Athan Anagnostopoulos and by Kimon Friar

SMALL SONG FOR ÉRI

The small mirror hanging on the wall nail
thrusts a small sky into the room —
this sky trembles at the sound of the cicada.
The rooms walk, they go out into the countryside —
our chairs on the plane trees,
our table on the white cloud,
my papers in the stream,
my coat on the shoulders of the bell-tower,
and my eyes — just look — in the swallow's nest,
two blue eggs, very blue, warmed;
and inside them two yellow birds
pecking and pecking with rosy beaks —
Éri, hurry up; hurry up, Éri,
they are longing to sing with you.

(K.F.)

THE IMPONDEROUS NIGHT

A leaf falls in the night. The silence is audible.
An insect whistles into the ear of the Great Bear.
The moon too has come out — it is small, very small,
smaller than the key to the cupboard. On the terrace
our table has remained empty — it is damp with dew;
the table glistens like a cistern. A white tree
leaps into the room from the open window,
wanders through the rooms with noiseless, dancing swirls.
Ah, tell me, how can we sleep tonight?

And how can we not wake up tomorrow? Éri, Éri,
do you want to dance a small mazurka with the tree?

(K.F.)

UNEXPECTEDLY

The door opens. Enters Éri. Two cherries
hang over her ears. "I am Spring," she says.
A noise is heard outside. The small motorboat
comes up out of the sea, enters our garden,
cuts across the rose bushes, leaps in through the window
and bumps into the armchair. The crystals tinkle.
Éri laughs. She looks at her father,
leaps on his knees, cuts off a smile from his lips
with two of her fingers—a red smile
like a wild rose that hung
unprepared and bewildered outside the trellis of his verses.

(K.F.)

SCHOOL HOLIDAYS

Two doors open directly onto the sky.
In the corridor the farmers' baskets are filled
with vineshoots and vineleaves. Childhood names,
apricots, peaches, grapes, pears, figs,
each with its distinguishing fragrance coloring
a large, turning glass sphere
like the colored globe of the earth on the bench of the closed school;
and outside, the undisciplined cicadas reciting
their same poems over and over again—and not for the
    examinations.

(K.F.)

REVIVAL

The day shone brand new, in contrast to your disbelief:
trees, mountains, door-windows—glitter and colors—what colors!
You can no longer deny them. Gleaming pebbles on the seashore,
rose-red, lemon-tinted, violet. A blossoming branch
leans on the shoulder of a roof—it claims a smile from you
as once more poetry passes by, adolescent, slender, thoughtless,
under the poplar trees, with a luminous yellow umbrella.

(K.F.)

CALM

Quiet little harbor—paintings, ships, colors,
green, yellow, and red. Hammering from the shipyards.
A girl with a pitcher. The sun leaves.
The balconies hang into the caïques. Nothing is
from yesterday or tomorrow. A speechless passing.
And a paper moon right in the middle of the day.

When the sun has set, I'll write you a poem.

(A.A.)

LYRIC POEM

The water flows, drenches the fields, flows, shines.
Blue sea, green trees, green.
Red roof, white cloud, shadowless.
And that bit of smoke? Tell me
what color may the dream have, what color

may the woman's step on the wet grass have
early in the morning, with the birds, when the bell's shadow
is half in your palm and half in the seashells?

(A.A.)

SEPARATION

The husband was cutting his toenails. The wife was preparing his
    bags
quietly, silently — his shirts, one by one, his undergarments, his
    handkerchiefs.
When he went out to the corridor for a moment,
she gathered up hurriedly the two cut nails from the large toes
and hid them in her pocket. When the man came back
she was busily sweeping the floor. In her pocket
she felt those two toenails like two tender, erotic half moons
for her future lonely nights when on her island the wind roars.

(K.F.)

INVISIBLE GLORY

Beautiful woman (nor does she know it) who has already reached
    forty,
matured now from love to affection, with her sweet intimacy
and the four seasons of the year; as she holds
in both her hands the large fruit bowl laden
with pears, peaches, grapes (the small drops of water on the fruits'
    skins
glitter in the light from the window), as she stoops
to place it on the white table — all the gleaming light gathers
around her head. O it is only now we recognize her — she is the
    priestess
who places the modest libations at the feet of a statue.

Samos, Athens, Dhiminio, 1960–1965   (K.F.)

ہ

PHILOCTETES

The Ultimate Mask
(1963–1965)

Translated by Peter Bien

(*Summertime on the deserted shore of an island—perhaps Lemnos.
Early evening, colors beginning to fade. A boat anchored in the rocky
cove. The crew, a little way below, washing, exercising, wrestling,
their shouts and laughter audible. Here above, two men are seated
before a stony cavern fitted out as a dwelling-place. One is hand-
some, bearded, mature, with a manly, spiritual face, the other a wiry
youth with fervent, inquisitive eyes filled with love. He has some-
thing of Achilles' features, but slightly more spiritualized, as though
he were his son Neoptolemos. Somewhere, a frazzled, indiscernible
moon shifts slowly, obscurely, across the sky, silver amid the pro-
tracted violet and pink reflections of the sunset. Apparently the older
man, after years of solitude and silence, has been speaking at length
to the youth, that unexpected visitor who arrived scarcely two hours
earlier. But now, silent once again, he is inscrutable and sated, weary
with yet another wearying grief—one of no greater avail than the
first, yet understandably human. A vague remorse clouds his broad
forehead; nevertheless, he continues to observe the youth's splendid
face, as though expecting something. Reflections from his weapons
gleam from time to time at the back of the cavern: his huge, well-
wrought shield with its depiction of Herakles' labors, and his three
famous, incomparable spears. The young man seems to be making a
difficult decision. He begins to speak*):

I was sure, my worthy friend, that you would understand
    profoundly. We of the younger generation,
called up at the very last minute, as they say, supposedly to reap
the glory that all of you prepared for us
with your arms, your wounds, your deaths:
we too recognize and know—yes, we too possess our wounds
elsewhere on the body, wounds unseen,
unrecompensed by pride or by respectable blood
shed visibly in the visible battles, visible competitions.

We could have done without such glory! Did we ever ask for it?
Fulfilling others' duties and paying off
their debts, we had not a moment for ourselves, no time even
to observe a tranquil hand unlatch a window across from us at
    dawn
and suspend a canary cage outside from the bracket on the wall
with the seemliness of a superfluous yet necessary gesture.

Our elders spoke of nothing but dead men and heroes.
Strange words followed us even into sleep, terrible words
that slipped beneath closed doors, out of the banqueting hall
where shouts and goblets flashed, and the veil
of an unseen dancing-girl fluttered soundlessly
like a transparent partition whirling
between life and death. It comforted
our childish nights somehow, that rhythmic,
throbbing transparency of the veil, dispersing the shields' shadows
inscribed on white walls by lingering moonlight.

They prepared food for the dead
together with our own food. Jugs
of honey and oil were taken from table at mealtime
and carried to unknown tombs. We never distinguished
funerary urns from amphorae of wine, never knew
what belonged to us and what to the dead. The tap
of a spoon on a plate became an unexpected finger
tapping our shoulder in rebuke. We turned to look. Nothing.

Drums and bugles outside our bedroom windows;
red sparks and muted hammer-blows in hidden smithies
where shields and javelins were forged day and night;
hammering as well in basement studios
for statues and busts of warring men and warring gods (never
    poets
or athletes); also tombstones by the hundreds
with handsome, naked youths standing invariably erect,
masking, with their vertical pose,
death's everlasting horizontal. Sometimes, to be sure,
they drooped their heads and gently arched their necks

like flowers at chasm-edge, but the chasm never showed, the artists
having learned (having been compelled, perhaps?)
to leave out chasms and all things similar.

We had a long, white corridor (and so it remained).
Tombstones lined it everywhere, yet to rest our gaze
upon the youths' well-shaped limbs for even a moment was
forbidden, or upon the marble ringlets which fell across their brow
    sometimes
as if tousled by the lips of sudden incense-bearing gusts
on a golden summer's noon — I think sun-warmed willow
perfumed the place, yes, and lemon blossoms. Great models
they bequeathed to us! Did we ever ask for them? If only we'd
    been left
to our littleness, our own restricted selves! We'd rather not
compete with models. All of you, besides: what have you gained?
    And what have we?

Worthy friend, I understand your dignified withdrawal.
Your excuse (acceptable to all): bodily woe,
not mental pain or spiritual. A fine excuse
that snakebite (the snake of wisdom, maybe?) for you
to stay alone, existing — you, none other,
even if not existing — . . . existing like a snake
curled into a ball, biting its tail (How often have I yearned for
    that myself!)

You studied revenge perhaps in your solitude,
recognition for yourself or at least for the significance
of your arms. And now, behold your vindication.
I have come for them (why not admit it frankly?) just as you
    predicted.
They'll bring victory to the Greeks at last
(on this the oracle is clear): your arms, in my hands.

But first of all I've come for you. I would never accept your arms
in exchange for recognition of myself, or for the "deliverance"
I offer you. What deliverance to take you with me in my ships

with all your incurable wounds and all your loneliness?
Such words are quite the fashion now. We've learned them —
what more can we say? No chance to see or speak.

Runners hurry through the night: their torches gild the streets.
Whiter than white, the statues of the gods shine a moment
like open gateways in giant walls; then
shadows fall again from their stony hands and overcast the road.
No one distinguishes clearly after that. I beheld
a frenzied mob one night raise a person to their shoulders
in acclamation. A torch fell on him.
His hair caught fire. *He* did not shout.
He was long since dead. The mob dispersed. The night
was left in solitude, garlanded with the golden leaves of the stars.

Impossible to choose, I think. And what alternatives were given
    us? I recall
my childhood: from the visitors' quarters of our house,
the manly, resonant voices of our guests would reach me
just before bedtime. Most likely they were undressing then, and
    surely
must have forgotten struggles, battle plans, and ambitions for a
    time —
sensual in their nudity; aroused and innocent; while
(most likely) they fondled their own chests as though by chance,
and dawdled at their bedsides with thighs spread wide,
knees forgotten beneath heated palms,
until they finished a brief, happy tale
embellished by laughter and the creaking of beds.

I heard this from the corridor as I perused
in stealth their polished swords and shields
which, propped against the wall, reflected mystically the moon-
    light striking them
through glazed doors. I felt so lonely then, so perplexed,
as though that very instant I was forced to choose for ever
between their laughter and their weapons. (Both belonged to
    them.) My father

made me tremble even more, lest he wake and find me in the
      corridor
touching those curious arms, but chiefly lest he realize
I had overheard their laughter and apprehend
my secret dilemma. I never dared approach the visitors' domain
but only heard their voices cross successive galleries
—or so it seemed—of alternating light
and dark. The din of horses' hoofbeats, outside in the courtyard,
      often
drowned them; indeed, a giant shadow
fell before my feet one time and startled me—at the glazed doors
a horse stood looking in, obscuring with its shade
the images hammered on the shields.

My father's shadow was just as large. He cast his gloom
throughout the house, shutting doors and windows from top to
      bottom.
I felt as though constrained sometimes to place my head
between his legs should I wish to see the sun.
That's what unnerved me most: the sensation of his thighs against
      my neck. I preferred
to stay indoors in the kindly semidarkness of the rooms,
with docile furniture surrounding me and curtains so yielding to
      the touch,
or else within the deserted sculpture hall. I loved the kouroi.

Quiet ruled in there, and coolness, while out-of-doors
in olive grove and vineyard cicadas raged
in noontime's golden swelter. Shadows from the sculptured forms
intersected tranquilly in concord upon the tiles,
shaping parallelograms of transparent blue. Emboldened by the
      calm,
a tiny mouse strolled leisurely
now and then across a kouros's foot, halted with suspicion
to contemplate the oblong windows with its pair of oil-drop eyes,
and on behalf of all the enmarbled—as their tiny partner—
fixed its pointed snout, like a flaccid arrow, upon the absolute.

My father did not care for statues. I never saw him

stand before one: he had turned perhaps
into the statue of himself already—a monument in bronze
of a horseman arrogant and unapproachable. Only
his friendship with Patroklos
brought him somewhat close to me, as though with massive
    strides
he had stepped off his pedestal
and vanished beneath the trees. How strange
to hear no creaking
from his knee-joints of bronze.

Mother—one more shadow, transparent too,
weightless and remote: a tenderness present
in her constant absence. Just before they reached the house,
returning from the hunt, the men would glimpse
the west window behind the trees, hanging
all alone in mid-air from a branch, it seemed,
and inside its sombre frame my mother
hanging too (it seemed) and powdered all with gold-dust,
as she peered far off into the sunset. They thought
she'd been awaiting them, devouring the road with expectation.
We understood much later: she was never there at all, but actually
    hanged.

Her face betrayed the noose's shadow imperceptibly as she
    corrected
her expression, once the hunters could be heard
along the road. Banishing with her hand
a coal-black curl on pretext it blocked her vision,
that noose's shade is what she pushed aside. We learned this later,
as horns blared out their last above the lake in twilight,
and stucco from our home's facade peeled off in noiseless bits,
as trees' blue phantoms joined pink and golden mists rising
    everywhere
above the plain, and exhausted dogs, despite their hanging
    tongues,
trod lightly, as though climbing in ecstasy to heaven.

Brilliant plumage quickly filled the evening; colorful feathers

of slaughtered birds lay there upon the tabletop of stone,
    outdoors,
with purple, red and amber grapes on overflowing platters,
and cooling water from the well. Mother always smiled with sorrow
    then;
"And to think you wanted to be a bird!" she'd say to me,
directing the servant-girls to pluck the fowl for dinner
in the yard behind the house, where mountain-shade already
fell like scintillating molten iron, and giant cypresses,
austere, reclusive, dark,
assumed a mute, inexplicable initiative.

The men, all this time—begrimed and sweaty from the hunt,
fuzzy burrs in their hair,
shoulders blotched with pollen from the pines—
were in the baths. The sound
of falling water reached outside, the smell of soap
mixed with garden scents: geranium and heated resin, rosemary
    and mint—
full, refreshing exhalations. Having placed his ample watering-pot
upon the stone settee, the gardener would seize the chance
to say a humble, bright "Good evening" to his worthy mistress,
blended with names of flowers, habits of seeds, and something
    else
concerning grubs and caterpillars, and the blights of leaves and
    fruit.

Thousands of songbirds atop the eucalyptus trees strained their
    throats like hawkers
at a market fair, madly giving praise while servants
beneath them plucked those other birds. Night came on,
tranquil, slow, irreversible, filled with fluffy green and golden
    down.
At its root each feather bore an imperceptible red blot.
Such a plume had settled once on mother's hair;
it shaded her completely. I approached her then a moment, slyly,
and removed it—to see her shaded by the sins of others
was more than I could bear. Despite herself she voiced
a tiny exclamation: you'd think a dagger had been taken from her
    breast.

Another evening, I remember, she curled her palms around the
    lamp
to guard the flame against a breeze. Her hands
became transparent and pink, like two enormous rose-petals—
a peculiar blossom, with the lamp-flame
an unlikely pistil. I saw
her keys abandoned then on the stone steps,
beside the hunters' satchels and their bows. I understood:
those hands—so set apart, so visible from every vantage point,
locked forever inside their very own transparency—could never
unlock anything again. When she spoke,
she always seemed to withhold the crucial point, and her lips
    protruded
scarcely beyond her long eyelashes' shadow.

I recall a certain afternoon as well. She was drinking water beneath
    the trees;
I noticed her hands again—more transparent than the glass
she held. That glass's shadow
struck the lawn—a circle of light, barely visible. Then a bee
alighted at the center of this circle and remained with wings
    illumined faintly—
beleaguered, so it seemed, by sensations of inexplicable bliss.
That was the final summer, before I too was called up, in my turn.

I have told you very much about my mother. Perhaps, my friend,
    in your hands I've discerned
a little of the luster found in hers. Everything she touched
was suddenly transformed to distant music; it could be touched no
    longer
but only heard—not even heard. Nothing at all was left:
unremembered sound, a vague sense . . .; no knowledge.

After that the lighting changed: fires at the bivouac, naked
    bodies
ruddy and scarlet from the flames: blood-smeared, so you'd
    think,
or flayed of all their skin; more sensual and beastly,
more shamelessly erotic, like a giant slaughterhouse

with guts and testicles suspended in the night from meat hooks
between stars made dim by our fires
while urine, semen, excrement, slops and blood
surged in ditches near us,
and shadows galloped far in glaring redness
until the moon appeared, soft and moist like a vagina,
and remorse commenced, repentance too, and creation.

The river's din beneath the trees refreshed
our hearing then, though no one asked about its course.
Campfires died slowly into embers; large birds, asleep
on branches, half-opened their eyes from time to time;
a feeble glimmer slipped between the leaves.

The men deloused their chests and inner thighs;
the lads, with scarce a body-hair upon them, so retiring you'd
    think they'd been offended,
often felt two potent twinges at the nipples of their chests
as though a pair of passion's darts had been nailed in them at
    midnight.
The muscles of their bellies tautened then around their waists, like
    ropes. The sentries,
removing both their sandals, rubbed two fingers between their
    toes
to make some greasy, blackish clods. These they kneaded endlessly
like mystic statuettes, pliant, comforting,
then slung them noiselessly into the night. Afterwards
— handsome, brutish, torpid — they smelled their fingers,
sniffed at them for hours, until they fell asleep.

On the ground where they'd been left, the massive shields
gave forth metallic, sluggish rumbles as the stars' far-off lances
battered them. Commands by generals
lay hidden and congealing in their hollows. The huge bare
    fishbone
of the Milky Way was sparkling above the tents. Again,
almost as in summers past, we feared
some thief unseen and undefined, if not the customary thieves
that might vault into our rooms from balconies or open windows.

We knew nothing then (or now) about self-protection. A
    mosquito's buzz
distracted us, as did the moonlight's hum
or stolen kisses resounding in the archways—
a woman, entrusted to seclusion, defecated tranquilly in the
    meadow,
feeling sharp pinches on her haunches from the grass and from the
    stars.

Oh, that sense of perpetual thievery—pillage rather:
secret, mute and steadfast pillage! In mid-heat
the bedroom curtain suddenly would leap in dance-step, thrice,
intending clearly to bring to our notice
gold-embodied hems on a woman's gown. Then it stood stock-
    still;
pale blue in the dead calm, and veiled a sculpture
—a granite one perhaps of Night, or one depicting Thievery in red
    stone—
and again we heard that seductive sawing of the crickets
and those reassuring croakings of the frogs
or sharp clacks from a cockroach circling inside a helmet.

We lacked the time to verify: before we'd counted
the constellations even once, we fell asleep. At dawn
an owl rummaged blindly, having fallen in the undergrowth
while its milky eyes sought another place;
and Oeta's shadow receded from the plain
like a monstrous tortoise drawing in its legs.

The sun resounded then on the horizon. The sixty-four hoofs
of its horses flashed high in the air
while oxcarts below reflected the rays. The gates swung open.
Hubbub in the marketplace—fruit sellers, merchants,
mountains of lemons, greens; farmers with their donkeys.

Awakened before his hour, a philosopher sauntered mutely
between two rows of slaughtered cattle. Potters
arranged their jugs in ranks along the road
like earthenware troops from another planet. In the gymnasiums,

cooled as yet by morning damp and lighted with slanting rays,
the earliest runners were emerging from the dressing-rooms and
    sprinting
short trial-laps—almost like birds in the air. Soldiers
in barracks courtyards scrubbed enormous cauldrons.

At their windows, some unkempt women shook out
bedsheets of startling whiteness. Temple metopes and the upper
tiers of stadiums glistened. This blind and blinding
luster seemed—precisely in its ostentation—
to be holding something back from us (which truly was the case).
That thievery perhaps? The massive jars
were in the gardens still and in the cellars,
as were the golden masks with their vacuous, searching eyes.
A moment's silence; the same ill-defined significance; a general
    conspiracy.

Beards, hair, fingernails and penises grew longer.
The news: forever concerning heroes and the dead, then still more
    concerning heroes.
Large horse-bones on the hillsides with the dry twigs.
Increasing stench from unwashed bodies. Far away, a woman
passed from time to time at close of day, a water jug upon her
    shoulder;
the breeze filled in the space where she had been. Sundown
was enfolded in a banner's tip. A certain star would cry
an incomprehensible "No!"—abruptly—whereupon
the horses' gallop vanished along the length of the night,
leaving the stars more silent above the river.

No one managed to remember any more, to think or question.
Constant shifting about. Everything curt, abortive, incomplete.
Wails and cheers acquired an increasingly similar tone.
Indistinguishable too the faces of friend and foe.
Only at night when battle ceased, when silence came flatly down,
the wounded's protracted groans were heard among the rocks
and the moon was like a slaughtered mare's dilated eyes:
only then did we realize that we still had not died.

Machination next sparked its myriad eyes in nighttime's every
    corner:
"Whatever they stole from us we should now take back—even
    commandeer!" Down below
on the bright seashore, our vessels—dark,
unmoving, turned to stone—were planning yet another voyage,
and if a wet oar briefly flashed at times, the pulses on our wrists
throbbed unexpectedly in response. Tiptoeing messengers
darted back and forth like slippery bats, and when by chance
a compromising trace remained upon the milk-white pebbles or
    among the thorns
—a black feather, bit of sandal-thong, a silver buckle—
at dawn we'd make sure that it had vanished.

We seemed to hear the secret axes already in the forest
cutting wood. We heard the giant thump when a tree
subsided to the ground; we heard the silence
hide in fright behind our backs. Already I seemed to view
the Trojan Horse gleaming in the starlight—hollow and huge,
dangerous, almost religious—while its shadow
spread fablelike across the walls. Already I sensed
myself inside the horse's cavity together with the others,
positioned awkwardly within its neck, alone,
watching through its vacant eyes the crystal night
as though I were suspended over chaos, and knowing that
the mane which waved above my nape
was not my own—nor the victory, of course. Nonetheless, I
    prepared myself
for the enormous, futile leap into the unknown.

High above, in this position inside the horse's plank-lined throat,
I must have felt swallowed; swallowed alive, however, in order to
    observe
the enemy camp, the fires, ships and stars,
the entire miracle (as it's called), the familiar, dread, incalculable
    miracle of the world,
as though I were a morsel stuck in the infinite's gullet, and
    concurrently a bridge
above two embankments equally precipitous and unknown—
a jerry-built bridge, to be sure, of wood and bitter scheming.

(From there on high, I think, in such a nightmare,
I first espied the soothing brilliance of your weapons.)

At various other times—during the long middays, an interval in
    the fighting,
while on march, or halting for rest—suddenly we felt that we were
    thirsty.
Nothing more—: only thirsty. We did not call the water or our
    thirst by name,
but just bent down in confusion, feigning to tie our sandal-
    thongs.
In this position, bending down, we gazed out into the distance
    and retained a topsy-turvy
view of landscapes, people and ourselves,
a view fallacious, forgiving, pellucid, diffracted,
as though mirrored in some water. There was no water. We were
    thirsty.

That road was ravaged along its entire length. Its wells on either
    side
were covered over, polluted by cadavers. The cobbles were
    splitting
from so much heat, the cicadas shouting. Seething lime
on the horizon; tongues of fire. Atop the coping of the walls
stood bits of broken glass that sparked in unrelenting sunlight as
    they divided
comrades, friends and fellow-fighters. Despite
the glorious, piercing brilliance, nothing was concealed: I saw
    courageous men
throw ashes in their hair and saw the ashes
mingle with their tears. Black furrows
dug into their beards, down to the chin.

Those who, naked on the seashore, used to wash their horses
and grease their manes with yellow oil, men and beasts alike
    resplendent
on brilliant mornings, those same who
danced at night above campfire flame, their bare soles
flashing vermilion—they cower now

amid the crags, they sulk and whine, they place their palms
before their thighs, they hide in shame as though they'd done
    some wrong
to others and all the others had done some wrong to them.
    Perhaps they also grudge
the young recruits their lovely absence of suspicion, their pluck,
their enthusiastic, rote grandiloquence, and most of all perhaps
their hair so thick and glossy, swollen out with health and sex.

Yet those too set forth one day to reform the world:
Charmingly naive, secretly vainglorious, they set forth together,
each one individually, and saw and looked, each for
a private reason, a distinct ambition sheltered
underneath a single great idea, a common purpose whose
    transparency
made that much clearer every man's fragmented self,
the wretchedness and contemptibility of the lot. How, my friend,
    could you have brought
some order to that chaos? How could you stand by them? Now I
    see.

During the night on the boats when the common soldiers,
    exhausted,
slept on deck like sacks heaped together,
so admirable for their youthful good faith,
asleep in their ignorance, their animalistic innocence and their
    fleshly beauty,
robust from the pursuit of useful employment in the fields, in
    workshops, on the roads,
subject to necessity and to facile hopes,
effortlessly universalizing their own guilelessness, like lambs
being led to slaughter for others' profit, yet
smiling in their sleep and babbling, snoring,
cursing a dream-born cow, or—half naked, with nocturnal
    erections—
whispering again and again a woman's name
while laved in the mystic sempiternity of ocean starlight—during
    those nights,

162

I heard, amid the splashing of the oars, our leaders'
shouts and squabbles over booty still to be acquired, titles
still to be decreed. And in their eyes I saw
hatred toward all, the savage passion for preeminence,
and deep deep within, like a fragile glowworm at the farthest end
    of a dark cave,
I saw their loneliness as well. Behind their beards
their fate was glinting in its nakedness, as, behind the leafless
    branches of a forest,
an arid plain sown with white bones sparkles in the moonlight.

This knowledge was a kind of happiness: a release,
a mitigating acceptance, an inert delight
from the touch of everlastingness and nothingness. Despite all
    that,
I managed still to have the privilege now and then
of discerning behind the shields and spears, or between them,
a bit of sea, a little twilight, a well-shaped knee,
and of liking this—yes, despite all the rest. A remission, though
    scant;
and all the countless, unknown fears were dispelled into the
    distance:
a dense and cheery cloud in fabulous infinitude.

I remember one night when we sailed beneath a full moon. On
    every face
the moonlight fixed a burial mask of gold.
The soldiers stood in place a moment and exchanged looks
as though they did not recognize each other or were meeting
for the very first time, then abruptly turned
and gazed up high at the moon,
immobile one and all upon the ever-mobile sea,
not speaking, in a spell, as though dead already and immortal.

Afterwards, as if they vaguely felt some guilt and could not bear
this huge, imponderous weight, they began to shout,
to joke, to gesticulate obscenely, to compare their penises,
to coat themselves with drippings from the roasts, to jump, dance,
    wrestle,

pretend to read amusing fortunes and dirty stories on the exposed
    shoulder blades of rams—
in order to forget, perhaps, that moment, that comprehension,
    that absence.

Perhaps you as well, on such a night, clearly heard
among the countervailing voices of your fellow combatants
the absence of your own voice—just as I did then, beneath the full
    moon.
Yes, I heard myself not shouting, and I remained
transfixed there among them all, companionless
even among my closest friends, companionless
in a giant circle of desolation, an alpine threshing-floor,
overhearing the others' voices with terrifying clarity and
    simultaneously
hearing my own silence. From there on high
I espied a second time the brilliance of your weapons. And I
    comprehended.

Perhaps you as well, my worthy friend, decided at some
    corresponding moment
to withdraw. I imagine you must have let yourself be bitten then
by the serpent at the shrine. Besides, you realized that our weapons
    alone
are what is needed and not (as you said) we ourselves.
You, however, *are* your weapons. Honorably earned
through labor, sacrifice and friendship, they were given you by the
    hand
that choked the seven-headed Hydra, that killed
the guardian of Hades. With your own two eyes
you have seen, you have experienced: that is your inheritance
and your consummate weapon. That alone gains victories.
Now please show me how to use them. The time has come.

It will be said perhaps that the triumph is mine alone; people will
    forget, perhaps,
who took possession of the arms and who first fashioned them.
    That no one would desire.

But what difference will this make to you? Reserved for you will
    be
the ultimate and only victory (as you said):
this knowledge — so sweet, so terrible — that victories do not exist.

You and no one but you hung your vacant shirt upon a tree
to misdirect those who passed, to make them say "He's dead!"
so that — concealed behind the bushes, hearing
yourself considered dead — you might experience
the fullness of your sensibility, and afterwards might
don again the shirt of your make-believe demise
until you became (as you have become) the great silence of your
    own being.

An old spear stained with blood — retired from the fray,
left standing by itself, tranquil, useless,
propped against a boulder with its bronze head
imprinted on the moon and diffracted in the rays —
will slowly crook itself like a compliant finger
on a lyre: the eternal lyre that you mentioned. Right now
I can sense, I think, precisely where your gratitude is directed.

I've just recalled a glorious dusk on the open sea, an astonishing
    dead calm
that I'd forgotten: the exposed infinitude
of sky and water; not a single islet or promontory;
the shadowy triremes only, soaring or gliding
in a dense and fabulous rose-garden, the noiseless oars
identical in shape, broad, oblique, like moistened sunbeams. A
    sailor
tried to sing; he remained that way,
his mouth spread open like a hole
in which the ocean's glitter reappeared.

I, in turn, removed my belt then; I felt
my movement placid, inescapable, inexplicable,
possessing the authenticity of metaphysics — as though I were
    removing
a primeval noose from round my neck. I held my belt a little,

then rested one end upon the water and watched it etch
a peaceful track within the infinite, while simultaneously
a motionless pulsation of uncommon buoyancy
resounded in my fingers. Afterwards,
I hauled my belt out of the water and secured it
tightly again, wet as it was, around my waist.

On occasion the light of twilight is enlightening, is it not?—
mirrored so dazzlingly in the water, united
with its own image, autonomous
in relation to night and day, a completely independent synthesis
of night and day. This glimmer
so brief and yet immortal is a cuirass of pure gold
secured around our breasts, and most of all
it's that thinmost layer of invulnerable air,
between the cuirass and our flesh, which turns inward again
the outward motion of our breath. Sometimes,
during the deepest inhalations, we feel the tips of our chest
covertly graze the cuirass' evening-cooled metal, feel them
contact non-existence with the extreme delight of tactile
        sensuality.

I can show you the belt's mark upon my body,
a small wheel stamped there, the engraving of the clasp.
Freedom—O, yes—is always buckled and taut
round the entire body, including without fail the heel.
The belt's tight embrace, in addition, obliges the chest to expand.
It's that deep and painful estrangement which grows tractable in
        time.

May the gods, however, keep us from falling prisoner
to even the most beautiful of revelations, lest we lose forever
the tender ingenuousness that transforms actuality,
and the ultimate action: speech. Perhaps this alone dismayed you
in your thoroughgoing isolation; also, I'd say, the lack of objects,
not for you to use but rather for coming into contact; for
        comparisons and representations;
for brotherly images of the illimitable and calculations of the
        incalculable.

Return with us, if only because of this. I shall betray to no one
the dignified sufferings of your uncompanioned saintliness.
No one will comprehend your freedom's unmarred joy
or be frightened by it ever. The mask of action,
which I have brought you hidden in my pack, will conceal
your remote, transparent face. Put it on. Let's be going.

When we get to Troy, the wooden horse I described to you
will be ready. I shall hide in it, together with your weapons. Such
    will be
my own disguise, my mask, and your weapons' mask as well. In
    this way only
shall we gain the victory. This subterfuge will be
my triumph—yours too, I mean to say. It will be the victory
of all the Greeks together and of their gods. What did you
    expect?
Such victories are the only ones. Let's be on our way.

The ten years are over now. The end is near.
Come to see what you foresaw. See for what variety of plunder
we exchanged so many of our dead, for what internal hatreds
we exchanged our former enemies. Amid the debris
whose smoke will rise in upright columns toward the sun,
amid the slain, the fallen shields, the chariot-wheels,
amid the groans of vanquisher and vanquished,
your affable, intelligent smile will be a light for us,
your clemency and silence a compass.

Come. We need you not just for the victory but after it especially,
when we board the ships again (those who have survived) to
    return
with Helen—a Helen ten years older,
her accent altered, different scenes in her vision,
concealing her expatriation and old age behind
long, gold-embroidered veils, concealing
our own expatriation too behind her veils, our remorse, despair,
and the huge inescapable fear of asking
why we went, why we fought, why we are going home—and
    where.

Even the most beautiful women become something like mothers, I
     suppose,
when they grow old, full of self-abasement and sorrowful
     persistence,
full of tenderness and parental affection—and that transmuted
into the supposedly categorical justice of unavoidable error,
unavoidable loss, the unavoidable ten years. Women
clutch the key-ring at their belts with both their palms then
in a gesture wholly common, as though racked by abdominal
     pangs—
beautiful women grown old, mythical mothers
in an ultimate gesture of unaffected saintliness,
lest we realize that those keys can never unlock anything again.

Helen's gaze: how shall we endure it
behind her sombre, sparkling veils,
amid the honeyed brightness of the stars in unfathomable night,
while the rowers hold their silence and the oars are beating
ocean's secret timbrels of return in the tempo of all things that do
     not return?

Remain with us, at least for now. This we need
even more than we need your weapons—as you yourself well
     know.
Here is the mask I've brought for you. Put it on. We're leaving.

(*The serene man with the beard takes the mask and rests it on the
ground. He does not put it on. Little by little his face is transformed.
It becomes younger, more positive, more present—it seems to dupli-
cate the mask. A long pause. Great expectation. A star shoots across
the sky. The youth feels a scant breeze on his face, and his hair is
parted neatly in the middle, spontaneously, as if by a fine golden
comb. The crew's song is audible from the shore below: an unassum-
ing folk song which encompasses hawsers, masts, rowers, stars, abun-
dant sorrow, gallantry and persistence, the whole murky sparkling
sea, the whole of infinity, in human dimensions. Perhaps it is the
same song that the anchorite came to know by other means. And
perhaps this is why he made his decision. He rises calmly, fetches his
weapons from the cave, hands them over to the youth, allows him to
go out in front, and follows him toward the shore. While advancing*

between stones and thistles, he sees his weapons glitter in the starlight as they precede him, and he hears the crew's folk song reverberate against their metal. Thus it seems that he is following not the youth but his weapons themselves, heading in the direction which their burnished, well-honed tips ceaselessly indicate: against death. The mask has remained up above on the stones, outside the cave. It too glitters in the mysterious nocturnal beatitude — with a curious, incomprehensible affirmation.)

Athens, Samos, May 1963–October 1965   *(P.B.)*

ﺣ

from

TESTIMONIES II
(1964–1965)

Translated by Kimon Friar

DISPLACEMENT

No matter how much he called them "harmless," there was always a
    danger
lurking in a color, a movement, when opening
a door in or out, when emptying
the glass ashtray out the window, for sometimes the wind
would blow the cigarette butts into the room, and the dust into his
    eyes,
and then he was obliged to gather them on his knees one by one.
It was in precisely this position we found him, as though he were
    praying,
and perhaps in truth he was. "No, no," he said,
and spread out his palm for proof, the cigarette butts
arranged in rows like those lead soldiers who, it is safe to say,
never took part in any battle. Nevertheless, we could see in his face
the extremely cunning triumph of the thoroughly defeated.

Samos, January, 1965   *(K.F.)*

AN INVALID'S DAY

All day an odor of damp, rotting floorboards,
drying and steaming in the sun. The birds
for a moment gaze from the rooftops, then leave.
In the neighboring tavern at night, the gravediggers sit
and eat fried minnows, drink, and sing

a song with many dark holes—
from which a quiet wind begins to blow,
and the leaves, the lights, and the shelfpaper quiver.

Athens, June, 1961   (K.F.)

THE SUSPECT

He locked the door, looked behind him distrustfully,
and thrust the key in his pocket. It was then they arrested him.
They harassed him for months. Until, one evening, he confessed
(and this was proved) that the key and the house
were his. But no one could understand
why he had hidden the key. And so,
though he was found innocent, he remained suspected by all.

1964–1965   (K.F.)

THE WIND'S BODY

I saw the full body of the wind, he said, its full body—
it slapped my cheeks, it grabbed
my chest and my groin, its knees
struck my knees; it tread
on my toes—I saw it, I tell you,
here, body to body, upright both of us. Now,
in my mouth I have a great desolation
and nine fleshy leaves around my neck.

Samos, December, 1964   (K.F.)

172

SMALL CONFESSION

I'd like to be cheerful, she said. All day
I seek to find something to rejoice in. Often I find nothing,
and then my clothes fall from me; I remain
clinging softly in the void, waiting
for someone to love me that I may exist. Before even
the slightest breeze blows, I feel it trembling
on my toenails. Then suddenly
a single dangling spiderweb
rips my cheek apart from top to bottom.

Samos, August 20, 1964   (K.F.)

UNTAMED

Not blue—she says—the sky is red
with yellow spots. This is what she says. She raises her hand,
takes the red apple from the shelf, cuts the apple,
throws plate and apple out the window,
stands before the mirror and combs her hair,
with her red shoes, green hair, blue breasts,
with the knife between her teeth like reins,
ready to jump over her image with her red horse—
and its mane flashed in a sudden toss deep in the mirror.

Samos, August, 1964   (K.F.)

AFTERNOON

She watered the flowers and heard the water dripping from the
    balcony.
The boards became drenched and worn. The day after tomorrow,

when the balcony shall topple, she will remain in the air,
quiet, beautiful, holding in her hands
her two big flower pots, her gardenias, and her smile.

Samos, August, 1964   (K.F.)

MESSENGER

His sandals, left on the sand, warping in the sun.
He couldn't be seen anywhere. Perhaps he had forgotten himself
down below, with a group of swimmers. The shape of the sandals
betrays the attitude of a young man's foot. Evident the imprint
of the rhythmical, strong toes. Yet, how strange,
the two familiar, distinctive wings at the ankles are missing.

1964–1965   (K.F.)

REVERSE SIDE

He said: "Even solitude is a correlation."
He paused. Considered: "To what?"
Moon, beautiful loss, exhaustion,
ancient coin, I shall turn you on your other side
to see the sculptured profile of a youth
shaded by a horse's tail and a helmet.

Samos, August, 1964   (K.F.)

AFTER THE CEREMONY

With the shouting, the noise, the beautiful multicolored garments,
we forgot ourselves completely, nor did we raise our eyes
toward the high temple pediments cleansed only a month ago
by workers on erected scaffolds. However, when night fell
and the tumult had quieted down, the youngest of our company
cut away from us, ascended the marble stairs and stood
alone in that empty space where the morning's ceremonies were held.
    As he stood there
(and we a bit behind him that we might not seem inferior) with his
    beautiful head
slightly raised, absorbed, drenched
by the June moonlight, he gave us the impression
of being part of the pediment. We approached him, therefore,
clasped one another by the shoulders, and once more descended
the many steps. Nevertheless, it was as though
he had remained there, naked, enmarbled, withdrawn,
amid the youthful gods and the horses.

Samos, January, 1965   (K.F.)

THE PEACOCKS OF PERILAMPES

Why in the world did Perilámpes, that man of taste, want to carry
    off
those peacocks from the court of the Persian king?
Inappropriate on Hellenic soil, swaggering
with their vulgar coats of many colors on Periktióne's
pure-white marble staircase. Of course, the crowd
admired them extravagantly. And perhaps Perilámpes
brought them to Athens not for their feathers
but for their one unique croak. Certainly Plato

knew why. Moreover, even then, did not the ancients paint
their speeches and water jugs and faces and statues?
Even though all these today seem dazzlingly white?

Samos, August, 1964   (K.F.)

THE FIRST SENSUAL DELIGHT

Proud mountains, Kallídromon, Oéta, Óthrys,
dominating rocks, vineyards, wheat fields and olive groves;
here they've dug quarries, the sea has withdrawn;
the heavy scent of mastic trees burnt by the sun,
and the resin dripping in clots. A large
descending evening. There by the bank, Achilles,
not yet an adolescent, as he held his ankle
while tying his sandal, felt that distant sensual delight. For a
    moment
his mind wandered as he stayed gazing at reflections in the water.
    Then
he went to the blacksmith's and ordered his shield—
he knew precisely its shape now, its scenes, its size.

Stylis, June, 1964   (K.F.)

CHOICE

His companions fell asleep over the ropes at the stern;
and then she came, took him by the hand and brought him
a little way up from the shore; she lay beside him
and told him everything, like a mortal woman to her husband; she
    hid nothing from him—
what hardships he would meet, what precautions he should take.
    Yet,
at the most critical point, she didn't offer him any advice,
merely information. He had to decide—she said—

by himself and all by himself, to choose. (What choice was possible
between the two worse evils?) Yes, by himself,
just as he had remained in the wild fig tree, hanging like a bat
over the black bowels of the gaping depths, awaiting
the next impending rush of the sea,
by himself, in his last leap into the ocean, and by himself later
on his thunderstruck mast. This glory,
at least, was exclusively his — and perhaps his only glory.

1964–1965   (K.F.)

AT NAUSICÄ'S HOUSE

When in the evening, she returned from the riverbank to the
     seafaring town
where the masts stumbled against the balconies and grape arbors,
her very own brothers came out of the palace, unharnessed the
     mules,
then from the cart took and carried to the house the washed clothes,
dry and fragrant from sun, laurel, and soap, at the hour when
the servant girls lit the oil lamps and set the table for dinner.
     Tonight
the maiden shone with a different beauty, trembled, bustling
     around,
lest her brothers sense from the weight of the washed clothes
that one garment was missing. No one, of course, could tell. The
     stranger
had stayed outside the watered garden, by himself. When he
     appeared,
only Aréte recognized the clothes of her son Laodámas
on the stranger, when he fell to his knees before her,
and at once she felt toward him as toward her son. "Rise" — she
     said — and put him in the best seat
beneath the pillar where the guitar of Demódocus was hanging.

1964–1965   (K.F.)

GRADATIONS

Euryálos' improper words wrongfully enraged Odysseus.
Improper he wanted them, so spoke them. A merchant, he said,
who cares only for his merchandise and illegal profits,
and not for noble contests. Thus did he speak, and he and
the other succeeded when Odysseus lifted up the large discus
and flung it beyond all the other marks, with such a whistling
that the long-oared Phaeacians cowered (without considering
that the invisible Goddess had grooved the mark a good bit
    beyond).
Even so, how many other improprieties have there not been,
and these without the noble intentions of an Euryálos,
plain improprieties that have never succeeded in arousing
our strength? One should feel sorry for all
this sleeping power, and not at all for improprieties.
And the worse of it is that one feels sorry *only* for these.

Athens, January, 1965   (K.F.)

TRIVIAL DETAILS

As Eumaeus, the swineherd, got up to attend to
the stranger, at whom the sheep dogs were barking,
from his knees fell the beautiful, well-worked
oxhide he was preparing for his sandals. Later,
as he set forth to slaughter the two pigs
in hospitality for the old man, he tightened his belt.
These things—the hide, his sandals, the belt tightening—
their secret meaning (beyond gods and myths,
beyond symbols and ideas), only poets can sense.

1964–1965   (K.F.)

MONTH OF CLEANSING

January sunshine; frozen, denuding translucency.
All the clouds vanished suddenly. On the wooded hills,
still dark from the long dampness, rises
the sky blue smoke of shepherds. And the mountain ridges farther
    back,
absolutely sky blue—that superb sky blue. No other color,
—he says—can fit in this great, limpid landscape
except a speck of red from the rooster they slaughtered
on the foundation stone. So he spoke. And by this he meant
the movement of two fingers uncovering
a naked shoulder, a wound, a fountain, or a dream.

1964–1965   (K.F.)

ORESTES
(1962–1966)

Translated by Philip Pastras and George Pilitsis

(Two young men in their twenties stood before the gates. The expression on their faces made it seem as though they were trying to remember or recognize something, and yet everything seemed so familiar, so moving to them, only somehow smaller—much smaller—than they remembered while they were in that strange land; as if they belonged to a different place, to a different time, —even the walls, the huge stones, the lion-gate and the palace beneath the shadow of the mountain, were all smaller. It is summer already. Night is falling. The cars and the big charter busses have gone. The place can breathe again in peace, —a deep sigh from the mouths of ancient graves and memories. A piece of newspaper, blown by an indefinite breath, fluttered on the burnt grass. The footsteps of the night watchman and then the large key that locks the inside gate of the tower are heard. Then the crickets, as if they found their freedom in the hot coolness of the night, beat their small drums. Somewhere behind the mountain, an uncertain light crawls—maybe it's the moon. And exactly at that moment, a woman's wailings, sharp, harsh, out of tune, were heard coming from the stone stairway. The two young men didn't look at each other. They hugged the lower wall like two shadows. After a while, one of them wiped the sweat of his forehead with his handkerchief. With a slackened finger, he pointed in that direction and said to the other, who always stood there compassionately mute and devoted like Pylades):

Listen, —she hasn't stopped, she's not tired yet. She's unbearable,
in this Greek night, —so warm, so peaceful,
so independent from us and so indifferent, allowing us
the comfort—to be in it, to look at it from within
and the same time from afar; to see the night
naked to the tiniest voices of her crickets,
to the tiniest horrors of her dark skin.

How could we, too, have found a way to stay independent in the
     wonderful
joy of indifference and tolerance, away from everything,

inside of everything, inside of ourselves, — alone, united,
    unbound,
without comparisons, antagonisms, criticism, without
being measured by the expectations and claims of others. So I
    only
want to see the strap of your sandal that keeps
your big toe, the blameless one, pointed in my direction,
toward a secret spot of my own, next to the rhododendrons,
with the silvery leaves of the night falling on your shoulders
and the sound of the spring water passing unnoticed under our
    fingernails.

Listen to her, — her voice covers her like a resonant dome
and she hangs there from her voice
like a bell's clapper that's struck as it strikes the bell,
and yet it's neither a holiday or a funeral, only the pure solitude
    of the rocks
and the humble peace of the valley down below that underline
this unjustified rage surrounded
by countless stars that stir like innocent children's kites
with the restless paper-rustle of their long tails.

Let's move a little further away from here, so the woman's voice
    won't reach us;
let's stop down there; — not among the ancestral graves;
no libations tonight. I don't want
to cut my hair, — your hand
often wandered there. What a beautiful night —
something of our own that moves away, detached from us, and we
    hear it
flowing toward the sea like a dark river,
now and then reflecting the starlight under the branches,
in this sovereign sunless summer,
with invisible, momentary pauses, with random skips (maybe
    someone's
skipping stones over the river) — such a tiny leap,
and the windowpanes of the vinegrowers flash down below.
    Strange,

all my life they prepared me and I prepared myself for this. And
    now,

before this gate, I feel totally unprepared; —
the two marble lions — did you see them? — they've become tame,
the same ones that in our childhood years started out unyielding,
almost wild, with their manes erect for a bold leap,
they've settled in reconciliation on the top corners over the main
    gate,
their hair lifeless, their eyes vacant — they don't scare anyone — with
    the look
of whipped dogs, certainly not sad,
but loyal, blind dogs, without resentment,
now and then licking the tepid paw of the night with their
    tongues.

Unready, yes; — I can't do it;
I lack that inevitable relation to
the place, the time, the objects
and events; — not cowardice, — unready
before the threshold of the act, a complete stranger
to this mission that others have arranged for me. How does it
    happen
that others determine our fate, little by little, that they impose it
    on us
and that we accept it? How does it happen that, with the smallest
    piece of thread
from some of our moments, they weave
our whole lifetime, harsh and dark, thrown
over us like a veil from head to toe, covering
our entire face and hands where they've placed
a strange knife — totally unknown — and its harsh
reflecting light falls upon a landscape that's not ours, —
that much I know: not ours. And how can

our fate approve of it and withdraw and look at us and our alien
    fate
like a stranger, mute, austere, resigned, aloof,
without even a pretense of magnanimity or stoicism,
without at least disappearing, without dying,
so that we can become the prey of an alien fate,
but one only — not wavering and divided. There she is: our fate
    stands
there, she looks drowsy; — her one eye closed and the other open,

letting us see her as she looks and observes
our perpetual wavering, without approving or disapproving.

It seems to me that two counterbalancing centers of gravity are
  matched with our legs,
and the one center keeps moving away from the other,
widening our stride to the point of splitting the body in two; and
  the head
is a knot that keeps the torn body together
while, I think, the legs are made to move
one at a time, on their own, both in the same rhythm, in one
  direction,
carrying our body intact on the plain below, next to the clusters of
  grapes,
to the horizon beyond that turns red; — could it be
that we were created for that long, terrifying stride
over that unknown void, over the graves and over our own graves?
  I don't know.

But behind the many layers of confusion and fear, I foresee
the endless spread of stillness, — a justice,
a self-perpetuating balance that includes us
in the class of seeds and stars. Did you notice? — at noon,
as we were coming this way, the shadow of a cloud dragged itself
  over the plain,
covering the wheat-fields, the vineyards, the olive groves,
the horses, the birds, the leaves, — a translucent sketch
of a distant landscape of the infinite, here on the ground;
and the farmer who was walking on the far side of the plain
looked as though he was carrying under his left arm
the whole shadow of the cloud, like an enormous cloak,
majestic and yet as plain as his own sheep-skin.

That's how the earth becomes intimate with the infinite,
by taking something from its azure and from its vagueness; while
  the infinite
takes something from the earth, chestnut-brown and warm,
  something from the leaves,
something from water jugs and roots, something from the eyes
of that patient cow (do you remember her?)

and from the sure feet of the farmer who vanished in the
    distance.

Meanwhile, this woman's not about to quiet down. Listen to her.
Can't she hear her own voice? How can she stay
closed in, suffocating in an instant of time that has long gone,
of feelings that have long gone? How can she, and with what
can she revive this passion for revenge and the voice of that
    passion
when every echo contradicts her, even mocks her? echoes
from the huge storage vases in the garden, from the caves of Zaras,
    the aqueduct,
from the horse-stables down below and the watchtowers of the
    guards on the hilltops,
from the folds of the statues of women in the front yard
and from the noble phalluses of the stone runners and discus
    throwers?

Even the vases in the house seem to resist her wailings
by a gesture of compassion from the few delicate roses
gracefully placed by Mother's hand
there, on the carved console, before the large ancestral mirror
in a double light, a reflection within a reflection, watery — I
    remember that
from my childhood years — that much remains unclouded for
    me —
a watery, refined, neutral light — an infinity —
timeless, sinless, — tender and excellent,
just like the down on girls' necks or above the lips of young men,
just like the scent of a freshly bathed body on the cool sheets
that have been warmed by the breath of a summer night full of
    stars.

She doesn't understand a thing; not even the echoes
that mock her untuned voice. I'm afraid; I don't have the
    strength
to respond to her call — so monstrous and so comic at the same
    time —
or to her bombastic words, old words, almost as if they've been
    exhumed
from the chests of "the good old days" (as the old folks say),

like old flags, unironed, whose seams
have been penetrated by mothballs, deception and silence — they're
    so old
that they don't suspect their own age at all, and they insist
on flapping in an old-fashioned way over unsuspecting passers-by,
busy or exhausted, over asphalt streets, modest streets
in spite of their width and size, with their elegant store windows
full of neckties, sets of crystal, bathing suits, hats, hand bags, hair
    brushes,
all suitable for the necessities of our time,
and, therefore, of the life that commands us.

And she insists on preparing mead and food for the dead
who are no longer thirsty or hungry and don't even have a mouth
or dreams of restoration and revenge. She constantly invokes
their infallibility (— what infallibility, really?) perhaps because she
    wants
to avoid the responsibility of her choice and decision —
when the teeth of the dead, completely exposed, scattered on the
    ground,
are white seeds in an endless dark valley,
growing only into the infallible, invisible, pure white trees
that glow in the moonlight, till the end of time.

Ah, how can she stand to let her mouth shape these words,
dragged out of old linen-chests, yes (like the ones decorated with
    large nails), dragged out
from Mother's old hats, the ones she doesn't stoop to wear any
    more — did you see her
in the garden this afternoon? — how beautiful she still is — she
    hasn't aged a bit,
maybe because she oversees time and uses
every moment, — I mean, she rejuvenates herself,
aware she's losing her youth — maybe that's why she takes it back.

And Mother's voice, so contemporary, casual, correct, —
can pronounce the longest words naturally,
or even the simplest ones, each in its broadest sense, such as:
"a butterfly came in from the window"
or: "the world is unbearably wonderful"
or: "more blueing should've been used for the linen towels"

or: "a note from this night's fragrance escapes me" and she
    laughs,
maybe to forestall someone who could've laughed.

Her deep sense of understanding and tender compassion
for everyone and for everything (almost a sense of disdain); — I
    always admired her and was terrified of her
and her conscious, lofty arrogance,
as she'd blend her small, sly and many-sided smile
with the small sound of a struck match and its flame as she was
    lighting
the hanging lamp in the dining room, and there she'd be, lit from
    below
by a light that focused on her well-defined chin
and delicate, pulsating nostrils which for a moment
stopped breathing and narrowed
as if to stay near us, to stand, to be still,
so that she wouldn't be dispersed like a column of blue smoke in
    the night-breezes,
so that the trees wouldn't snatch her away with their long
    branches,
so that she wouldn't wear the thimble of a star for an endless
    embroidery—

That's how Mother always found her most precise movement and
    pose,
exactly at the moment of her absence, — I was always afraid
that she'd disappear before our eyes; better yet, that she might
    rise, — whenever she would bend
to tie the sandal that left her fine,
painted, rose-colored toes exposed, or when she would fix
her hair before the large mirror
with a stroke of her palm, so charming, youthful and light,
as if she were rearranging three or four stars on the forehead of the
    universe,
as if she were placing two daisies close enough to kiss each other
    by the water fountain,
or as if she were watching with affectionate boldness two dogs
fucking in the middle of the dusty road

on a blazing hot summer noon. That's how plain and convincing
   Mother was,
and strong, too, imposing and mystifying.

Maybe my sister never forgave her—for her perpetual
   youthfulness—
that old kid, sensible by contrast, given to the denial
of beauty and joy;—ascetic, repulsive in her prudence,
alone and desolate. Even her clothes
are stubbornly the clothes of an old woman, loose, untidy, aged,
and the cord around her waist is unflattering, worn out,
like a vein without blood around her belly (and yet she tightens
   it)
like the cord of a fallen curtain that neither opens nor closes
showing, slantwise, a landscape of an always harsh austerity
with sharp rocks and huge trees, naked, that branch out
over conventional, pompous clouds; and there, in the distance,
the obscure presence of a lost sheep,
an animate white stain, a grain of tenderness—it doesn't show—
and my sister, herself a rock, upright,
locked in its toughness;—she's unbearable. Listen to her,
almost trifle; she carefully watches Mother and gets absolutely
   furious
when she puts a flower in her hair or in her cleavage,
whenever she walks the hallway with her footsteps full of certainty
   and music,
whenever she tilts her head to the side with sorrowful ease
letting a deep sound fall from her long earring to her shoulder,
a sound that only she can hear,—that's her sweet privilege. And
   the other one becomes furious.

She sustains her rage with the intensity of her own voice—
(if she lost that, what else would she have left?)—I think she's
   afraid to carry out
the punishment, since she'd have nothing left. She never
heard the night-grass rustle secretly with the passing
of a graceful, invisible animal outside the windows at dinner
   time;
she never saw the rope ladder leaning, for no reason,
against the tall and bare wall on a holiday; she never paid
   attention

to that "for no reason"; she never noticed
the tuft of a corn stalk scratching the sole of a tiny cloud's foot,
or the shape of a water jug against the starry sky, or a sickle
left alone, next to the spring, one afternoon,
or the shadow of the loom in the closed room, when they sprinkle
    the vineyards with sulphur
and the voices of the farmers are heard down below on the plain,
while, left alone in this world, some sparrow,
pecking at small flies, seeds, or some bread crumbs in the yard,
is trying to spell out his freedom. She saw nothing.

She's totally blind, a prisoner in her blindness. But how can she
live a life only by opposing someone else,
only by hating someone else, and not by love
for her own life, without making a stand of her own? And what
    do they want?
What do they want from me? "Revenge. Revenge," they shout.
Let them do it themselves, since they feed on revenge.

I don't want to hear her any more. I can't stand it. No one
has the right to rule over my eyes, my mouth, my hands,
and over these feet that tread the earth. Give me your hand. Let's
    go.

Long summer nights, absolute, our own,
a blend of stars, damp armpits, broken glasses, —
an insect buzzes gently in the ear of silence,
lizards warm themselves at the feet of youthful statues,
slugs on park benches or even inside the closed blacksmith's shop
wander about on the huge anvil and leave
white lines of sperm and saliva on the black iron.

If we could only leave the land of Mycenae again; — here the
    ground smells like
rusted copper and dark blood. Attica is lighter, isn't it? I feel
now, at this particular moment, the moment
of my final resignation. I don't want
to become their topic of conversation, their agent, their
    instrument, not even their leader.

I've a life of my own, too, and I must live it. No revenge; —
how much could death lose by one less death,
especially a violent one? — what would that add to life? Years have
    gone by.
I don't feel hatred any more; — maybe I've forgotten? Am I tired? I
    don't know.
I can even feel some compassion for the murderers; — she carefully
    calculated the risks,
a great knowledge opened her eyes wide in the darkness
and she sees, — she sees the inexhaustible, the impossible, the
    inevitable. She sees me.

I, too, want to see Father's murder as part of the soothing totality
    of death,
to forget him in the wholeness of death
that awaits us, too. This night has taught me about the innocence
of all usurpers. All of us are usurpers of something, —
some, usurpers of people; some, of power,
some, of love, or even death; my sister
a usurper of my only life; and I of yours.

My dear friend, how patiently you share
the strange, foolish affairs of others. Anyhow, my hand
is yours; take it; you too can usurp it; — it's yours,
and so it's mine, too; take it; hold it tight; you expect it
to be free of my punishments, revenge, memories,
free; — that's how I want it, too,
to belong to me completely, that's the only way
I'd give it entirely to you. Forgive this
mysterious solitude and sharing of mine — you know about it —
that tears me in half. What a beautiful night —

A damp smell of oregano, thyme, caper, —
or is it geranium? — I confuse the smells; sometimes,
blood smells like sea-brine, and sperm smells of the forest; —
a willful transposition, perhaps, — that's what I need tonight,
as that soldier was telling us one night in Athens:
the seashore echoed the clashes and groans,
and he, hidden in the burned bushes, above the shore,
was watching, in the moonlight, the wavering shadow of his penis
    on his thigh

in an uncertain erection that he was trying to sustain, testing
his will on his own body, trying to remove himself
from the battlefield of death to the hope of a doubtful
    self-reliance.

Let's go further down; I can't listen to her; her wailing
shatters my nerves and my dreams, just as
those oars were striking the floating corpses
that the torches from the battleships and the shooting stars of
    August illuminated,
and all of them were shining, young and passionate, unbelievably
    immortal,
in a watery death that was cooling their backs, their ankles, their
    arms and legs.

How quietly the seasons change. Everywhere night is falling.
A straw chair stays alone, forgotten under the trees,
in the light humidity and the vapors that the ground gives out.
It's not grief; not even an expectation; it's nothing.
A motionless motion is spread over yesterday and tomorrow.
The turtle is a rock in the grass; it will move soon —
calmly unexpected, secret complicity, happiness.

A small spot of emptiness stays in your smile; — maybe
because of what I've said to you or what I'm about to say, though I
    don't know what that is yet,
I still haven't found the rhythm of the word that walks
ahead of my thoughts — way ahead, — it shows me
my rhythm and myself. Like that time in track,
when the runners arrived drenched in sweat, I noticed someone
who had a piece of string tied around his ankle
by chance, for no particular reason. And it was exactly that.
    Nothing else.

Sacrifices, she says, and heroic deeds — what kind of change is
    that? Years and years the same. Maybe we came
to make these small discoveries of the great miracle
that has nothing to do with great or small, murder or sin.

All a single passion — an enchantment and dazzle (as Mother used
    to say),

when the night's leaves, broad, fleshy, refreshing,
touch our foreheads and the fruit that falls
is a fixed and untranslatable message
like the circle, the triangle or the rhomb. I'm thinking
about a saw rusting in an abandoned carpenter's shop,
and the numbers on the houses move far in the horizon—
3, 7, 9—the countless number. Listen: she's finished.

Impossible, this great stillness;—I picture thousands of jet-black
     horses
climbing the slopes toward Tretó in the dark, while on the other
     side
a golden river flows down toward the plain
with its dried-up springs, vacant barracks, and the stables
where the straw gives off vapors from an ancient warmth of lost
     animals,
and the dogs, with their tails between their legs, vanish
like ink-black spots in the silvery depth of the night.

At last she's stopped;—silence;—what a relief. That's beautiful.
Look, the shadows of fleeting insects on the wall
leave behind a drop of moisture or a tiny bell
that sounds a little while later. Far away, a blaze—
a prolonged suspicion, purple—the moon,
a small, solitary fire behind the trees, the chimneys of the houses
     and the weather vanes,
burns the big thorns and yesterday's newspapers,
leaving behind this confirmation—almost a praise—
of the unexpected, the hopeless, of the proven futility,
far into the bold wilderness, to the end of the road
with the ghostly, violet passage of a cat.

When the moon rises, the houses shrink in the plain below,
the corn creaks with the morning chill or with the laws of growth,
the whitewashed tree-trunks glow at their bases like columns
     reaped
in a noiseless war, while the signs of the small stores
hang down like prophesies fulfilled over closed doors.

The farmers must have fallen asleep by now with their large hands
     on their bellies

and the birds with their small hands hooked over branches in their
    sleep,
as if they were not trying to hold on, as if such effort meant
    nothing,
as if nothing had happened, nothing was going to happen—
light, light, as if the sky had come under their wings,
as if someone walks on the long, narrow hallway with a lamp in
    his hand
while all the windows are open and outside in the country you can
    hear
the animals ruminate peacefully as if in eternity.

I like this fresh silence. Somewhere nearby, on a patio,
a young woman should be combing her long hair
and near her, underwear hung out to dry will breathe fresh air in
    the moonlight.
Everything is liquid, slippery, happy. Large water jugs in the bath
    house,
I suppose, are pouring water over the necks and breasts of young
    girls,
small, aromatic bars of soap slide on the tiles,
bubbles tear through the noise of water and laughter,
one woman slipped and fell,
the moon slipped down on the skylight,
everything slides from the soap—you can't hold them
or yourself;—this sliding
is the rhythm of life coming round again; the women laugh,
shaking the white, airy turrets of soap
on the small forest of their pubic hair. Is happiness like that?

This night of expectation allows me an opening to see outside
and inside as well. I don't see things clearly. Maybe they are
large, abysmal masks, metal clasps;
the sandals of the dead are warped from humidity,
they move by themselves, as if they walk without feet—they don't
    walk,
and the large net in the bath—who wove it?—
knot by knot,—it can't be untied—black,—Mother didn't weave
    it.

An endless shadow spreads over the arches;
a stone comes loose and falls down the ravine — but no one was
    walking there —
after that, nothing; and again, a branch that breaks away
from the airy weight of the sky. Tiny frogs
leap softly and noiselessly on the young grass. Silence.

Gray mice jump in the wells and drown,
compact constellations move slowly; that's where
the drinking parties throw water-jugs, cups, mirrors and chairs,
bones of animals, lyres and wise dialogues. The wells never fill.

Something like fingers of fire and dew run continuously over our
    chests
and trace circles that search around the nipples,
and we ourselves are spinning, circle after circle,
around an unknown, indefinite and yet definite center; — endless
    circles
around a mute scream, around a stabbing; and the knife,
I think, has pierced our hearts, making a center of our hearts
like the pole in the middle of the threshing-floor up there on the
    hill,

around it the horses, the wheat, the winnowers, the cart drivers,
and the women reapers, next to the hay stacks, the head of the
    moon on their shoulders,
hear the neighing of the horses in the furthest reaches of their
    sleep,
hear the bulls pissing on the willow trees and the berry-shrubs,
the thousand feet of the centipede on the water-jug,
the crawling of the tame snake in the olive grove
and the creaking of the heated rock that cools and contracts.

A word of love remains unspoken, always locked in our mouths,
like a pebble in our shoes, or even a nail; you don't feel like
taking the time to stop and take it out, to untie the laces
and waste time; — you've been captivated more by the secret pace
    of your journey
than by the arrogance of the pebble or
the stubborn reminder from your exhaustion,
from your procrastination; and still it's

a kind of small, thorny delight and recollection
that you carried from a beach that you're fond of,
from a pleasant walk with fine reflections and watery images,
when the conversations of the tobacco merchants
along with the sailors' song and the song of the sea
could be heard far, far away, lost, close, strange, ours, in the
   tavern by the sea.

The poor woman's quiet now. In her silence, I can hear that she's
   right, —
she's so unprotected in her wrath, so wronged,
her bitter hair hangs loose on her shoulders, like weeds on a
   tomb,
walled off in her narrow justice. Maybe she fell asleep,
maybe she's dreaming of an innocent place with kind animals,
with whitewashed houses, with the aroma of freshly-baked bread,
   and with roses.

I've just remembered — I don't know why — that cow
we saw that evening, in a field in Attica — do you remember?
She was standing, unyoked from the plow, and was looking far
   away,
two small streams of vapor coming from her nostrils,
misting the purple, violet, golden sunset, mute, wounded
on her sides and back, marks from a flogging on her forehead,
maybe she knew about denial and submission,
things irreconcilable, and hostility within the agreement.

Between her two horns, she was carrying
the heaviest piece of the sky, like a crown. A while later
she lowered her head and drank water from the stream,
licking with her bloody tongue the other
cool tongue of her image in the water, as if she were licking
broadly, peacefully, affectionately, like a mother,
her own inner wound from the outside, as if she were licking
the silent, large, round wound of the world; — maybe she
   quenched her thirst —
maybe only our own blood can quench our thirst — who knows?

Later, she raised her head from the water, without touching
   anything,

untouched herself and calm as a saint,
and only between her legs, as if they'd been rooted in the river,
the blood from her lips gathered and was changed into a small
    lake,
a red lake, in the shape of a map,
that little by little broadened and dispersed; it disappeared
as if her blood flowed far away, free and painless,
into an invisible vein of the world; she was calm
for this very reason, as if she'd learned
that blood is not wasted, that nothing is wasted,
nothing, nothing is wasted in this great nothing, inconsolable,
    unmerciful, incomparable,
so sweet, so consoling, so nothing.

That nothing is our familiar vastness. In vain this panting,
this anxiety, this praise. That's the kind of cow
I drag along with me, in my shadow — not tethered;
she follows me on her own; — she's my shadow on the road
when the moon's out; she's my shadow on a closed door; and you
    know it always:
the shadow is soft, bodiless; and the shadows of those two horns
could be two spearlike wings, and you can fly,
or maybe you can pass through that locked door in another way.

I've just remembered (even though this doesn't mean anything)
the cow's eyes, — dark, blind, huge, arched,
like two mounds of darkness or of black glass; on those mounds
a steeple and the blackbirds that sit on its cross are dimly reflected;
    and then, someone shouted
and the birds flew from the cow's eyes. I think the cow
was the symbol of an ancient religion. Keep
such ideas and abstractions away from me. A common cow
for the villagers' milk and for the plow, with all the wisdom
of work, perseverence and usefulness. And yet,

the last minute, just before the herd returned to the village —
    remember? —
she sounded such a harrowing cry at the horizon
that the branches around her, the swallows, the sparrows,
the horses, the goats and the farmers

196

scattered in all directions, leaving her alone in a completely empty
    circle
from which the group of constellations
was rising higher and higher in space, until the cow ascended; no,
    no,
I think I could make her out in the dark
as she climbed the path with the bushes, silently, submissively
toward the village, at the hour when the lamps were lit in the
    yards, behind the trees.

Look, it's dawning. There, the first rooster's crowing on the fence.
The gardener's up; a small tree takes root in the garden. Familiar
    noises
of tools — saws, hoes —
and the running water in the yard; someone is washing himself;
    the ground smells;
the water is boiling in the coffeepots; quiet columns of smoke over
    the rooftops;
a warm aroma of sage. We've survived this night, too.

Now let's lift this urn that's supposed to keep my ashes; —
the recognition scene is about to begin.
Everyone will find in me the one they've been expecting,
they'll find the just man, according to their laws,
and only you and I will know
I really carry my true ashes in this urn; — only the two of us.

And when the others triumph through my act, the two of us
will cry over the bright, bloody sword, the one worthy of praise,
we'll cry over these ashes, this dead man whose place was taken
by someone else, completely covering his flayed face
with a golden, auspicious, venerable mask,
maybe even useful with its rough-hewn shape,
as a piece of advice, an example, a delirium of the masses, a fear
    of the tyrant, an exercise
that perpetuates history, slowly, heavily, with successive deaths and
    triumphs,
not with a terrible knowledge (impossible for the masses)
but by a difficult act and an easy faith,
an unyielding, necessary, unhappy faith,
falsified a thousand times, and again that many times held

for dear life by man's soul;—ignorant faith
that secretly accomplishes great things in the dark.

And I, the infidel, chose this faith (the others don't choose me)
knowingly, however, in my case. I choose
the knowledge and the act of death that raises life. Let's go
      now—
not for my father, not for my sister (maybe
he and she both will be gone some day), not for revenge, not for
      hatred—not at all for hatred)
not for punishment (who'd punish who?)
but maybe for the fulfillment of an appointed time, to keep time
      free,
maybe for some useless victory over our first and last fear,
maybe for some "yes" that shines, vague and blameless, apart from
      you and me,
so that (if possible) this place can breathe. Look how
beautiful daybreak is.

In the morning it's a little humid in the Argolid. The urn
is almost frozen, with some dew-drops
as though rosy-fingered dawn, as the saying goes, sprinkled it with
      her tears,
as she held it between her knees. Let's go. The time
has come already. Why are you smiling? Are you nodding in
      approval?
You knew about it and didn't say anything?
This fair ending—yes?—after the fairest combat?

Let me kiss your smile for the last time,
as long as I still have lips. Let's go now, I recognize my fate. Let's
      go.

(*They walked toward the gate. The guards moved out of the way as if
they were expecting them. The old doorkeeper opened the large
door, his head kept humbly bowed, as if he were welcoming them.
Minutes later, the deep groaning of a man was heard and then the
frightening, painful scream of a woman. Again, deep silence. In the
plain down below, the sparse gunshots of hunters and the countless
chirpings of invisible sparrows, finches, bee-eaters and blackbirds.
The swallows flew stubbornly in circles over the north corner of the*

palace. The guards, undisturbed, took off their caps and wiped off the inside leather rim with their sleeves. Then right in the middle of the lion gate, a large cow stood, looking the morning sky right in the eyes with her own huge, pitch-black, motionless eyes.)

Bucharest, Athens, Samos, Mycenae,
June 1962–July 1966   *(P.P. & G.P.)*

జు

from

TANAGRA FIGURINES
(1967)

Translated by Kostas Myrsiades

THE POTTER

One day, he finished the pitchers, the flower pots, the cooking pots.
　　Some clay
remained. He made a woman. Her breasts
big and firm. He returned home late.
His wife complained. He didn't reply. The next day
he kept more clay and even more the following day.
He did not go home. His wife divorced him.
His eyes burn. He's half-naked. He has a red sash around his waist.
All night long he lies beside clay women. At dawn
you hear him singing behind the pottery wall.
He's removed his red sash. He's naked. Stark-naked. And around
　　him
the empty pitchers, the empty cooking pots, the empty flower pots
and the beautiful, blind, deaf-mute women with the bitten breasts.

(K.M.)

METHOD OF SALVATION

Night. A major storm. The lonely woman hears
the waves ascending the stairs. She's afraid
that they'll reach the second storey, that they'll put out the lamp,
that they'll drench the matches, that they'll hide under the bed.
　　Then
the lamp in the sea will be like a drowned man's head
with a single yellow thought. This saves her.
She hears the waves receding again. There, on the table,
she sees the lamp — its glass somewhat clouded by the salt.

(K.M.)

MARINE

Skillful, proud, handsome, with a sturdy knife,
he sliced the big fish on the wharf—
he threw the tail and the sword in the sea.
The blood seethed on the planks, shining.
His feet, his hands were red.
One woman said to another: "His knife is red, how well it matches his
    black eyes—."
Red, black, red. On an upper narrow sidestreet,
on an antiquated black scale
the fishermen's children weighed fish, coal.

(K.M.)

NIGHT RITUAL

They butchered the cock, the dove, the goat. With the blood
they smeared their faces, their necks, their shoulders. One
turned towards the wall and smeared his penis. Then
the three women, on the corner, wearing white veils
screamed out as if being butchered. On their bellies,
a long incision full of blood appeared. The men,
as if not hearing, as if not seeing, wrote on the floor
with chalk, with uncoiled snakes, and with ancient arrows. Outside
the fiery drums were heard throughout the neighborhood.

(K.M.)

FACE OR MASK?

"I carved this statue in the stone—he said,
not with a chisel; with my bare eyes, my bare fingers,
with my bare body, my bare lips. Now I forget
who is me and who the statue."
                              He hid behind it;
he was repulsive, repulsive—he embraced it, lifted it by the waist,
and together they walked away.

Later he would tell us that perhaps
this statue (truly admirable) was he; or even
that the statue walked unaided. Who believes him?

(K.M.)

THE ONE-ARMED MAN

Ancient clay lamps lay beside the grave;
beyond some pitchers and stone statues; farther off
a clay hand. A villager passing by on his horse
stopped abruptly. "That hand is mine — he said —
I lost it on the mountain," motioning in that direction with his
    head.
He took the hand and put it in its place. With precisely this hand
he hit his horse's rump and both disappeared
on a field-lined plain where smoke rose from several houses.

(K.M.)

ACROBATICS

He placed his hands on the floor; he stood upside down; not merely
with ease, perfectly vertical, but he even walked, in a manner
which made the past present and vice versa. Until a hole opened
and swallowed him whole. We were confused. Just then the door
    rang.
We rushed, anxious. We could be accused of murder. We opened it.
It was him, with a basket of oranges under his right hand.

(K.M.)

ESTEEM

Gunny sacks and bushels in rows standing in the courtyard.
The scale was in the warehouse. The warehouse locked.

The caretaker had forgotten the keys
under his wife's pillow. His wife,
making the bed (10 a.m. by now) found them —
ugly, bulky keys. She stood at the window;
she tossed them in the river. Only a bit of rust remained on the
    sheet.

(K.M.)

SUBJECT FOR AN OIL PAINTING

On the third day, when we unlocked the room, we found nothing.
Everything arranged to perfection, serene, unexplored. Only
a few drops of spermaceti on the purple velvet
of her old armchair. And the silver candlestick,
lofty in its solitude — a neglected trident
beside the music book and the bowl of apples.

(K.M.)

THE OLD HOUSE

The house unoccupied for years. When the newylweds leased it,
before moving their furniture, they came to air out the rooms.
    Wooden stairs,
carved trelliswork, wardrobes, hallways, echoes in the void.
On the walls large square areas of a darker color, pistachio, morose,
from old discarded oil-paintings. In the long narrow salon upstairs,
the heavy purple drapes full of dust. They removed them. Beyond:
a plaster statue, and the skeleton of a large bird. The woman
screamed and froze. The man approached
and stuffed a key in the statue's mouth.

Karlóvasi, Samos, January, 1967   *(K.M.)*

from

STONES
(1968)

Translated by Kimon Friar, N. C. Germanacos,
and by Gwendolyn MacEwen and Nikos Tsingos

UNACCOMPLISHED

Clouds on the mountains. Who is to blame? What is to blame?
    Silent, tired,
he looks ahead, turns back, walks on, stoops.
The stones are below, the birds are above. A pitcher
on the windowsill. Thorns in the fields. Hands in his pockets.
Pretenses, pretenses. The poem is slow in coming. Emptiness.
The word is marked by what it must pass over in silence.

May 15, 1968   *(K.F.)*

SIGNALS

Later, the statues were totally hidden by the weeds. We couldn't tell
if the statues got smaller or the weeds got taller. Only
one great bronze hand was visible over the mastic trees
shaped like an awful and unfitting eulogy. The woodcutters
passed by along the lower road — they didn't turn their heads at all.
The women didn't lie with their men. At night we heard
apples dropping one by one into the river; and later,
the stars, sawing quietly away on that upraised bronze hand.

May 16, 1968   *(G.M. & N.T.)*

UNANSWERED

Where are you taking me from here? Where does this road go? Tell
    me.
I can see nothing. It's not a road. Stones only.
Black beams. Streetlamp. If only at least
I had the cage—not that birdcage, but the other one
with the large wires, with the naked statue. Now I know:
the last thing that dies is the body. Speak to me, then.
Where are you taking me from here? I can see nothing. It's a good
    thing I can't see.
For me there is no greater obstacle for thinking to the end than
    glory.

May 19, 1968   *(K.F.)*

THE UNACCEPTABLE MAN

He withdrew from our company little by little, as though he were
    somewhat sad,
as though somewhat strangely serene, as though he had discovered
something great or incommunicable—a headless statue, a star, a
    truth,
a final and only truth.—"Which?" we asked him. He
never answered, somehow as though he knew we could not even have
    wanted to learn.
                    The first stone
was cast by his friends. Not that his adversaries
had to be restrained. At the trial
they questioned him again and again. Not a word. Then the judge
rang the bell loudly, shouted, became enraged; he commanded
    silence
so that the silence of the accused might not be heard. The verdict,
    guilty, was unanimous.
We returned one by one and leaned our heads against the wall.

May 24, 1968   *(K.F.)*

TOWARD WHAT?

As the years passed by, he began to speak bitterly; (how strange, he
    who had been so dedicated, or rather so submissive); not of
    course
about persons or events—but somewhat generally and vaguely, at any
    rate, uncomfortably,
and perhaps even somewhat fearfully.
                               His hands
were contorted like the roots of trees in an alien land,
in a land deeply our own.
                        No one
believed him any longer or looked him in the eyes—let him say what
    he will.
Not that we were ever afraid of this frightened man—not at all. A
    windowpane
high up on the fifth floor cast on him an affable glow,
lit up his face as though he were wearing a glass mask.
                            And we
put up our hands to our faces, as though we wanted to hide
or to hold up a leaning wall. Between our fingers
pieces of plaster fell, stones, soil, bronze coins;
we stopped and gathered them—we were not kneeling before him.

And in the mirror opposite, something white, infinitely white—
a glass of water, and inside it an old comb made of bone,
and the crystal gleam of the water in the glass, in the mirror, in the
    air.

May 24, 1968   (K.F.)

METHOD FOR OPTIMISM

A rancorous man—he would remember all that was gloomy—this is
    what he underlined;
indeed, he would generalize, somewhat arbitrarily and persuasively
    together—a system

that was profound, obscure, and probably foreseeing. Everything was
    dark, almost black—
furniture, faces, windows, time. For all that, his face
remained luminous, suffused with a certain secret happiness—
    perhaps because he had the ability
of discerning in the dark, of discerning the dark itself, and even
the four bronze bullets gleaming in the distance, on the large bed
where the two beautiful dead reposed in a position of sexual
    intercourse.

May 26, 1968   (K.F.)

WITH THESE STONES

A strong wind blew. The heavy shutters creaked.
The leaves rose from the ground. They fled, they fled.
Only the stones remained. It is with these we must make do now;
with these, with these, he keeps repeating. When night descends
from the large jet-black mountain and casts the keys into the well—
O stones—he says—my stones, one by one I shall hew
my unknown faces and my body, with one of my hands
clenched tight, raised up high above the wall.

May 30, 1968   (K.F.)

DOUBLE CONDEMNATION

So that's it? Just that? Shall our pride—he said—depend
on the errors of others? What pride? What justification? And not
on our own virtues? Master, Master, we've seen through your
    miming
well enough: justice, freedom; and that smile of yours—
heavenly is what we'd called it—when the doors opened and the
    crowds ran,
ran after you clamoring, leaving their homes wide open

to the sun, the wind, to thieves. And when, the following night,
the thirteenth man raised his glass, we knew now:
everything had happened already. The dead lay in the beds,
and under the beds your own cardboard boots,
red, imperial, with small mirrors stuck all round.

June 6, 1968   (N.C.G.)

SILENCE

Another body inside his body, large, inscrutable,
dumb—an omnipotent dumbness. At noon
or evenings, at the table, with the quiet lamp, as he slowly
and carefully lifts the fork to his mouth, he knows
he is feeding that other, that unknown, gluttonous mouth.

July 27, 1968   (N.C.G.)

cĀ

from

BARRIERS
(1968–1969)

Translated by Kimon Friar, N. C. Germanacos, Kostas Myrsiades, and by
Gwendolyn MacEwen and Nikos Tsingos

THE FINAL OBOL

Difficult hours, difficult in our land. And this proud,
naked, defenseless, feeble man allows them to help him;
they mortgage him off, take certain rights, set up claims;
they speak on his behalf, adjust his breathing and his steps;
they give him alms, dress him in other clothing, slack, hanging
    loose,
and tighten his waist with a ship's cord. He,
in clothing not his, does not speak or even smile
for fear of revealing (even when sleeping) the final obol
he is tightly gripping between his teeth (his sole property now),
his naked, glittering, obdurate death.

November 7, 1968   *(K.F.)*

TRICKS

He and I—he says—do two jobs totally similar in their
    dissimilarity—
he takes a face, strips it of flesh, of eyes,
makes naked skulls, lines them up on shelves; they gleam at night
under the green light-bulbs, almost beyond pain. Even in daytime,
in sunlight, they're white, disciplined, prohibiting. The dust
plays in gold particles in the hollow of their eyes. On the other hand,
    I
take back the skulls, stick on their hair, ears and nose with fishglue,
put colored glass for eyes, paint in their cheeks and mouth
carefully, tastefully; I put them at the windows; they stare outside—

211

"That's Peter." "That's Mary," the passers-by say, "That's Helen."
They smile, wave to them. Then pass on, go down to the beach.
"Ah"— he says—"What I need myself, I want to give to others too.
I'm not deceiving anyone—here is my handkerchief, and here my
    buttons."

February 2, 1969   (N.C.G.)

NEWS REPORT

Evening clouds; the lighted clock in the church in the square;
bald trees; cold; garbage. From the hilltops
gunfire could still be heard. A while later
Yiorgos arrived on a bicycle. He laid down
a guitar with broken strings. "We hauled the dead—he said—
into the storeroom. No time for prayers or flags.
But hide this list at least, so in the future we'll remember
their names, their ages—I've even got the measurements of their
    legs.
The three marble-workers were killed too. All that's left
is that stone angel, without a head—you can put any head
you like on it." With that he left. He didn't take the guitar.

February 4, 1969   (G.M. & N.T.)

ROUGHLY SQUARE

He had no arguments, yet always insisted on the same position.
He drew a square on the floor with chalk; stepped inside it—
that's the door—he drew—the window here; the woman in the
    corner;
another window; the light enters; the crystals of the chandelier
    sparkle.
We watched; there was neither a woman (and we knew it: she'd be
    naked)

nor any chandelier. He left the chalk on the table,
looked at the ground and dug his hands in his pockets, clearly
    bothered
he had not convinced us, and above all by that dry chalk-dust.
We realized he was secretly wiping his fingers
in his pockets, though feigning the immobility of statues.

February 18, 1969   (N.C.G.)

LAST WILL AND TESTAMENT

He said: I believe in poetry, in love, in death,
which is precisely why I believe in immortality. I write a verse,
I write the world; I exist; the world exists.
A river flows from the tip of my little finger.
The sky is seven times blue. This purity
is once again the prime truth, my last will.

March 31, 1969   (N.C.G.)

THE READY MAN

Oh, his death sure was a neat trick; he played dead
to save himself from our hassels. Lying there on the bed
in his best suit, arms folded, eyes shut,
so withdrawn and oblivious, he lay in wait. And had anyone
rung the front doorbell or a bird pecked on the pane,
he'd have been the first to dash out and open the door—his toes
twitched in his shoes, on the alert (they showed),
and maybe that's why he'd worn his best suit.
He kept his toothbrush in his vest pocket.

May 15, 1969   (G.M. & N.T.)

BLOOD

After, a bloodstain appeared in the asphalt;
the stain grew, spread out, swallowed
the courtyard, the chair, the well, the bucket;
a meter of rope was left—only that.
The clock of the church in the square turned red;
also the Post Office. The stain spread out,
swallowed the houses, the telegraph poles, the sun,
and us—it concealed us in its redness.
And only when we realized its size could we once again feel
beautiful, simple, back in place, absolved.

May 17, 1969   *(G.M. & N.T.)*

THE TIGHTROPE WALKER

No, he doesn't want to let go; the rope shakes; he shuts his eyes.
The depths, below, black with silence. There's no end to the rope.
His eyes open, dilate, float, drift upwards,
holding onto a cloud, a leaf; they change, grow circular,
become two great links; he hangs on by his eyes—look at him,
he lets go of the rope, somersaults in the air, eases down,
his hat falls off, so does the flower in his lapel—look at him again
as he feels for the rope with his fingertips; mounts the stairs,
balances, smiles; a final bow. Nobody's around
to applaud him. Just one voice: Hang on, hang on,
hang on by your eyes. Who's calling him? Where are they calling
    from?

May 19, 1969   *(G.M. & N.T.)*

THE CRAFTSMAN

He takes clay, molds the face, the body
beautiful, naked, serene—with what prototypes?—
Those in the coffeehouse, the temple, or the demonstration?
And that tall oarsman?
                        The sun
enters shining from the door and emphasizes
hollows and projections, places shadows
of the body on the body.
                        And the craftsman
blows his breath into the clay mouth—
a taste of earth remains on his lips;
afterwards he takes his hat, walks out into the street
with a guilty smile of secret happiness
as though he were playing the part of a deaf-mute, which in fact
    he is.

May 30, 1969   (K.F.)

ONE WORD

When he'd exhaust everything around him and inside himself
and felt as if in a slump—then he'd remember to utter
only one word: *statue* (and, of course, he meant
a Greek statue, naked). And immediately, all around him
island names would unfold; a knee shone opposite
on the sea; the young archer's quiver
could be discerned buried below a knoll of fine sand.
He'd dress and go to the Market. "Good morning," he'd say.
Butcher shops, pottery shops, fruit shops. He'd buy grapes,
liberating that deep, serene, and inexhaustible
gesture of a severed, marble forearm.

May 24, 1969   (K.M.)

RENAISSANCE

No one had taken care of the garden for years. And yet
this year—May, June—it had burst into bloom again by itself,
and all of it blazed up to the fence—a thousand roses,
a thousand carnations, a thousand geraniums, a thousand
      sweetpeas—
colors, color-wings—so that the woman once more appeared
with her old watering can to care for them—beautiful once more,
serene, with a vague good faith. And the garden
hid her up to her shoulders, embraced her, won all of her,
and raised her in its arms. And then we saw, on the drop of noon,
that the garden and the woman with her watering can were taken up
      into the heavens—
and as we raised our heads high, a few drops from the watering can
fell softly on our cheeks, our chins, our lips.

Karlóvasi, Samos, June 3, 1969   *(K.F.)*

from

REPETITIONS
(1968–1969)

Translated by Kimon Friar and Karelisa Hartigan,
N. C. Germanacos, Thanasis Maskaleris, Kostas Myrsiades,
and by Gwendolyn MacEwen and Nikos Tsingos

THE GRAVES OF OUR ANCESTORS

We should guard our dead and their power, lest at some hour
our opponents disinter them and take them away. And then,
without their protection, we will be running a double risk. How will
     we live any more
without our houses, our furniture, our fields, especially without
the graves of our ancestors, the warriors and the wise? Let us
     remember
how the Spartans stole the bones of Orestes from Tegéa. Our
     enemies
must never know where we have them buried. But
how will we ever know who our enemies are
or when and from where they will appear? No, therefore, no grand
     monuments,
no showy ornaments — such things arouse attention and malice. Our
     dead
have no such needs — temperate, modest, and now silent,
they are indifferent to the hydromels, the votive offerings, the vain
     honors. Better
one bare stone and a pot of geraniums, a secret sign,
or even nothing. To be more certain, we may hold them within us, if
     we can,
and better still if even we don't know where they lie.
The way things are in our times — who knows —
we ourselves may disinter them, one day we ourselves may throw
     them away.

March 20, 1968   *(K.F. & K.H.)*

AFTER THE DEFEAT

Later, after the utter destruction of the Athenians at Aegospotámi,
    and a little later,
after our own final defeat, then our free discussions ceased, then the
    Periclean glory also ceased,
the flowering of the Arts, the Gymnasiums, the Symposia of our wise
    men. Now
there is heavy silence and gloom in the Agorá, and the license of the
    Thirty Tyrants.
Everything (and especially what is most ours) happens by default,
    without
any possibility at all of any recourse, any protection or defense,
let alone any formal protest. Our papers and our books are in the
    fire,
and the honor of our fatherland in the trashbin. And if we should
    ever be permitted
to bring as a witness an old friend, he would not accept, out of fear
of suffering the same fate as we—and the man would be quite right.
    For this reason
it's good to be here—we may even acquire a new contact with
    nature,
looking from behind the barbed wire at a little bit of sea, some rocks,
    plants,
or some cloud in the sunset, deep, violet, moved. And perhaps
one day a new Kimon will come, secretly guided
by the same eagle, to dig and find the iron tip of our spear,
rusted, also worn thin, and he will carry it ceremoniously
in a procession, either mournful or triumphant, with music and
    garlands, to Athens.

March 21, 1968   *(K.F & K.H.)*

ALCMÉNE

She, who on the first night had lain with a god without knowing it,
—only by his world-heavy odor and his broad bushy chest,
almost like her husband's, but how different too, as though
she'd guessed at something, sensed something—well, how could she
    now lie
with a mortal? And why should she care for Amphitrýon's gifts, and
    even
her son's twelve tasks and his immortality, together with her own?
    She
recollects one night only, only one night does she wait for, late, at the
    hour
when, out in the garden, the Bear descends and close by Orion
shows his silver back (dear God, how fragrant the roses)—
she, all ready, when her husband's out at the chase, always ready,
    bathed,
naked, puts on her earrings again, and her bracelets, and dallies at
    the mirror,
combing her long hair, rich still, though dry and tinted.

March 23, 1968   (N.C.G.)

THE APPLES OF THE HESPERIDES I

We never liked the demi-gods, the gods, the super-heroes, the
    over-complicated myth
with too many angles—we couldn't grasp its meaning;
we simply reckoned how much of it was trivial, obscure; it lacked
that stark clarity of the unknown and inexplicable. But still
we liked the place—that place where day meets night
and the apple trees grow white with blossoms, or get
laden down with their golden apples. And we liked how
the Argonauts saw from their ship a little beyond the lake
or Tritonídha, the Dragon's corpse and the sad Hesperides. But most
    of all
we liked that little 'pillow' which Hercules asked for to rest his head

219

from the weight of heaven. That small cunningness,
so human, which triumphed over the ill-will of Atlas,
let us grasp the entire myth, and lent to it as well
a kind of vague, familiar light, an aesthetic sort of brilliance.

March 31, 1968   *(G.M. & N.T.)*

THE APPLES OF THE HESPERIDES II

Such a lot of confusion, so many killings for nothing. The hero
of Tiryns took the golden apples to Euristheus. He gave them back.
Then *he* presented them to Athena. Then *she* returned them
to the Garden of the Hesperides—their source. Perhaps they meant
    in this way
to show how futile the Labours were, the endless circle—dull
    philosophies.
We, meanwhile, had come to imagine those apples gleaming
in a white bowl, on the wide, beautifully-set table
with an embroidered linen tablecloth,—at some Greek summer
    noon
when the unchangeable light streams through the windows and
    outside
the frantic cicadas are heard, and the swimmers down on the beach.
With something still left over: the two jars of Medeas and
    Achemoros.

March 31, 1968   *(G.M. & N.T.)*

220

AFTER THE BREAKDOWN OF THE TREATY BETWEEN THE LACEDAEMONIANS AND THE ATHENIANS

According to Thucydides

Corinth, Argos, Sparta, Athens, Sicyon, and how many other smaller
    city-states—
the Greeks became a thousand fragments; the great treaty was
    shattered;
everyone was angry with everyone else—new councils, deliberations,
    conferences;
those who scarcely yesterday were friends and neighbors will not greet
    each other in the street—
ancient grudges have come to the fore; new allies,
entirely opposite from the former, sound each other out, make
    preparations. Embassies
meet secretly at midnight; others leave. Statues of heroes
are untended in the squares and in the gardens are dunged by the
    sparrows.
Groups here and there in the Agorá, with sobriety, with exaltation,
    with passion,
discuss our affairs—Who nominated them? Who appointed them?
We, anyway, did not elect them (and besides, how? and when?—
New masters again? We can do without them!)—April has come;
the small pepper trees on the sidewalks turn green—a green
gentle, tender, childish (it moved us) although
rather dusty;—the Municiple Services are in confusion;
they don't even go out in the afternoons to sprinkle the streets. But
    today
at the peristyle of the closed Councilhouse the first swallow appeared
    suddenly
and all the people cried out, "A swallow; look, a swallow; look, a
    swallow!"
all with one voice, even those most opposed, "A swallow!" And
    suddenly
all became silent, feeling alone, separated from the others, as free
    men,
as men united by the extent of time, in a public isolation. And then,

they understood that their only freedom is their solitude, but that
    even this
(although visible) is unprotected, vulnerable, trapped in a thousand
    ways, alone.

April 4, 1968   (K.F. & K.H.)

THE NEW DANCE

Not only pretences, but actual motives and great results—
sufferings, profits, dangers, fears—Pasipháe, Minotaur,
Labyrinth, and Ariadne with her beautiful, erotic thread
branching out as a guide in the rocky darkness. And later,
the return of Theseus triumphant. At Delos he stopped,
and there around the Kératon (the famous altar constructed entirely
of animal horns—the left ones only), Theseus danced,
with the Athenian ephebes as his companions, a new
exciting dance, with crisscrossing steps which perhaps depicted,
in the powerful midday light, the dark turns of the Labyrinth, and
    perhaps—
who knows what—the birds and the cicadas were shrilling from the
    small pine wood—
you don't understand—the sun makes you dizzy and the reflections
    from the sea,
fragments of thin glass—and the bright movements of the naked
    bodies—
a wonderful, true dance. And later we forgot entirely
the Minotaurs, and Pasipháes, and Labyrinths, even unhappy
    Ariadne
abandoned all alone to die in Naxos. The dance, however,
spread quickly, and remained. We still dance it today. And since then
a palm has been decreed as the prize at the Delian gymnastic contests.

April 6, 1968   (K.F. & K.H.)

PHILOMEL

Thus, even with her tongue cut out, Philomel narrated her torments
by weaving them one by one on her tunic with patience and faith,
in modest colors—violet, grey, white and black—as always happens
with works of art—there is black in abundance. All the rest—
Prócne and Tiréas with his axe and their pursuit in Daulís,
even the cutting out of the tongue—we regard as insignificant, we
     forget. That tunic of hers
is enough, secret, precise; and her metamorphosis
at the critical moment into a nightingale. Yet, we say: without all the
     rest,
the things held of no account now, would there perhaps have been this
     superb tunic and the nightingale?

April 9, 1968   (N.C.G.)

NIOBE

This statue, of excellent craftsmanship, of unusual stone,
no sculptor has carved—a proud, unsubdued woman
above her seven slain young sons, the arrows still in their chests,
and her seven slain daughters. Here, when she had exhausted
her last appeal, her last curse against gods and men,
going up the staircase of silence and immobility, step by step,
she became the final statue of herself—a pitch-black rock
with two pure streams rolling down her great face
so that on summer noons the small shepherds on barren Sipylus might
     have some water,
their sheep, distressed musicians and lost travellers. Today, of course,
many alledge that the streams from her eyes are nothing more
than the water of the neighboring streams which, through thin,
     hidden pipes,
is channeled to her eyes; and there are others again who persistently
     propose

that we tear down the marvellous statue itself—the pride of our poor
    land—
if only for the pleasure of discovering the clever mechanism.

April 10, 1968   *(K.F. & K.H.)*

THE GOLDEN FLEECE

What did we want with the golden fleece?—a new trial—perhaps the
    greatest;
deaths, the Symplegades, murders; and Heracles forgotten at Mysia,
and the beautiful Hylas drowned in the spring; and neither a new oar
nor any rest at all. Colchis, Aeétes, Medea. The bull with the brazen feet.
The potion and the vain contests. And later Aspyrtos—bit by bit
his father gathered him from the sea.
                        And that fleece—
a goal now completed—another fear: lest a mortal or a god steal it from
    you
at times, holding it in your hand, its golden fur would brighten you during
    your nights;
at times, on your shoulder, it would illuminate you entirely, pointing
    you out—a target
for this man and for that; and it would never allow you even a
    moment in shadow;
in one smallest corner of your own to hide, to strip bare, and to exist.

Nevertheless, what would our life be without this golden (as we say)
    torment?

May 5, 1968   *(K.F. & K.H.)*

224

TALOS

Repetitions—he says—repetitions without end;—what fatigue, my
    God;
the entire change in tints only—Jason, Odysseus, Colchis, Troy,
Minotaur, Talos—and in these very tints
all the deception and the beauty too—a work that's ours.
                                I still
retain the image of that giant from the race of bronze men,
a single vein from his throat to his heels—just one vein,
plugged with a bronze nail right at the end. When they knocked
that nail out, his blood and life spilled out.
                        And perhaps, I say,
we all have but one vein, sealed with a nail,
and all of us have the same fear.
                 Opposite, on the great whitewashed wall,
on nails hammered in a row (from unplugged veins perhaps?) we
    hang
our coats, hats, umbrellas, underpants and masks.

May 6, 1968   (N.C.G.)

ACHILLES AFTER DEATH

He was all in;—what use to him were glories now?—enough.
He'd got to know enemies and friends well—friends supposedly;—
behind love and admiration, they hid their own interests,
their own suspect dreams, the foxes, the innocents.
                               Now,
on the Isle of Leuce, alone at last, serene, without claims,
without duties and tight-fitting armor, without, above all,
the base hypocrisy of heroism, he can, for hours and hours, relish
the evening brine, the stars, and silence, and that feeling,
gentle and limitless, of the general futility of things, with only
wild goats for company.
                   But here, too, even after his death,

new admirers have pursued him — usurpers of his memory this time —
who've erected altars and statues to him, prayed, left. Only
seabirds have stayed with him; — each morning, they fly down to the
    shore,
wet their wings and hurriedly return to wash
the floor of his temple with easy, dancing motions. Thus,
a hint of poetry stirs the air (perhaps his only justification)
and a condescending smile crosses his lips, for everyone and
    everything,
as once again he awaits new pilgrims (and he knows he likes it)
with all their noise, canteens, eggs, gramophones,
as now he waits for Helen — yes, the selfsame one for whose beauty
of flesh and dream so many Achaeans and Trojans (himself included)
    were annihilated.

September 19, 1968   (N.C.G.)

PENELOPE'S DESPAIR

Not that she didn't recognize him in the fireside light; nor was it
the beggar's rags, the disguise; no: transparent signs —
the scarred knee, the sturdiness, the craftiness in the eye. Startled,
leaning her back against the wall, she sought some justification,
a short reprieve from having to respond,
and be betrayed. Were twenty years wasted for him then?
Twenty years of dreams and anticipation, for this wretch,
these white whiskers soaked in blood? She sank mute onto a chair,
slowly she gazed at the slaughtered suitors on the floor, as if seeing
her own muffled aspirations. And she uttered, "Welcome,"
heeding her own strange and distant voice. In the corner her loom
veiled the ceiling in trelliswork shadows; and those birds, woven
against green foliage in striking red yarn, suddenly
turned black and gray on this homecoming night,
hovering in the unbroken sky of her final perseverance.

September 21, 1968   (K.M.)

MARPESSA'S SELECTION

It was no accident Marpessa preferred Ida to Apollo,
in spite of all her passion for the god, in spite of his incomparable
    beauty,
which made the myrtle bloom and tremble at his passing. She
never dared to raise her eyes higher than his knee;—
from his toe-nails to his knee, what an inexhaustible world,
what superb routes and discoveries—from his toenails to his knee.
    Yet,
at the ultimate moment of selection, Marpessa panicked: what would
    she do
with such a great gift? She, a mortal, would one day age.
She thought suddenly of her comb, with a tuft of white hair,
    forgotten
on some chair, beside the couch where the immortal, resplendent,
    rested;
she thought, too, of the fingerprints of time on her thighs, her fallen
    paps
before the black metal mirror. Ah, no; and like one dead she leant
on Ida's mortal shoulder. And he raised her in his arms like a flag
and turned his back on Apollo. But as he was leaving, almost
    arrogantly,
something like a crackling was heard, the sound of cloth tearing (a
    strange sound)—
an edge of the flag was caught, pinned under the god's foot.

October 28, 1968   *(N.C.G.)*

THE FLUTE-PLAYER

How good it is, the hollow reed—giving us the marvellous sounds
of the fountain and the wind we miss. That 'Ahh!' so often breathed:
contentment, joy.
                    But the one who's blowing the reed
grows ugly;—his cheeks swell up, his eyes get smaller

love's invitation; — others accept it, and give away
the love the flute-player's asking for.
                                        And so he
throws the reed into the water; gazes around; — nobody's there.
He stares at his face in the fountain, solitary, carved up
by the flute which shimmers on the bottom, gleaming like a knife.

October 29, 1968   *(G.M. & N.T.)*

THE ACTUAL CAUSE

No, it's not that Apollo took back his pledge
and that spitting on Cassandra's mouth removed
all persuasion from her speech, thus rendering her
prophetic words ineffective for herself and others — no. Only that
no one wants to believe the truth. And when you see
the net inside the bath, you think it was prepared
for your fishing trip on the following day and you don't hear at all,
      within you
and without, ascending the castle's marble stairs,
the dark augury in ill-fated Cassandra's pleas.

June 7, 1969   *(K.M.)*

THE CONJUNCTION "OR"

Then brazen Ares bellowed as loud as nine
Or ten thousand men who scream as they clash in battle.
                                        —Illiad

When the spear of Diomedes, guided by the hand of the goddess,
pierced into the side of the savage god, then helmeted Ares
bellowed so loudly that both the Achaeans and the Trojans were
      terrified,

228

because it was (says the Poet) as though *nine* or *ten* thousand
frenzied warriors had roared together.
Oh that "or" —
an expression of both mocking and noble accuracy,
the ambigious smile of an uncommunicable and unparticipating
    wisdom
that turns derisively against itself and others
knowing full well that accuracy is unachievable,
that accuracy does not exist (and this is why
the pompous tone of certainty is unforgivable — may God help us).

"Or," conjunction, humble consequence of the mystery of
    ambiguity,
deep correlation among the multiplicity of essences and
    phenomena,
it is with you we adjust to the difficulties of life and dream,
to the many nuances and versions between black to invisible white.

June 18, 1969   *(K.F.)*

THE MODELS

Let us never forget — he said — the good lessons we have learned
from the art of the Greeks. Always, the celestial side by side
with the everyday. Side by side with man: the animal and the thing —
a bracelet on the arm of the nude goddess; a flower
fallen to the floor. Remember the beautiful presentations
on our clay urns — gods with birds and animals,
together with the lyre, a hammer, an apple, the box, the pliers;
ah, and that poem where the god, on finishing his work,
takes his bellows from the fire, gathers up his tools one by one
and puts them in his silver chest, then with a sponge wipes
his face, his hands, his sinewy neck, his bushy chest.
And so, scrubbed clean, he goes out in the evening, as is his habit,
    leaning

on the shoulders of golden adolescents—the works of his hands
that have strength and thought and voice—goes out into the street,
the most majestic of all, the limping god, the worker god.

June 23, 1969   (K.F.)

MEMORIAL SERVICE AT POROS

The gods are always being forgotten; and if tonight we've
    remembered Poseidon,
roaming the empty shores of Kalavria,
it's because there, in the sacred grove, one night in July,
while oars glittered in the moonlight, and the guitars
of ivy-crowned youths sounded from rowboats,
here, in this pinewood, Demosthenes took poison—
he, the stutterer, who labored till he became the first orator of the
    Greeks,
and then, condemned by Macedonians and Athenians, in one night
learned the most difficult, the greatest art: to be silent.

June 26, 1969   (N.C.G.)

TO ORPHEUS

This summer, under the constellation of the Lyre, we remain pensive.

What was the use of enchanting Hades and Persephone with your
    song?
Of their consenting to return Eurydice to you? You, doubting your
    own strength,
turned back to re-assure yourself, and she was lost again to the
    kingdom of shades under the poplars.
          Then, bent by attempting the impossible, you declared
to the Lyre solitude as the ultimate truth. For this neither
gods nor men have forgiven you. The Maenads tore your body

to pieces on the banks of Hebros. Only your lyre and your head
    reached Lesbos
swept by the current.
                        What then, is the justification of your song?
The momentary merging (itself a false image) of light and darkness?
Or, perhaps, that the Muses hung your lyre at the very center of the
    stars?

Under this constellation, in the summer of this year, we remain
    pensive.

Karlóvasi, Samos, June 27, 1969   (T.M.)

cho

AGAMEMNON

(1966–1970)

Translated by Philip Pastras and George Pilitsis

(Once again, from the head of the marble staircase, completely covered with purple carpets, the warlord, with a motion almost of anxiety, greets the shouting crowd. In the crystalline winter sunlight drums are heard in the square furtherest below, along with the noise of the horses' hooves, the flapping of flags and the shouts of the slaves who are unloading the spoils from the wagons. At the porticos, the guards alone remain motionless, as though they belonged to another world. An acrid odor from the many trampled laurels ripples through the air. Every so often, the loud prophetic cries of a raving woman lying in a heap at the base of the stairs stand out from the applause and the general uproar—inexplicable cries, in a foreign tongue. The warlord and his wife have withdrawn. They have passed through the long corridor. They enter the hall where the table has been set for breakfast. He strips off his military uniform. He places his large helmet with the horsetail crest on the console, before the mirror. The mirror reflects the helmet, and it's as though two empty, disfigured metal skulls have been keeping each other company. He slumps into a sofa. He closes his eyes. Outside, the applause of the crowd and the shouts of the foreign woman can still be heard. He covers his ears with the palms of his hands. His wife, beautiful, austere, imposing, bends with a humility that doesn't match her demeanor, to untie his sandals. He places his left hand on her hair, careful lest he spoil her beautiful coiffure. She pulls away. She stands upright, a little further away. His smile appears distant, weary. He speaks to her. You don't know if she is listening).

Tell them to be quiet, I beg you. Why are they still shouting?
Who are they applauding? What are they cheering about? Maybe
    their executioners? Their dead?
or to make sure that they have hands and can clap them,
that they have voices and can shout to hear their voices?

Make them be quiet. Look, an ant is coming down the wall—
how surely and plainly he walks that perpendicular,

without the least bit of arrogance, as if he's performing a feat —
    maybe because he's alone,
maybe because he's unimportant, weightless, almost
    non-existent; — I envy him.

Leave him alone; don't chase him away; he's climbing up the
    table; he took a crumb;
his load is larger than he is; — look at him, — that's right,
the burden we carry is always larger than we are.

They'll never be quiet. And the fires at the altars — this smoke
and the smell of roasting; — seasickness, — no, not at all from the
    storms at sea —
something bitter in the mouth, a fear
at the fingertips, on the skin; like that time one night during the
    summer
when I was shaken from sleep — a crawling slime over my whole
    body;
I couldn't find the matches; I stumbled; I lit the flashlight:
on the tent, on the ground, on the sheets, on the shield, on my
    helmet,
thousands of slugs; with my bare feet I stepped on them; I went
    outside — there was a little moonlight,
naked soldiers were playing war, laughing, joking
with those disgusting crawlers — the soldiers themselves were ugly;
    their penises
stirred like slugs. I fell into the sea; the water didn't wash me;
the moon dragged itself along my left cheek like mucus, too,
yellow, yellow, thick. And now those cheers —

Have a hot bath ready for me, very hot; — you've done it already?
with leaves of myrtle and medlar? I remember their aroma,
bracing, tonic — a letting go; as if you caught the scent once more
of childhood, with trees, with rivers, with cicadas. Our daughters
seemed to me like lost creatures; — did you notice? — one of them
held my chin through my beard as if she were blind. You did
    right
to send them away to their rooms — I couldn't stand seeing them.

As for the spoils, keep them all or share them — I don't want
    anything.
And that woman who's howling at the staircase keep her as your
    maid
or as a nurse for our son (— where is he, really? — I didn't see
    him) — she's not for my bed, no,
now I need a totally empty bed to sink in, to lose myself, to be,
to sleep unobserved at least, not to care
if my face is as austere as it should be, or whether
the muscles of my belly and my arms have gone slack. Now
only the memory of love works erotically, cancelling
that great disproportion (not very flattering) between
the withering of the body and the obstinacy of desire.

And yes, I give up our bed to you. I'd never want
to testify to the changes that time makes on your beautiful figure,
on your thighs and breasts. I have no hate to feed
on such a show. On the contrary, yet, I'd like
(for my sake, not yours) to keep
your sensuous figure intact, beyond time, like a fine statue
that somehow preserves both the dazzle and the splendor of my
    own youth.

I only want (if it's still around) that ashtray with the sculptured
    tripod base,
where sometimes, at night, I'd leave my cigarette alone to burn
like a faraway smokestack on a tiny Ithaca, or like a
star of my very own, while you slept by my side.

Keep the rest; even the heavy, diamond-studded scepter —
that more than anything — I don't need it; — it's unbearable. Today
    I feel
the anger of Achilles; it wasn't at all because of the dispute
    between us — it was fatigue,
a prophetic fatigue, one that leveled victory and defeat,
life and death. All alone down at the beach,
with his companion the black dog that attached itself to him
    unexplainably
one autumn night with a full moon (so they said).

Maybe he needed that dumb presence
that doesn't ask, doesn't deny, but always believes and approves
by wagging his tail, blinking his eyes,
or by sometimes resting his muzzle gratefully
on his master's sandals, by waiting with the same happiness
for either petting or abuse; at other times, by panting, not from
    the chase,
but from devotion, dangling his red tongue
as though he held a bloody piece of his soul between his teeth
and wanted to give it away. Such boundless devotion, I imagine,
could save a man or even a god. Patroclus was jealous;

and maybe that's why he was urging Achilles to return to the
    battle
and maybe that's why he was killed. How much blood was
    spilled—
I never learned why—I don't know;—there have been times I
    didn't dare
touch bread—the bread was red. And that dog
wandered alone at the beach when Achilles was killed,
looked at the ships, the clouds, sniffed the rocks
where his master's feet had stepped, sniffed his clothes in the
    tent,
fasting, starving—who would take care of him?—he got in the
    way,
tripping our feet up; many of us kicked him; he sat
and watched the soldiers at their dinner hour; he didn't growl.

One day, someone threw him a bone; he didn't eat it;
he grabbed it with his teeth and vanished. Not long after that,
    they found him
at Achilles' grave,—he'd left the bone there
like a small offering; he was crying huge tears,
maybe because he'd lost his master, or maybe he was ashamed of
    his hunger.
Later, he took the bone again, hid behind the rocks
and started gnawing. Along with the gnawing we heard
his whining,—it could have been the groan of everlasting hunger.

How strange your eyes are; and your voice was strange, when you
     said:
"Servants, why are you standing around like that? You've forgotten
     my orders, then?
I told you to unroll the carpets from the chariot to the house, and
     to let the road become
completely red for my lord to pass." In your voice
a deep river ran, and I felt I was floating in it. When I stepped
on the purple carpets, my knees buckled. I turned back
and saw the dusty tracks from my sandals on the great purple
like the fishermen's corks that float
over the hidden, sunken net. Ahead of me, I saw the servants
unrolling even more of the red carpets, as though they were
     pushing
the red wheels of fate. A chill
ran down my spine. That's why I asked you
to have a warm bath ready. That chill — glassy, glassy — you know,
no one wants to die, however tired.

This fatigue is my place now, it's my own self; as though I was
     climbing
without effort, almost without using my feet, up the sky-blue
     mountain
where I'll gaze (I see them already) at
the hills, meadows, cities down there — a little smoke turns golden
     in the sun — harbors
and the boats of our bitter return on the half-circle
of the deserted beach — white boats, distant, diminished
like the nail-clippings of children — like those of our other
     daughter — you remember? —
you were clipping them for her at the bathroom door; — she didn't
     want it; she cried out; — so many years ago.

How we let time slip away, foolishly trying to secure a place
in the eyes of others. Not a single
moment to ourselves, in such ample summertimes, to watch
the shadow of a bird on the wheatfields — a small trireme
on a sea all of gold; we could've set sail there
for quiet rewards, more glorious conquests. But we didn't set sail.

From time to time, I think I'm a dead man who calmly watches
my own existence; with his empty eyes, he follows
my movements, my gestures; — just like that one winter night
down there, outside the walls, in an indescribable chilly
    moonlight
when everything seemed marble, made of moon and whitewash.

I watched everything around me with the detachment of an
    immortal who hardly
fears death or concerns himself with his own immorality. Yes,
    like a
handsome dead-man who strolls around in night's white light and
    looks
at the plaster-of-paris ornaments on houses, wrought iron fences,
the shadows of masts at the seaside. At that very instant, an arrow
whistled past my ear, thrust itself into the wall and vibrated
like a lone string on an unknown instrument, like a nerve
in the body of the void, sounding with incomprehensible delight.

Exactly like that, sometimes, something would stop us, over
    there — no one knew what was happening —
a reflection from the sunrise on a sword, the miniature
mirror-image of a still cloud on a helmet,
or Patroclus' habit of touching the tip of his ear
with his two fingers whenever he became quiet and steeped
    himself in a lonely,
erotic daydream. One day, Achilles grabbed his hand, looked
at his fingers like a seer, and then looked at his ear. "Autumn is
    coming," he said;
"We'll have to reform our forces." And that "reform"
had an odd relation to the handsome motion of Patroclus.

And then Patroclus came out of the tent, went near his friend's
    horses,
Válio and Xántho, stood between them, and passed both his arms
around their delicate necks, and so the three of them, face to
    face,
stood perfectly still, watching the sunset. I think I've seen

that image as a bas-relief on some pediment, and suddenly I
    understood
how it is possible to sacrifice a person for a little favorable wind.

Little by little, everything was stripped and became calm,
    glasslike;
the walls, the doors, your hair, your hands—
a fine, glassy transparency—not even death's breath clouds it; you
    can make out
the indivisible nothing behind the glass—something whole, at
    last—
that original unity, invulnerable, like non-existence.

Before I put my hand on the doorknob, before I open the door,
before I enter the hall, I've already seen the couch and the chairs
and the mirror that reflects the opposite wall with a painting
of some ancient sea-battle. Before I enter the bath
I see the myrtle leaves floating on the water and the swollen faces
of the vapors rising to the ceiling, to crowd against the skylight.
    Somehow
I can see even the hour of my death.

Forgive that vision, above all that confession—
it's a way of letting all of you see me, so we can be of equal
    strength—as we already are—
all of us unarmed, in other words. And yet, right now, I ask
    myself again
what can I possibly gain, or avoid, or hide
with that confession of mine;—what possible new mask
of unbreakable glass on my glassy, fragile face—
a large, hollow mask, an extension of my features, my expression,
hung high, before the palaces, on the metope of the gates,
my own coat of arms, not dynastic. Sometimes I think
that everything has happened only so that I could remember it
    some day
or, rather, so that perhaps I could discover its immortal vanity.

A favorable time—and I welcome it. I look at my hand—
it's not for the sword or for caresses;—alone, given

—given where?—to some unseen strings, like the hand
of the rhapsode on a large lyre—and if you hold his hand for
just an instant, the music will stop, puzzled,—and the half-
finished sound forgives neither of the two; like a silver
ring hung in the air by a thread, it strikes your shoulder
    unexplainably.

The others fell—truly brave young men (but who knows
how much bitterness, how much fear even they felt). I didn't envy
    their deaths.
If I praised their heroism, I did it to hide
my secret gratitude that I was still alive—not a hero at all.

Here I am, then, and I've not even given you that pleasure—the
    glory of many names, as they call it,
which maybe could've redeemed, alas!
our silent sterling decade with thunderous and counterfeit
    coinage,
thousands of murders, both open and concealed, thousands of
    errors and graves.

I can do without such heroism;—someone else, now,
noiseless and invisible, nods to me. Once, at dusk,
I saw the last golden leaf on an all-black tree
and it was the naked shoulder of a calm, handsome athlete who,
    bending,
lifted the weight of us all, to set it softly down on the ground. At
    that moment
a new hunger, another appetite made my mouth water
and from the corners of my mouth I felt
the sweet, soothing milk of gratitude flowing. Unwillingly
I raised my hand to the spot to wipe it,
before I gave myself away, before my men could see my second
    childhood,
my new suckling at the first nipple of creation.

Then they'd have realized how powerful, how powerless I am—
a provocation in either case. Late one afternoon I was strolling
    along at the beach;

a golden calm; rose-colored sea; an oar flashed. On a boulder
they had stretched a large red sail. From the encampment, up
   above,
a lonely, sorrowful song reached me,
warm and steaming like a garment just shed by a fine body —
a war song. I was holding it in my hands as I was strolling
in the coolness of the evening, close to the ships. Everywhere,
an aroma something like roasted corn and seaweed.
A little boiling water must've fallen on a burning log. Outside the
   tents,
great fires had been lit for the evening mess.

Death seemed so easy. I remembered quiet Philemon: one night,
when all the drinkers in the tent were babbling on and on
about games, women, horses, Antilochus provoked
Philemon's calmness and sobriety with mockery. And Philemon: "I
   am preparing myself," he said; nothing more;
and he stayed like that, bowed, without drinking, his elbows on
   the table,
holding his face in his hands. Behind his fingers
a strange smile gleamed, "I am preparing myself." At daybreak,
Antilochus left the tent, turned toward the east, and recited
his prayer to the sun with the grace of an actor and with youthful
   impiety.

How I managed to remember his last words I don't know. "O
   sun," he said,
"You who with your finger open a golden hole in the black wall
and from which two birds fly out, the one red, the other blue —
the red one sits on my knee, the blue one on my shoulder —."
   And in fact,
at that moment, two large birds flew at him —
two crows, they were. Neither he nor Philemon returned.
On a white urn we engraved two beautiful birds — the red and the
   blue.

O our life together will surely be difficult. Tomorrow already
I'll retire to my estate. Don't give it a thought. I know:
maybe someday they'll forgive us everything, yet

if they knew that you see them and that you see yourself,
no one—not foe or even friend—can forgive that. And
you can't hide yourself, either: in the center of your forehead is
    that third eye
which, however much it's hidden or closed, marks you with the
    brightness
of loneliness and singularity—the ultimate arrogance and
    humility.

The years are passing. We're leaving. We're growing old;—not
    you. You know, when the city fell,
Helen sat for hours on end before the large mirror
that she made them carry over especially for her in the ship;— a
    strange mirror:
two sly golden cupids, carved on the sides of the frame,
naked, without quivers, without bow, look with disbelief
at whoever looks in the mirror. Well then, Helen

makes up her face now according to the model in her memory—
    maybe even more beautiful
with memory, knowledge and desire (and stubborn as well)
with mystic dyes—a complete alchemy—with ocher, rose, mauve,
    silver,
with heavy black all around the gray of her eyes,
with deep cherry-red on her soft, fleshy lips.

She paints her mouth large now, as though she was going to
    shout
an unexplainable "no" from the balcony, or kiss a god. But no
    matter what, her face
is no longer the one we set out for, the one we fought for,
sowing sea and plain with broken hulls, with wheels and skulls.
Already it's another face—maybe it's more her own—another,
    anyhow.
Beneath the fine tints of her feminine craft
it's as though she hides or bitterly puts her own death to sleep.
    And she knows it.

One day, at the victory banquet, down at the beach,
after we had buried the dead, and from one end to the other the
    city

was still smoking in the calm autumn twilight, Helen,
holding the glass to her lips, shouted:
"Listen to the sound of my bracelet; I am dead" —
and from her teeth fell a pure white light, and suddenly
everything became marble and bone. Hands and voices were fixed
    in the air.

All white, pure white — even the masts and the sea; a gull,
as though hit by an unseen arrow, fell noiselessly
in the center of the table, near the amphorae. Helen
took it in her hands, looked at it without saying a word,
wetted her little finger in its blood and drew
a perfect circle on the tablecloth — maybe a zero, maybe
    everything. Later,
plucking with a motion of unbelievable grace a tuft of feathers
from the bird's breast and laughing, she scattered them in our
    hair. We forgot.
Only a taste of whiteness and that unexplainable circle remained.

During our return, in the Aegean Sea, the night of a great sea-
    storm,
the rudder broke. Just then I became aware of a terrified freedom
right in the midst of this driftless state. I was searching
in the darkness with unbelievably sharp vision. I made out a
    life-preserver being thrown into the waves. I could even
make out the word "Lachesis" in the dim light of the torches.

And that life-preserver, that name, and the fact that I had seen
    them
gave me a strange strength and calmness; and I said to myself:
"If nothing else is to be saved but that life-preserver, nothing's
    been lost."

The next day, the Aegean became calm. I saw the life-preserver
    floating
among the castaways and the broken planks. I gathered it up.
I still have it in my bag, like a secret life-preserver. If you want,
you can hang it as a keepsake in some room
or else throw it away — I don't need it any more — "Lachesis" it
    says.

All things are inconceivable, deceptive; — that Wooden Horse, implacable
before the walls; with those huge glass eyes of his reflecting the
    sea —
a horse made of wood, with blue eyes of life. You'd have thought
the very same sea was watching herself with the eyes of the horse,
was watching at the same time even the insides of the horse,
    pitch-dark, hollow,
with the warriors, armed to the teeth, closed inside. Anyhow, I
    preserved
that blue image of the sea, boundless,
compassionate, exhausted. Not the least resentment over fate:
only the sense of a strange undeterred law which has abolished
the errors and sins of each of us personally and the responsibility
    of us all.
Sometimes even fatigue leaves you with an intuition of the
    imperishable — isn't that so?

At a drinking party, down there, during a three-day truce
when all who were drunk (not so much from wine as from death)
were smashing their glasses on the rocks, it seemed to me as
    though I was seeing the broken glasses
shine, whole once more, without even a crack, in a perfect line to
    the edges of the horizon
sparkling in the flames of the torches; at the very end
the half-moon shone — a silver cup, steaming peacefully
full of lukewarm milk.
                              And then Ion, the twenty-year-old,
threw off his tunic and, completely naked like a god, leaped onto
    the table,
kicked plates and amphorae, poured a pitcher of wine over his
    curly hair,
drenched himself from head to toe, and he was dripping, he was
    shining. "The indestructible exists,
the indestructible exists," he shouted. He threw his glass down — it
    didn't break;
they gave it back to him; he took aim at an anchor; he threw it
again; a fourth, a fifth, a tenth time, — it didn't break; (maybe it
    was made
of another substance — a fake — who knows? — or again maybe
our own drunkenness forced us into the sway of the unattainable).

244

The next day
Ion was killed in battle. I looked for his glass in the tent, in his
   knapsack;
I searched everywhere. I didn't find it. But I do remember those
   words of his.

I don't think you're listening; — it looks like you're in a hurry. But
   of course, we're all in a hurry
for someone else to stop, so that we can speak. And each of us
hears only his own words. What's the use of words? Only the
   deed
counts and is counted by others — as you always stressed.
                                        Do you think
the water you've drawn for me has turned cold? You don't have to
   come with me;
I can get along by myself — I got used to it over there; and maybe
   it's better that way.
Also, I have to say, I think I'd be ashamed in your presence.

So many years have passed — out of sight, out of mind. The body
(not only the soul) seems to have lost that old sense of certainty:
closely-knit and erect in its own joy to exist and be seen. Now
(distrustful and old) it sees only with different eyes
the trustful and ageless beauty of the world, which belongs to it
   no more.
No one forgives that vision. And really it's so independent,
so deep and self-sufficient and limitless, I think it impedes
us and the others alike — useless.

                                This chill — not glassy now,
down my spine here — it's different. Only a while ago,
everything was glassy — faces, bodies, objects, landscapes, you, I,
   our children —
glassy, uncovered, shining — of hard, clear glass. I watched their
   insides with interest,
with joy, almost — like the movement of beautiful, small, strange
   fish in an aquarium
or even of large, ugly, sullen and bloodthirsty fish — always strange.
   And then, suddenly,

it's as though the glass has softened—it doesn't hold its shape, it
    loses transparency,
as though it never had form or transparency—it fell down in a
    heap,
together with what it contained—a turbid mass, like a dirty sack
where people have carelessly gathered dirty underwear to wash one
    day
and they don't wash them—they get bored; they forget them there
    (they want to forget them), thrown
on the floor, near the door;—they trip over them, they kick them
    as they leave
and again as they enter the house. They really did forget them,
and what'll they do to remember?—the clothes have decayed
    already, closed
in their own smell of ancient sweat, urine and blood. To the bath,
    to the bath,
the water will turn cold, it will have turned cold. I'm going. You
    stay;—it's not necessary. You insist?—Come on.

(*The man stands up. He proceeds—evidently toward the bathroom.
Speechless, the woman follows him. They leave. The hall, empty
now, appears larger. Breakfast remains untouched on the table. The
glasses somehow have become opaque. The helmet always there
before the mirror. A heavy silence inside and outside of the house.
An ant takes a stroll again on the white tablecloth. Following the ant,
you notice an embroidered circle in the center of the table—a wreath
of red flowers. Suddenly, the voice of the foreign woman is heard
from outside, by the marble staircase, in clear Greek: "Citizens of
Argos, citizens of Argos, the large goldfish in the black net, and the
sword raised. Citizens of Argos, the sword raised, double-tongued,
citizens of Argos, citizens—." Loud drums, trumpets, noise, drown
her voice. A man, handsome, bare-headed, in battle dress, with a
large, blood-stained sword in his hand, enters the empty hall. With
his left hand, he takes the helmet from the console. He puts it on
backwards. The horsetail in his face. Like a mask. He leaves. The
voice of the raving woman: "Citizens of Argos, it's already too late,
too late, citizens of Argos—." She stops. The drums become louder.
The first woman enters the hall. Pale, tall, extremely beautiful. She*

climbs up on a chair. She hangs a life-preserver on a nail in the wall. "Lachesis" it says. Then she draws near to the mirror and fixes her hair.")

Athens, Sikyon, Heraion, Samos,
December 1966–October 1970   *(P. P. & G. P.)*

from

GESTURES
(1969–1970)

Translated by N.C. Germanacos and by Minas Savvas

NEW PRETEXTS

He recalled the young newsboys, in winter, in the subway station;
the swallows in schoolyards in front of the steamed window panes;
those small beds in the children's hospital—so blameless;
it was the day before Christmas, raining, they were singing carols
    down below in the town.
"What's the matter with me?" he asked. There was no one to answer.
    The question
was staring elsewhere. So does poetry—elsewhere—with her kitchen
    apron,
heating up yesterday's meal for us. "Yes, poetry, too," he said,
"or rather the few words with the long intervening pauses."

(M.S.)

SLIGHT AILMENT

This morning he was almost sick.
The night before they had burdened him with heavy words.
He can't endure them; he can't shake them off.
The house across the street is being painted excessively white,
unsuitably white. The voices of the plasterers can be heard
very loud in the winter sun. One of them
on the rooftop has embraced the chimney, standing
as though fucking it. Drops of whitewash
spurt thickly on the black soil with the rotten leaves.

(M.S.)

SPINELESSLY

The flags were put in mothballs. That was arrogance — he said —
arrogance in the science of insignificance. — Even here then? — Why
    do you ask now?
To delay, perhaps (for how long?) the only,
the ultimate certainty? Spineless colors, words,
spineless gestures.
        They undressed. They did not turn out the light.
They left their watches on the table, lay down,
and beneath them felt, or rather remembered, that the legs
of the bed were four, strong, iron.

(N.C.G.)

GENERALIZATION OF DISTRUST

A mighty wind was blowing. The deep, dark cypress
swayed back and forth. And yet the statue did not sway.
The stone smile immovable. "This immobility
is the secret of art," he said. He was misleading us
with a host of decorative elements — the statue, the cypress,
and that feigned smile.
        So, he put his gloves on,
frayed, brown leather, with the all-too-clear intention
not to touch the words carnally, not to let them touch him.

(N.C.G.)

DEPARTURES I

They leave one by one. The rooms empty, grow.
The furniture stands in the void like scattered islets. Soon
secret groups gather in a corner; they prattle out their news.
The chairs turn their backs to the door. The shadows
walk sideways to dodge some blow. At night,
when you turn off the switch, from the outer corridor, you hear
the secret agents of some foreign power shuffling and shoving
in rubber tin shoes; then the creaking
in the wall joints, for, while the rooms are growing,
the house narrows, and behind the mirror in the parlor,
the mercury moults in small silver leaves, leaving behind
dark stains or holes on the faces of those who never return.

(N.C.G.)

DEPARTURES II

Those that leave us, possibly linger for awhile,
there, further down, at the turn in the road, near the tall electric
pylon (perhaps to appear small in relation
to its height — that their disappearance may not seem important) —
they pause, stare at the house to retain an image of it a little longer,
for even memory collapses bit by bit — and where would the time and
    means be found
for repairs and whitewashing? — the silence installs itself
outside the walls and inside; and if someone is about to speak,
he puts his hand immediately to his mouth, expecting to hear
the noise of the uncorking of a gigantic glass bottle —
like that, his hand before his mouth, as though to hide a yawn.

(N.C.G.)

DEPARTURES III

Little by little, things empty, like those large bones
we come upon in summer on the beach—bones of horses
or prehistoric animals; they lose their inner stuff, the marrow;
only a solid white remains, like lack of color, with invisible holes,
like that color of rooms in winter, when outside
it's raining hard. At such times, you hold the handle of the door
    or the handle
of the teacup, not knowing whether you are holding them or they are
    holding you
or whether they or you can be held. And suddenly, as you try
to drink your tea, you see the porcelain handle between your fingers
by itself—the teacup's missing; you examine this handle: so white,
so weightless, almost like bone—and you find it lovely, shaped
like a half nought—it seeks its complement, while opposite, on the
    wall,
from a deep fissure, rises the warm steam of the tea you didn't drink.

(N.C.G.)

THE FATE OF THE OBSERVER

The protests multiplied—protests of actors,
prompters, propmen, spectators, electricians—
in fact, a silence strike was called; and all because of him
who was not playing any role. He was simply totally alone,
leaning on the cardboard wall of the stage, upright,
motionless, like an ancient, stopped pendulum, observing
the actors, electricians, spectators. "Get him out of here," they
    shouted, "Get him out of here."
But he wouldn't budge. Till one day they strung him from the
    chandelier
and carried on with their performance. Yet, from up there,
in the midst of so much crystal, he seemed to be observing them
more closely than before; which is perhaps why the electricians,
    annoyed,

kept dimming the lights or turning them off, and the theatrical
    stichomythias
filled with long pauses, inaugurating a new logos.

September, 1969–May, 1970   (N.C.G.)

☙

CORRIDOR AND STAIRS
(1970)

Translated by N.C. Germanacos and by Minas Savvas

ONLY

I cannot pretend any more — he said;
chairs, people, my children, my cigarettes,
it is death, you are death, I am death;
I snap the soiled toothpick on the saucer;
it is death; he looks at me, I look at him — death only;
the potted geraniums, the caged canaries —
don't fool yourselves — corridor, paraffin-lamp,
old photos on the wall, black umbrellas,
muffled waters under the floor; the house is leaving
together with the tenants, together with the long divan —
the house is leaving, it's disappearing, has disappeared — where is it
    going?

(N.C.G.)

THE UNHIDDEN

Nights, streets, faces, lights —
masks of death;
a door opens, a window shuts;
the dead woman's icebox full of food;
blind men line up in the subway station;
"Let's buy a new apartment";
"Let's buy a new motorcar";
the shadow hides behind the curtain;
the circus has set up in the square;
the loudspeakers blare;
people run, stop,

eat on their feet, copulate on their feet;
"They multiply death," he said,
(turning to the wall), only the dead
stay awake where they lie — only they;
their eyes phosphoresce,
drill holes in the night; we look;
through these holes we see —
faces, lights, bayonets, buses,
the clay basin, the iron stairs,
the bread, the knife, the excrement, the sperm, the bone,
the woman with the big, stone-dead fish,
the broken basin and the inverted stairs.

                                                            (N.C.G.)

WHAT'S THE USE?

Everything ages, wears out, becomes useless — he said —
clandestine smoke, closed rooms,
flags, men killed, proclamations, statues —
the white curtain has turned yellow,
the mirror's scratched along with the face,
moths have settled
on the lovely dress you wore that night,
the corner coffeehouse has closed down,
the balcony's fallen face-first in the nettles,
the statues in the garden without a phallus —
so what's the use of sorrow, what's the use of hatred,
of freedom, the absence of freedom,
the silver coffee-spoons, the bank account,
the gold dentures of the dead woman, the sun,
the two candlesticks on the table, the aspirins,
what's the use of love and of poetry?

The sun was shining — it was the month of July —
they were folding the bread in the napkin,

the small boat was leaving,
they were burning the newspapers in a straw hat
in the middle of the water.

(N.C.G.)

INEVITABLY

Along the back street, on the other side, on the iron stairs,
there, with the broken flower-pots, the broken pitchers,
there, with the dead dogs, the worms, the green flies,
there, where the blacksmiths piss, the butchers, the turners —
the children are afraid at night; the stars shout too much,
they shout from very far, as though everybody's gone —
don't speak to me again about the statues — he said — I can't bear it, I
    tell you;
no more excuses — down in the large cellar
slim women with long hands scrape soot from the pots,
smear their eyes, their teeth, the kitchen door, the pitcher,
and fancy in this way they become invisible or at least
    unrecognizable,
while the mirror in the corridor, osseous, advances towards them
at the moment when they secretly enter or leave, hugging the wall,
and the spotlights transfix them in the middle of the yellow lawn.

(N.C.G.)

COMPROMISES

The barbed wire, the plaster, the fallen windows.
The woman shouts from the terrace, "Katína! Katína!"
The green-grocer scratches his balls.
Five more have been summoned to the Police Station.
Another ten carted to the cemetery.
Two new apartment buildings have gone up.

257

The trees don't understand a thing — they stare.
"One way or another, we all die," he said.
"It's not the same," the other protested.
"Protest is just another pretext," the first said.

Then a gust of wind blew up.
Paper napkins scattered from the restaurant.
The waiters watched from doorways.
"Aren't they like birds?," and he pointed to the napkins.
The first accepted the compromise. He said nothing.

                                        (N.C.G.)

WHY THE QUESTION?

Will the moment come again
for you to say the words once more, so long ago exhausted,
to lengthen your stride as though you were advancing,
as though you did not know the road was closed,
to knock at the same door patiently
when no one is there to open,
when you have neither the means nor disposition to force it,
when the clay statues in the garden
stand in a row behind the railing,
eaten away by creeping vines and caterpillars
perforated, many-eyed, blind,
with their glass eyes fallen
down, deep, in the hollows of their feet,
further down, deeper still, in the rotting water and the earth?

                                        (N.C.G.)

CHARIOTEER 1970

Here is the bronze youth
with the straight band around his forehead,
with his motionless eyes —
concessive and alien,
holding the broken reins
in a quiet hand,
upright
above the absence of his chariot —
upright, did you say?
upright. The rest
under the stones and years,
unredeemable, unreturnable, lost.

"Only Nothing is indivisible," he said,
and, licking his two fingers,
touched the bronze tunic of the Charioteer.

(N.C.G.)

INDISCRIMINATELY

Behind the ancient wall,
amid the battlements,
amid the holes left by fallen stones,
the dead,
with wild, dilated eyes,
watched
the young hunter pissing
on a broken pediment.

So, then, if life is lying,
death is lying, too.

(N.C.G.)

THE SAME MEANING

Experienced words, dense, defined,
indefinite, insistent, simple, mistrustful—
useless memories, pretexts, pretexts,
the stress on modesty—stones supposedly,
dwellings supposedly, weapons supposedly—the handle of the door,
handle of the pitcher, table with a vase,
tidy bed—smoke. Words—
you beat them on air, on wood, on marble,
you beat them on paper—nothing; death.

Knot your tie more tightly. Like that.
Be silent. Wait. Like that. Like that.
Easy, easy, in the narrow niche, there
behind the stairs, flat against the wall.

(N.C.G.)

THE UNACCEPTABLE

He stands at the marble table. He persists,
chipping at a block of ice with a hammer.
Bits fly off, melt. The cold
masters his fingers, his body. He persists.
A statue, he says, of warmth—of absent warmth,
of willed warmth, he says. The ice melts. The statue melts.
The water runs off the marble. It gurgles
in the pipes in the walls, under the floor,
under the black and white kitchen tiles, outside
in the clay drain in the garden, under the earth
among the gluttonous roots. The sick woman
calls from the back room. He
wipes his hands hastily on a towel,
lights the lamp. The match trembles.
"It's ready," he says. "I'll bring it in a minute."

The light flickers over the large bed
and the tattered, moulting blankets.
The water runs deep in the sewers. They both know it

THE BIASED MAN

With the bias of one disobediant to death,
wily, hypocritical, obstinate,
he underlines trivial or nonexistent things —
the down of the shot bird on the thorns,
a window cut in the blank wall,
the cracks on the wall — the design on an urn —
the handsome archer with the large lilies,
that invisible something the archer is aiming at in the distance,
while the two dead, with backs turned,
carefully raise before the window
the white, square, stretched sheet.

THE FUNDAMENTALS

Clumsily, with a thick needle, with thick thread,
he sews the buttons on his jacket. He talks to himself:

Have you eaten your bread? Have you slept in peace?
Have you been able to speak? To stretch out your arm?

Did you remember to look out of the window?
Did you smile at the knock on the door?

If death always is—it is second.
Freedom is always first.

(N.C.G.)

PERFORATION

Under the houses there are immemorial graves.
Under the graves there are more houses.
A huge stone stairway traverses
the houses and graves. The dead ascend,
the living descend. Their ways cross;
they do not greet each other—perhaps they do not recognize
    each other,
perhaps they are even pretending. The smell
of an invisible orange-grove on the hill. The children
roll down barrel hoops. Two women
chat at the spring. Their voices pass
into the pitcher along with the water. At nightfall
they return between two rows of cypresses,
carrying the pitcher like an illegitimate infant.
Above them the stars glitter connivingly.

(N.C.G.)

MEMORIAL SERVICES

The adolescent stone hand on the chair;
the headless torso before the mirror;
the sole of a foot solitary in its marble sandal
walking elsewhere (not unsuspecting) among
disused objects, paper roses,

fresh asphodels.
                    "These things, at least" — he said —
"these things have not been lost; not everything is lost, you know."
"Nothing is lost," he added (the strain
showed in his hands).
                    "Nothing is lost,"
the old women kept saying, as they cleaned wheat
in large white dishes, and boiled the wheat
in the broad copper pot. "Nothing, nothing,"
they repeated and wept, leaning their heads on
the shoulders of the motionless steam in the kitchen.

Aunt Laho brought in the tray and sugar,
put it on the table, stood aside,
turned toward the wall and licked her fingers.

                                        (N.C.G.)

IN THE OLD GARDEN

After many years, the sick woman got up,
went into the garden. Winter sunshine. Enclosed serenity —
on it float the thuds of nails driven into new, invisible
scaffoldings. The grass is fragrant. Flower-pots, terraces,
eaten away by hairy plants and roots. The pomegranate tree
taller than the cypress. The well closed. Yellow dust
like the dust that falls behind icons full of holes. And suddenly
the distant, nuptial smell of cool orange-blossoms
beautifully arranged around a silver tray
on the pedestal of a proud statue that is absent.

                                        (N.C.G.)

SHELTERS

Naked, marble, invisible statues lined up
on both sides of the road. Every now and then
we hid behind them for awhile, on sunny days
when the masked mail-clad men went by or when
the long narrow cart drawn by four horses dressed
in white, embroidered sheets, raised dust. At other times again
we wore a statue from head to toe, motionless,
holding our breath, observing the road gleaming
in the distance with an apocalyptic, dissembling, deadened light,
knowing that at any moment we might be betrayed by
the smoke of a cigarette, a light cough, an erection.

(N.C.G.)

CALCULATED BEHAVIOR

He was measuring his gestures, his expressions, his words,
even at night when, alone, in his narrow room
he was arranging his shoes, his clothes, moving
from his bed to the closet. And if occasionally, at midnight,
he would undress completely and stare erotically at his nudity
before the mirror, he would do so in order to pretend
he did not know that the big voyeur and eavesdropper
in the empty, unrented room next door,
with nails on its walls, was always watching him
through invisible holes in the door or in his own body.

(M.S.)

CORRIDOR

Austere space. Measured words. No hint of color,
A corridor—closed doors to right and left. Muffled sounds
behind the doors (each with his own) combining
in a common secrecy—the tray falls on the boards,
the plate falls, the comb, the shoe, the mirror,
the treasured obol. The sound turns elsewhere. At night
the three sleepwalkers cross the silence of the corridor,
disappearing down this oblong uniformity. The large clock
on the far wall stopped; it reveals nothing, not even
the relativity of time. Behind the dim pane,
invisible, the landlady—mute, fleshy, bulky,
spinning her keys like an iron spindle, working out
the new evictions of her tenants and the Lovely Helen—
takes the chewing-gum from her mouth and sticks it on her
     forehead.

(N.C.G.)

NORMAL OCCURENCE

Now and then he assures himself he didn't see, he doesn't know;
he preserves the naturalness of his chin, his lips, his eyes;
he knots his tie tastefully before the mirror,
puts the keys in his pocket, goes out, walks along—
doesn't look back at all, greets the passers-by. Yet
he knows with a terrible certainty that behind the door,
in the house, in the mirror, he has left behind, locked up,
the same handsome, dark prisoner, and that, on his return,
he will find his slippers somewhere else, and the three fluffy towels
will be wet, tossed over the back of the chair.

(N.C.G.)

PROVINCIAL SPRING

Time is slow. The light smooths surfaces, penetrates
into old wardrobes, drawers, under beds,
dries the pillow wet with saliva, abolishes the spiral of the stairs,
puts words into iambic order. And he,
who had only a long, old coat to hide
his inglorious scars, his grizzled body-hair, is now forced
to stand naked in the light, as if feigning
to be a youthful statue on whose stone hair
a silly passer-by plants a battered straw hat
with ribbons and wax cherries from immemorial summers.

(N.C.G.)

WHITEWASH

With the years, purely by chance, with nothing in mind, they replaced
the white of marble with the white of whitewash—a somewhat
more blinding white, of course, more on the outside—it was needed;
the words and drawings on the walls were too many. Now,
one after the other, they whitewash courtyards, flowerpots, stones,
even the trees, up to the middle—it gives a certain radiance, a cleanness;
it smells of health—and so, sidewalks and churches shine
with a new classical simplicity—something that's ours. In the evening
they put a pot of geraniums on the whitewashed wall
and look out to sea. On the doorstep across the way, Dame Pelayía
looks angry—her black dress spattered
with drops of whitewash, as though blooming with small daisies.

(N.C.G.)

EXPERIENCES

With the years—he says—colors abandon me, I abandon them;
white stone seems to me more appropriate.
With the tips of my fingers, with my whole palm, my lips,
I chip at a white body, antithetical to night, matching night—
it stands out clearly in the darkness; it shines. I leave my tongue
voluptuously in its marble mouth. Now at last
I have the right to fall silent and close my eyes.

(N.C.G.)

THE STAIRS

He ascended and descended the stairs. Little by little
the going up and the coming down blurred in his tiredness,
took on the same meaning—no meaning at all—the same point
on a revolving wheel. And he, motionless,
tied to the wheel, with the illusion he was traveling,
feeling the wind combing his hair back,
observing his companions, successfully disguised
as busy sailors, pulling nonexistent oars,
plugging their ears with wax, though the Sirens
had died at least three thousand years before.

January-June, 1970   *(N.C.G.)*

ᏨᎠ

267

HELEN

(1970)

Translated by Gwendolyn MacEwen and Nikos Tsingos

(*Even from a distance the wear and tear showed—crumbling walls
with fallen plaster; faded window-shutters; the balcony railings
rusted. A curtain stirring outside the window on the upper floor,
yellowed, frayed at the bottom. When he approached—hesitantly—
he found the same sense of desolation in the garden: disorderly
plants, voluptuous leaves, unpruned trees; the odd flower choked in
the nettles; the waterless fountains, mouldy; lichen on the beautiful
statues. An immobile lizard between the breasts of a young Aphro-
dite, basking in the last rays of the setting sun. How many years had
passed! He was so young then—twenty-two? twenty-three? And she?
You could never tell—she radiated so much light, it blinded you; it
pierced you through—you couldn't tell anymore what she was, if she
was, if you were. He rang the doorbell. Standing in the place he once
knew so well, now so strangely changed with its unknown entangle-
ment of dark colors, he heard the sound of the bell ringing, solitary.
They were slow to answer the door. Someone peered out from the
upper window. It wasn't her. A servant, very young. Apparently
laughing. She left the window. Still no answer at the door. After-
wards, footsteps were heard inside on the stairway. Someone
unlocked the door. He went up. A smell of dust, rotten fruit, dried-
up slop, urine. Over here. Bedroom. Wardrobe. Metal mirror. Two
tottering carved arm-chairs. A small cheap tin table with coffee cups
and cigarette butts. And she? No, no, impossible! An old, old
woman—one, two hundred years old! But five years ago—Oh no!
The bedsheet full of holes. There, unstirring; sitting on the bed; bent
over. Only her eyes—larger than ever, autocratic, penetrating,
vacant*):

Yes, yes—it's me. Sit down for a while. Nobody comes around
    anymore. I'm starting
to forget how to use words. Anyway, words don't matter. I think
    summer's coming,
the curtains are stirring differently—they're—trying to say
    something—such stupidities! One of them
has already flown out of the window, straining to break the rings,

to fly over the trees—maybe to haul the whole
house away as well—but the house resists with all corners
and me along with it, despite the fact that for months I've felt
        liberated
from my dead ones, my own self, and this resistance of mine,
incomprehensible, beyond my will, strange to me, is all I
        possess—my wedlock
with this bed, this curtain—is also my fear, as though
my whole body were sustained by the ring with the black stone I
        wear on my forefinger.

Now I examine this stone very closely; now, in these endless hours
        of night—
it's black, it has no reflections—it grows, it grows, it fills up
with black waters—the waters overflow, swell; I sink,
not to the bottom, but to an upper depth; from up there
I can make out my room down below, myself, the wardrobe, the
        servants
quibbling voicelessly; I see one of them perched
on a stool and with a hard, spiteful expression,
polishing the photograph of Leda; I see the duster leaving behind
a trail of dust and delicate bubbles which rise and burst
with quiet murmuring all around my ankle-bones or knees.

I notice you also have a perplexed, dumbfounded face, distorted
by the slow undulations of black water—now widening, now
        lengthening your face
with yellow streaks. Your hair's writhing upwards
like an upside down medusa. But then I say: it's only a stone,
a small precious stone. All the blackness contracts, then
dries up and localizes in the smallest possible knot—I feel it
here, just under my throat. And I'm back again
in my room, on my bed, beside my familiar phials
which stare at me, one by one, nodding—only they can help me
for insomnia, fear, memories, forgetfulness, asthma.

What are you up to? Still in the army? Be careful. Don't distress
        yourself so much
about heroism, honors and glories. What'll you do with them? Do
        you still have

that shield on which you had my face engraved? You were so
     funny
in your tall helmet with its long tail—so very young,
and shy, as though you'd concealed your handsome face
between the hind legs of a horse whose tail hung all the way
     down
your bare back. Don't get mad again. Stay a little longer.

The time of antagonism is over now; desires have dried up;
perhaps now, together, we can observe the same point of
     futility—
where, I think, the only true encounters are realized—however
     indifferent,
but nonetheless soothing—our new community, bleak, quiet,
     empty,
without much displacement or opposition—let's just stir the ashes
     of the fireplace,
now and then making long thin lovely burial urns
or sit down on the ground and beat it with soundless palms.

Little by little, things lost their meaning, became empty; did
they ever mean anything perhaps?—slack, hollow;
we stuffed them with straw and chaff, to give them form,
let them thicken, solidify, stand firmly—the tables, chairs,
the bed we lay on, the words; always hollow
like the cloth sacks, the vendors' burlap bags;
from the outside you can already make out what's inside them,
potatoes, onions, wheat, corn, almonds, or flour.

Sometimes one of them catches on a nail on the stair
or on the prong of an anchor down in the harbor, it rips open,
the flour spills out—a foolish river. The bag empties itself.
The poor gather up the flour in handfuls to make
some pies or gruel. The bag collapses. Someone
picks it up from the bottom; shakes it out in the air;
a cloud of white dust enfolds him; his hair turns white;
his eyebrows especially turn white. The others watch him.
They don't understand a thing; they wait for him to open his
     mouth, to say something.
He doesn't. He folds up the bag into four sections; he leaves
as he is, white, inexplicable, wordless, as though disguised

as a lewd naked man covered with a sheet,
or like a cunning dead man resurrected in his shroud.

So, events and things don't have any meaning—the same goes for
    words, although
with words we name, more or less, those things we lack, or which
we've never seen—airy, as we say, eternal things—
innocent words, misleading, consoling, equivocal, always
trying to be correct—what a terrible thing,
to have named a shadow, invoking it at night in bed
with the sheet pulled up to your neck, and hearing it, we fools
    think
that we're holding our bodies together, that they're holding us,
    that we're keeping our hold on the world.

Nowadays I forget the names I knew best, or get them all mixed
    up—
Paris, Menelaus, Achilles, Proteus, Theoklymenos, Tefkros,
Castor and Polydeuces—my moralizing brothers, who, I gather
have turned into stars—so they say—pilot-lights for ships—
    Theseus, Pireitheus,
Andromache, Cassandra, Agamemnon—sounds, only formless
    sounds,
their images unwritten on a window-pane
or a metal mirror or on the shallows of a beach, like that time
on a quiet sunny day, with myriads of masts, after the battle
had abated, and the creaking of the wet ropes on the pulleys
hauled the world up high, like the knot of a sob arrested
in a crystalline throat—you could see it sparkling, trembling
without becoming a scream, and suddenly the entire landscape,
    the ships,
the sailors and the chariots, were sinking into light and
    anonymity.

Now, another deeper, darker submersion—out of which
some sounds emerge now and then—when hammers were
    pounding wood
and nailing together a new trireme in a small shipyard; when a
    huge
four-horse chariot was passing by on the stone road, adding to the
    ticks

from the cathedral clock in another duration, as though
there were more, much more than twelve hours and the horses
were turning around in the clock until they were exhausted; or
    when one night
two handsome young men were below my windows, singing
a song for me, without words—one of them one-eyed; the other
wearing a huge buckle on his belt—gleaming in the moonlight.

Words don't come to me on their own now—I search them out as
    though I'm translating
from a language I don't know—nevertheless, I do translate.
    Between the words,
and within them, are deep holes; I peer through them as though
I'm peering through the knots which have fallen from the boards
    of a door
completely closed up, nailed here for ages. I don't see a thing.

No more words or names; I can only single out some sounds—a
    silver candlestick
or a crystal vase rings by itself and all of a sudden stops
pretending it knows nothing, that it didn't ring, that nobody
struck it, or passed by it. A dress
collapses softly from the chair onto the floor, diverting
attention from the previous sound to the simplicity of nothing.
    However,
the idea of a silent conspiracy, although diffused in air,
floats densely higher up, almost levelled out,
so that you feel the etching of the lines around your mouth grow
    deeper
precisely because of this presence of an intruder who takes over
    your position
turning you into an intruder, right here on your own bed, in your
    own room.

Oh, to be alienated in our very clothes which get old,
in our own skin which gets wrinkled; while our fingers
can no longer grip or even wrap around our bodies
the blanket which rises by itself, disperses, disappears, leaving us
bare before the void. Then the guitar hanging on the wall,
with its rusty strings, forgotten for years, begins to quiver
like the jaw of an old woman quivering from cold or fear, and

you have to put your palm flat upon the strings to stop
the contagious chill. But you can't find your hand, you don't have
    one;
and in your guts you hear your own jar shaking.

In this house the air's become heavy and inexplicable, maybe
due to the natural presence of the dead. A trunk opens
on its own, old dresses fall out, rustle, stand up straight
and quietly stroll around; two gold tassles remain on the carpet; a
    curtain
opens — revealing nobody — but they're still there; a cigarette
burns on and off in the ashtray; the person who
left it there is in the other room, rather awkward,
his back turned, gazing at the wall, possibly at a spider
or a damp stain, facing the wall, so the dark
hollow under his protruding cheekbones won't show.

The dead feel no pain for us any more — that's odd, isn't it? —
not so much for them as for us — that neutral intimacy of theirs
within a place which has rejected them and where they don't
    contribute
a thing to the upkeep, nor concern themselves with the run-down
    condition,
them, finished and unchangeable, just somewhat bigger.

This is what sometimes confounds us — the augmentation of the
    unchangeable
and their silent self-sufficiency — not at all haughty; they don't try
to force you to remember them, to be pleasing. The women
let their bellies slacken, their stockings sag, they take
the pins from the silver box; they stick them in the sofa's velvet
one by one, in two straight rows, then pick them up
and begin again with the same polite attention. Someone who's
    very tall
emerges from the hall — he knocks his head against the door;
he doesn't make a single grimace — and neither could the knock be
    heard at all.

Yes, they're as foolish as we are; only quieter. Another one of
    them

raises his arm ceremoniously, as though to give a blessing to
    someone,
pulls off a piece of the crystal from the chandelier, puts it in his
    mouth,
simply, like glass fruit—you'd think he's going to chew it, to get a
    human function
in motion again—but no; he clenches it between his teeth, thus,
to let the crystal shine with a futile brightness. A woman
takes some face-cream from the little round white jar
with the skilled movement of two of her fingers, and writes
two thick capital letters on the windowpane—they look like L and
    D—
the sun heats the glass pane, the cream melts, drips down the
    wall—
and all this means nothing—just two greasy, brief furrows.

I don't know why the dead stay around here without anyone's
    sympathy; I don't know what they want,
wandering around the rooms in their best clothes, their best shoes
polished, immaculate, yet noiselessly as though they never touch
    the floor.
They take up space, sprawl wherever they like, in the two rocking
    chairs,
down on the floor, or in the bathroom; they forget and leave the
    tap dripping;
forget the perfumed bars of soap melting in the water. The
    servants
passing among them, sweeping with the big broom,
don't notice them. Only sometimes, the laughter of a maid,
somewhat confined—it doesn't fly up out of the window,
it's like a bird tied by the leg with a string, which someone is
    pulling downward.

Then the servants get inexplicably furious with me, they throw the
    broom
here, right into the middle of my room, and go into the kitchen; I
    hear them
making coffee in big pots, spilling sugar on the floor—
it crunches under their shoes; the aroma of the coffee
drifts through the hallway, floods the house, observes itself

in the mirror like a silly, dark, impudent face, covered with
    uncombed tufts of hair
and two false skyblue earrings, that blows its breath on the
    mirror,
clouds the glass. I feel my tongue probing around in my mouth;
I feel that I've still got some saliva. "A coffee for me too," I call to
    the servants;
"a coffee," (that's all I ask for; I don't want anything else). They
act as though they don't hear. I call over and over again
without bitterness or rage. They don't answer. I hear them
gulping down their coffee from my porcelain cups with the gold
    rims
and the delicate violet flowers. I become silent and gaze at
that broom flung on the floor like the rigid corpse
of that tall, slim young grocer's boy, who, years ago,
showed me his big penis between the railings of the garden gate.

Oh yes, I laugh sometimes, and I hear my hoarse laughter rise
    up,
no longer from the chest, but much deeper, from the feet; even
    deeper,
from the earth. I laugh. How pointless it all was,
how purposeless, ephemeral and insubstantial — riches, wars,
    glories,
jealousies, jewels, my own beauty.
                              What foolish legends,
swans and Troys and loves and brave deeds.
                                   I met my old
lovers again in mournful night feasts, with white beards,
with white hair, with bulging bellies, as though they were
already pregnant with their death, devouring with a strange
    craving
the roasted goats, without looking into a shoulder blade — what
    should they look for? —
a level shadow filled all of it with a few white specks.

I, as you know, preserved my former beauty
as if by miracle (but also with tints, herbs and salves,
lemon juice and cucumber water). I was just terrified to see in
    their faces

the passing of my own years. At that time I was tightening my belly muscles,
I was tightening my cheeks with a false smile, as though
propping up two crumbling walls with a thin beam.

That's how I was, shut in, confined, strained — God, what exhaustion —
confined every moment (even in my sleep) as though I were inside
freezing armor or a wooden corset around my whole body, or within
my own Trojan Horse, deceptive and narrow, knowing even then
the pointlessness of deceit and self-deception, the pointlessness of fame,
the pointlessness and temporality of every victory.
                                        A few months ago,
when I lost my husband (was it months or years?), I left
my Trojan Horse down in the stable forever, with his old horses,
so the scorpions and spiders could circle around inside him. I don't tint my hair anymore.

Huge warts have sprouted on my face. Thick hairs have grown around my mouth —
I clutch them; I don't look at myself in the mirror —
long, wild hairs — as though someone else has enthroned himself within me,
an impudent, malevolent man, and it's his beard
that emerges from my skin. I let him be — what can I do? —
I'm afraid that if I chased him away, he'd drag me along behind him.

Don't go away. Stay a little longer. I haven't talked for ages.
Nobody comes to see me anymore. They were all in a hurry to leave,
I saw it in their eyes — all in a hurry for me to die. Time doesn't roll on.
The servants loathe me. I hear them opening my drawers at night,
taking the lacey things, the jewels, the gold coins; who can tell
if they'll leave me with a single decent dress for some necessary hour

or a single pair of shoes. They even took my keys
from under my pillow; I didn't stir at all; I pretended I was
    asleep—
they would have taken them one day anyway—I just don't want
    them to know that I know.

What would I do without even them? "Patience, patience," I tell
    myself;
"patience"—and this too is the smallest form of victory,
when they read the old letters of my admirers
or the poems great poets dedicated to me; they read them
with idiotic bombast and many mistakes in pronunciation,
    accentuation, metre
and syllabification—I don't correct them. I pretend I don't hear.
    Occasionally
they draw big moustaches with my black eyebrow pencil
on my statues, or stick an ancient helmet or a chamber-pot
on their heads. I look at them cooly. They get angry.

One day, when I felt a little better, I asked them again
to make up my face. They did. I asked for a mirror.
They had painted my face green, with a black mouth. "Thank
    you," I told them,
as though I hadn't seen anything strange. They were laughing.
    One of them
stripped right in front of me, put on my gold veils, and just like
    that,
bare-legged, with her fat legs began to dance,
leapt up on the table—frenzied; danced and danced, bowing
in imitation, as it were, of my old gestures. High up on her thigh
she had a love-bite from a man's strong, even teeth.

I watched them as though I were in the theatre—with no
    humiliation or grief,
or indignation—for what purpose?—But I kept telling myself:
"One day we'll die," or rather: "One day you will," and that
was a sure revenge, fear and consolation. I looked
everything straight in the eye with an indescribable, apathetic
    clarity, as if
my eyes were independent of me; I looked at my own eyes
situated a metre away from my face, like the panes

of a window far removed, from behind which someone else
sits and observes the goings-on in an unknown street
with closed coffee, photograph and perfume shops,
and I had the feeling that a beautiful crystal phial
broke, and the perfume spilled out in the dusty showcase.
    Everyone who passed,
pausing vaguely, sniffing the air, remembered something good
and then disappeared behind the pepper-trees or at the end of the
    street.

Now and again, I can still sense that aroma—I mean, I remember
    it;
isn't it strange?—those things we usually consider great, dissolve,
    fade away—
Agamemnon's murder, the slaughter of Clytemnestra (they'd sent
    me
one of her beautiful necklaces from Mycenae, made
from small gold masks, held together by links
from the upper tips of their ears—I never wore it). They're
    forgotten;
some other things remain—unimportant, meaningless things; I
    recall seeing one day
a bird perching on a horse's back; and that baffling thing
seemed to explain (especially for me) a certain beautiful mystery.

I still remember, as a child, on the banks of the Eurotas, beside
    the burning leanders,
the sound of a tree peeling off its bark alone; the strips
falling gently into the water and floating away like triremes,
and I waited, stubbornly, for a black butterfly with orange stripes
to land on a piece of bark, amazed that although it was immobile,
    it moved,
and this broke me up, that butterflies, although adept in air,
know nothing about travelling in water, or rowing. And it came.

There are certain strange, isolated moments, almost funny. A man
takes a stroll at midday, wearing a huge hamper on his head; the
    basket
hides his whole face as though he were headless or disguised
by an enormous eyeless, multi-eyed head. Another man,

strolling along, musing in the dusk, stumbles over something,
 curses,
turns back, searches—finds a pebble, picks it up; kisses it; then
remembers to look around; goes off guiltily. A woman
slips her hand inside her pocket; finds nothing; takes her hand
 out,
raises it and carefully scrutinizes it, as though it were breathed on
 by the powder of emptiness.

A waiter's caught a fly in his hand—he doesn't crush it;
a customer calls him; he's absorbed; he loosens his fist; the fly
escapes and lands on the glass. A piece of paper rolls down the
 street
hesitantly, spasmodically, attracting nobody's
attention—enjoying it all. But yet, every so often
it gives off a certain crackle which belies it; as though looking for
an impartial witness to its humble, secret route. And all these
 things
have a desolate and inexplicable beauty, and a profound pain
because of our own odd and unknown gestures—don't they?

The rest is lost, as though it were nothing. Argos, Athens, Sparta,
Corinth, Thebes, Sikion—shadows of names. I utter them; they
 re-echo as though they're sinking
into the incomplete. A well-bred, lost dog stands
in front of the window of a cheap dairy. A young girl passing by
 looks at it;
it doesn't respond; its shadow spreads wide on the sidewalk.
I never learned the reason. I doubt it even exists. There's only
this humiliating compulsive approval (by whom?)
as we nod "yes," as though greeting someone
with incredible servility, though nobody's passing, nobody's there.

I think another person, with a totally colorless voice, one evening
 told me
the details of my life; I was sleepy and wishing deep inside
that he'd finally stop; that I could close my eyes,
and sleep. And as he spoke, in order to do something, to fight off
 sleep,
I counted the tassels on my shawl, one by one, to the tune of
a silly children's song of Blindman's Bluff, until

the meaning got lost in the repetition. But the sound remains —
noises, thuds, scrapings — the drone of silence, a discordant
      weeping,
someone scratches the wall with his fingernails, a scissor falls onto
      the floor boards,
someone coughs — his hand over his mouth, so as not to awaken
      the other
sleeping with him — maybe his death — stops; and once again
that spiralling drone from an empty, shut-up well.

At night I hear the servants moving my big pieces of furniture;
they take them down the stairs — a mirror, held like a stretcher,
reveals the worn-out plaster designs on the ceiling; a windowpane
knocks agains the railings — it doesn't break; the old overcoat on
      the coat-rack
raises its empty arms for a moment, slips them back into the
      pockets;
the little wheels of the sofa's legs creak on the floor. I can feel
right here on my elbow the scratching on the wall made by the
      corners of the wardrobe
or the big carved table. What are they going to do with them?
      "Goodbye," I say
almost mechanically, as though bidding farewell to a visitor who's
      always a stranger. There's only
that vague droning which lingers in the hallway as though from
      the horn
of downfallen hunting lords in the last drops of rain, in a
      burnt-out forest.

Honestly, so many useless things collected with so much greed
blocked the space — we couldn't move; our knees
knocked against wooden, stony, metallic knees. Oh, we've really
got to grow old, very old, to become just, to reach that
mild impartiality, that sweet lack of interest in comparisons,
      judgements,
when it's no longer our lot to take part in anything except this
      quietness.

Oh yes, how many silly battles, heroic deeds, ambitions, arrogance,
sacrifices and defeats, defeats, and still more battles for things
that others determined when we weren't there. Innocent people

poking hairpins into their eyes, banging their heads
on the high wall, knowing full well that it wouldn't fall
or even crack, just to see at least from a little crevice
a slight shadowless sky-blue free from time and their own shadows.
    Meanwhile—who knows—
there, where someone is resisting, hopelessly, perhaps there
human history begins, so to speak, and man's beauty
among rusty bits of iron and the bones of bulls and horses,
among ancient tripods where some laurel still burns
and the smoke rises, curling in the sunset like a golden fleece.

Stay a little longer. Evening's falling. The golden fleece we spoke
    of—Oh, thought
comes slowly to us women—it relaxes somehow. On the other hand,
    men
never stop to think—maybe they're afraid; maybe they don't want
to look their fear straight in the eye, to see their fatigue, to relax—
timid, conceited, busybodies, they surge into darkness. Their
    clothes
always smell of smoke from a conflagration they've passed by or
    through
unwittingly. Quickly they undress; fling
their clothes onto the floor; fall into bed. But even their bodies
reek of smoke—it numbs them. I used to find, when they were
    finally asleep,
some fine burnt leaves among the hairs on their chests
or some ash-grey down from slain birds. Then
I'd gather them up and keep them in a small box—the only signs
of a secret communion—I never showed these to them—they
    wouldn't have recognized them.

Sometimes, oh yes, they were beautiful—naked as they were,
    surrendered to sleep,
thoroughly unresisting, loosened up, their big strong bodies
damp and softened, like roaring rivers surging down
from high mountains into a quiet plain, or like abandoned
    children, At such times
I really loved them, as though I'd given birth to them. I noticed
    their long eyelashes
and I wanted to draw them back into me, to protect them, or in
    this way

to couple with their whole bodies. They were sleeping. And sleep
    demands respect
from you, because it's so rare. That's all over, too. All forgotten.

Not that I don't remember anymore—I do; it's just that the
    memories
are no longer emotional—they can't move us—they're impersonal,
    placid,
clear right into their most bloody corners. Only one of them
still retains some air around it, and breathes.
                                    That late afternoon,
when I was surrounded by the endless shrieks of the wounded,
the mumbled curses of the old men and their wonder of me, amid
the smell of overall death, which, from time to time glittered
on a shield or the tip of a spear or the metope
of a neglected temple or the wheel of a chariot—I went up alone
onto the high walls and strolled around.
                            Alone, utterly alone, between
the Trojans and Achaeans, feeling the wind pressing my fine veils
against me, brushing my nipples, embracing my whole body
both clothed and naked, with only a single wide silver belt
holding my breasts up high—
                        there I was, beautiful, untouched, experienced,
while my two rivals in love were dueling and the fate of the long
war was being determined—
                        I didn't even see the strap of Paris' helmet
severed—instead I saw a brightness from its brass,
a circular brightness, as his opponent swung it in rage
around his head—an illumined zero.
                        It wasn't really worth looking at—
the will of the gods had shaped things from the start; and Paris,
divested of his dusty sandals, would soon be in bed,
cleansed by the hands of the goddess, waiting for me, smirking,
pretentiously hiding a false scar on his side with a pink bandage.

I didn't watch anymore; hardly even listened to their war-cries—
I, high up on the walls, over the heads of mortals, airy, carnate,
belonging to no one, needing no one,
as though I were (I, independent) absolute Love—free
from the fear of death and time, with a white flower in my hair,

with a flower between my breasts, and another in between my lips
    hiding
the smile of freedom for me.
                                    They could have shot
their arrows at me from either side.
                                    I was an easy target
walking slowly on the walls, completely etched
against the golden crimson of the evening sky.
                                    I kept my eyes closed
to make any hostile gesture easy for them—knowing deeply
that none of them would dare. Their hands trembled with awe
at my beauty and immortality—
                                    (maybe I can elaborate on that:
I didn't fear death because I felt it was so far from me).
                                    Then
I tossed down the two flowers from my hair and breasts—keeping
    the third one
in my mouth—I tossed them down on both sides of the wall
with an absolutely impartial gesture.
                                    Then the men, both within and without,
threw themselves upon each other, enemies and friends, to snatch
the flowers, to offer them to me—my own flowers. I didn't see
anything else after that—only bent backs, as if all of them
were kneeling on the ground, where the sun was drying the
    blood—maybe
they had even crushed the flowers.
                                    I didn't see.
                                    I raised my arms
and, risen on the tips of my toes and ascended,
let the third flower drop from my lips.

All this still remains with me—a sort of consolation, a remote
    justification, and perhaps
this will remain, I hope, somewhere in the world—a momentary
    freedom,
illusory, too, of course—a game of our luck and our ignorance. In
    precisely
that position (as I recall), the sculptors worked on
my last statues; they're still out there in the garden;
you must have seen them when you came in. Sometimes (when the
    servants are in good spirits

and hold me by my arms to take me to that chair
in front of the window), I can see them also. They glow in the
    sunlight. A white heat
wafts from the marble right up to here. I won't dwell on it any
    longer.
It tires me out, too, after awhile. I'd rather watch a part of the
    street
where two or three kids play with a rag ball, or some girl
lowers a basket on a rope from the balcony across the way.

Sometimes the servants forget I'm there. They don't come to put
    me back in bed.
I stay all night gazing at an old bicycle propped up
in front of the lit window of a new candy store,
until the lights go out, or I fall asleep on the window-sill. Every
    now
and then I think that a star wakes me, falling through space
like the saliva from the toothless, slack mouth of an old man.
                                                              Now
it's been ages since they've taken me to the window. I stay here in
    bed
sitting up or lying down—I can handle that. To pass the time
I grasp my face—an unfamiliar face—touch it, feel it, count
the hairs, the wrinkles, the warts—who's inside
this face?
            Something acrid rises in my throat—nausea and fear,
a silly fear, my God, that even the nausea might be lost. Stay a
    little longer—
a little light's coming through the window—they must have lit the
    street lamps.

Wouldn't you like me to ring for something for you? —some
    preserved cherries
or candied bitter orange—maybe something's left in the big jars,
turned to congealed sugar by now—if, of course the greedy servants
have left anything. The last few years I've been busy
making sweets—what else is there to do?
                              After Troy—life in Sparta
was very dull—really provincial; shut up all day at home,
among the crowded spoils of so many wars; and memories,
faded and annoying, sneaking up behind you in the mirror

as you combed your hair, or in the kitchen emerging
from the greasy vapors of the pot; and you hear in the water's
    boiling
a few dactylic hexameters from the Third Rhapsody
as a cock crows discordantly, from a neighbor's coop close by.

You surely know how humdrum our life is. Even the newspapers
have the same shape, size, headlines—I no longer read them. Over
    and over
flags on balconies, national celebrations, parades
of toy soliders—only the cavalry maintained something improvized,
something personal—maybe because of the horses. The dust rose
    like a cloud;
we closed the windows—afterwards you'd have to go about dusting,
    piece by piece,
vases, little boxes, picture frames, small porcelain statues, mirrors,
    buffets.
I stopped going to the celebrations. My husband used to come back
    sweating,
fling himself on his food, licking his chops, re-chewing
old, boring glories and resentments gone up in smoke. I stared at
his waistcoat buttons which were about to pop—he'd become quite
    fat.
Under his chin a large black stain flickered.

Then I'd prop my chin up, distractedly, continuing my meal,
feeling my lower jaw move in my hand
as though it were detached from my head and I was holding it
    naked in my palm.
Maybe because of this I got fat too. I don't know. Everybody
    seemed scared—
I saw them sometimes from the windows—walking on a slant,
sort of limping, as though they were concealing something under
    their arms. Afternoons
the bells rang dismally. The beggars knocked on the doors. In the
    distance,
as night fell, the white-washed facade of the Maternity Hospital
    seemed whiter,
farther away and unknowable. We lit the lamps quickly. I'd alter
an old dress. Then the sewing machine broke down; they took it
into the basement with those old romantic oil paintings

full of banal mythical scenes—Aphrodite's rising from the sea,
    eagles and Ganymedes.

One by one our old acquaintances left. The mail diminished.
Only a brief postcard for special occasions, birthdays—
a stereotyped scene of Mount Taygetos with ridged peaks, very
    blue,
a part of the Eurotas river with white pebbles and rhododendrons,
or the ruins of Mistras with wild fig trees. But more often,
telegrams of condolences. No answers came. Maybe
the recipient had died in the meantime—we don't get news
    anymore.

My husband travelled no more. Didn't open a book. In his later
    years
he grew very nervous. He smoked incessantly. Paced around at
    night
in the huge living room, with those tattered brown slippers
and his long nightgown. At noon, at the table, he'd bring up
    memories
of Clytemnestra's infidelity and how right Orestes' actions were,
as though he were threatening someone. Who cared? I didn't even
    listen. Yet
when he died, I missed him much—most of all I missed his silly
    threats,
as though they'd frozen me into an immobile position in time,
as though they'd prevented me from becoming old.
                                    Then I used to dream
of Odysseus, him with that same agelessness, with his smart
    triangular cap,
delaying his return, that crafty guy—with the pretense of imaginary
    dangers,
whereas he'd throw himself (supposedly ship-wrecked) at times in
    the arms of a Circe, at times in the arms
of a Nausicaa, to have the barnacles taken off his chest, to be
    bathed
with small bars of rose soap, to have the scar on his knee kissed, to
    be anointed with oil.

I think he also reached Ithaca—dull, fat Penelope must have
    muffled him up

in those things she weaves. I never got a message from him since
    then—
the servants might have torn them up—what does it matter
    anymore? The Symblygades
shifted to another, more inner place—you can feel them,
immobile, softened—worse than ever—they don't crush,
they drown you in a thick, black fluid—nobody escapes them.

You may go now. Night's fallen. I'm sleepy. Oh, to close my eyes,
to sleep, to see nothing outside or inside, to forget
the fear of sleeping and awakening. I can't. I jump up—
I'm afraid I'll never wake again. I stay up, listening to
the snoring of the servants from the living room, the spiders on the
    walls,
the cockroaches in the kitchen, the dead snoring
with deep breaths, as though sound asleep, calmed down.
Now I'm even losing my dead. I've lost them. They're gone.

Sometimes, after midnight, the rhythmic hoofbeats of the horses
of a late carriage can be heard, as though they are returning
from a dismal show at some broken-down theatre in the
    neighborhood
with its plaster fallen from the ceiling, its peeling walls,
its enormous faded red curtain drawn,
shrunken from too many washings, leaving a space below
to reveal the bare feet of the great stage manager or the electrician
maybe rolling up a paper forest so the lights can be shut off.

That crack is still alight, while in the auditorium
the applause and the chandeliers have long since vanished. The air
is heavy with the breath of silence, the hum of silence beneath
the empty seats, together with shells from sunflower seeds and
    twisted-up tickets,
a few buttons, a lace handkerchief, and a piece of red string.

... And that scene, on the walls of Troy—did I really undergo an
    ascension,
letting fall from my lips—? Sometimes even now,
as I lie here in bed, I try to raise my arms, to stand
on tiptoe—to stand on air—the third flower—

288

(She stopped talking. Her head fell back. She might have been asleep. The other person got up. He didn't say Good-night. Darkness had already come. As he went out into the corridor, he felt the servants glued to the wall, eavesdropping. Motionless. He went down the inner stairs as though into a deep well, with the feeling that he wouldn't find any exit—any door. His fingers, contracted, searched for the doorknob. He even imagined that his hands were two birds gasping for want of air, yet knowing at the same time that this was no more than the expression of self-pity which we usually compare with vague fear. Suddenly, voices were heard from upstairs. The electric lights were turned on in the corridor, on the stairs, in the rooms. He went up again. Now he was sure. The woman was sitting on the bed with her elbow propped up on the tin table, her cheek resting in her palm. The servants were noisily going in and out. Somebody was making a phone call in the hall. The women in the neighborhood rushed in. "Ah, ah," they cried, as they hid things under their dresses. Another phone call. Already the police were coming up. They sent the servants and the women away, but the neighbors had time to grab the bird cages with the canaries, some flower pots with exotic plants, a transistor, an electric heater. One of them grabbed a gold picture frame. They put the dead woman onto a stretcher. The person in charge sealed up the house—"until the rightful owners are found," he said—although he knew there weren't any. The house would stay like that, sealed up for forty days, and after, its possessions—as many as were saved—would be auctioned off for the public good. "To the morgue," he said to the driver. The covered car went off. Everything suddenly disappeared. Total silence. He was alone. He turned and looked around. The moon had risen. The statues in the garden were dimly lit—her statues, solitary, beside the trees, outside of the closed house. And a silent, deceitful moon. Where could he go now?).

May–August, 1970   *(G.M. & N.T.)*

THE WALL IN THE MIRROR
(1967–1971)

Translated by Andonis Decavalles and by N.C. Germanacos

EXULTATION

Since things have grown empty bit by bit
he has nothing to do any more. He sits alone,
looks at his hands, his fingernails — they are alien —
he touches his chin time and again, he notices:
another chin, so very simply alien,
so deeply and so naturally alien, that he himself
starts enjoying his intangibility.

November, 1967–January, 1968   (A.D.)

MUTUAL CONCESSIONS

His eyes, expressionless and fixed — he affected blindness. In
   a patched,
discolored jacket, too large for him, with a stick in his hand, he
   advanced,
fumbling at the walls. And everybody — children, athletes, old men,
lovely women, officers — offered eagerly to lead him,
not where they wanted but strangely enough where he asked them
   to,
exactly there. In return, he, with exquisite manners,
almost never spoke of what he noticed. And if he spoke,
he always took care to change the place, the names, the dates

hiding all of them, and hiding himself too behind the hidden
(or was he by chance revealing, on the contrary, the unknown they
   had in common?).

November, 1967–January, 1968   *(A.D.)*

UNFAMILIAR INSTRUMENT

He no longer loved things, words, or birds that had become
slogans or symbols; (and almost nothing had escaped
that fate). So he preferred to shut his mouth,
using, like the mutes, some strange movements,
calm, equivocal, bitter and somewhat amusing. But even they,
some years later, were reduced to slogans.

November, 1967–January, 1968   *(A.D.)*

MODERATION

Words are much like stones. You can build
peaceful houses with white furniture, with white beds,
provided only that somebody is found to inhabit them or at least
to stand and look through the garden railings at the moment
when the windowpanes are in inflamed maroon, and up on the hills
the evening bells are ringing, and after a while
the slack bell rope beats on the wall by itself.

November, 1967–January, 1968   *(A.D.)*

OUR LAND

We went up the hill to view our land —
shabby, scant fields, stones, olive trees.
Vineyards stretch down to the sea. A little fire
is smoking near the plough. With grandpa's clothes
we've made scarecrows for the jackdaws. Our days set out
in search of a little bread and much sunshine.
A straw hat glimmers under the poplar trees
The cock is on the fence. The cow is in the yellow.
How was it that we set our house and life in order
with a stone hand? On our door lintels
soot has gathered, year after year, from Easter candles —
tiny black crosses the dead have traced
on their return from the Resurrection. This land is much loved
with patience and with pride. Every night from the dry well
the statues come out cautiously and climb the trees.

November, 1967–January, 1968   (A.D.)

NEED TO EXPRESS

With time and fatigue — he said — words die too.
Nothing is left him to express nothingness. His fingers
have grown very thin. His ring slips off. He ties it to a string,
drops it into the well, lifts it up again. Desolation. The well
has no more water now, nor does the string have any meaning.
    Anyway, the striking
of that ring on the stones as though it were counting something,
something that should be counted, that it might result at evening
in the same odd number written on the back of the door.

November, 1967–January, 1968   (A.D.)

WAX DUMMIES

He entered the hall. There was little light. He scrutinized
the naked, beautifully painted wax dummies—he liked them:
a certain emotion, almost erotic. Bodies exquisite, as if all were
    made
from the same model, in various ages. As he raised his eyes,
he recognized his face in their faces. At that moment
he heard steps in the corridor. He undressed quickly, then stood still.
They entered, ran through the hall and finally stood in front of him.
    "This one
looks the least natural," said a woman, and pointed at him.
He heard his eyelashes lowering. They closed.

November, 1967–January, 1968   (A.D.)

EVENING PROCESSION

Meager earth, very meager, burnt bushes, stones;
we loved these stones, we worked them. Time passes.
Resplendent sunsets. A cherry-glow on the windowpanes.
Behind the panes, the flower pots, unmarried girls.
Mists rise from the olive grove. When evening falls,
the processing of the veiled ones ascends behind the cypress trees;
they walk a little stiffly, with an ancient, sad pride;
it's immediately clear from the walk: their knees
are marble, broken, stuck together with cement.

November, 1967–January, 1968   (N.C.G.)

RETURN

First the statues left. A little later
the trees, the people, the animals. The land
was left totally deserted. A wind was blowing.
Newspapers and thorns ran down the streets.
In the evening the lights went on by themselves.
A man returned alone, looked around,
took out his key, stuck it in the earth
as though entrusting it to some underground hand,
as though planting a tree. Then he ascended
the marble stairs and looked down over the city.
Warily, one by one, the statues were returning.

November, 1967–January, 1968   (N.C.G.)

DANGERS

The dead nailed to the walls, next to the advertisements
of state bonds; the dead propped on the pavements,
on the wooden platforms of the notables, with flags, with helmets,
cardboard masks.
    The dead
have nowhere to hide anymore, they can't command
their dry bones (negotiable deaths, boxes
lifted by winches, yellow paper with pins). The dead
are more endangered.
    And he, prudent, with his umbrella,
walking high on the electric wires, a tightrope walker
above the parade, with a handkerchief tied over his eyes,
as the first raindrops began to fall.
    Then the storm burst.
The trumpeters were shouting to the women to wring the flags dry,
but they had locked themselves in the basements and had swallowed
  their keys.

March-October 1971   (A.D.)

THE YARD

A peaceful yard, silent. The sickly trees, sad,
far away in time. The smell of mould,
the lizard, the dry well, the pulleys. There
the lame boy comes out in the evening. At the other door,
across the way, the one-handed boy stands, looking afar.
They do not greet each other. They clench their teeth. They want to
    forget
the killed bird they had buried together one evening when
the one still had his leg and the other his hand,
and the straw chair near the rose-bush
was warm with the sun, with nobody sitting there,
and everything was pointless, sad, immobile,
and therefore immortal, in a city
of long ago, naively nailed to the future.

March–October, 1971   (A.D.)

PRESENCE

Tall mountains, taller clouds, meeting
among trees and myths, on precipitous slopes,
there where the healthy omnipotent logos
echoed without fear of emphasis, while further down,
in the yellow clouds of blossoming crops,
in two facing rows, the statues had fallen silent,
stark naked above death, with nipples erect.

March-October, 1971   (N.C.G.)

INVENTION OF THE CENTER

They locked him up in a circle. He still insisted
on thinking and observing. He kept pacing
within the circle, close to the wall in the yard
of the circular jail. He did not speak. In the evening
he continued his rounds, his head bent down. Perhaps he
    meditated;
perhaps he learned that every circle has a center
(or do all circles have the same center?).
                                 Anyhow,
he would smile now and then, feeling on his back,
exactly on the large number they had stamped there,
the most secret, the most white bird sitting.

March–October, 1971   *(A.D.)*

NOT EVEN

Not even poetry, then, not even poetry.
You knew it in advance when from the seventh heaven
you lowered, tied with a rope,
that old kitchen basket
with the shaving machine, the bread, the shoes,
with the little mirror and the mute canary.
You left it there then; you did not raise it up. Little by little
the nettles smothered the basket. Nevertheless,
you still keep the rope tied to your bed rails.

March–Oct. 1971   *(A.D.)*

THE SECRET PAIN OF THE DECOR

To rescue his truth, he spoke a thousand lies.
Finally he could no longer recall what he wished to save.
Others, before going to bed, put their shoes
in the closet; most people, the simpler ones,
put them under the bed; some, more infrequently,
put them on the chair; yet all, without exception,
died one day or another (or at night).
One pair of ladies' shoes, white, has been left
in front of an open window. The air blows gently.
The long white curtain touches them every so often.

March–October, 1971   (A.D.)

FORBIDDEN GROUND

He always searched, without reason, without need.
In the ashes he found little inhabited islands
with their old churches full of wind.
Outside one of the churches, there was a chair.
Down below, on the rocks, big sea-urchins
shadowed by a standstill cloud. Afterwards,
he had nothing to add. It was obvious that he was carefully
avoiding to mention the word *death*.

March–October, 1971   (A.D.)

INEVITABLES

An evening as dark as an empty pocket. Deep in the pocket,
a hole, soft and downy. Through it
you secretly pass one of your fingers, touch your thigh
as if touching another, large, alien body—

298

the deep body of your death or of the night.
Through that hole all the coins slip,
in particular those golden ones with the lovely profile
of the adolescent Prince of the Lilies.

March–October, 1971   (A.D.)

ↄ

HINTS
(1970–1971)

Translated by Kimon Friar

In your empty pocket an ancient coin, forgotten —
your touch recognizes blindly the naked limbs of the god.

*

The tree, the statue, the garden, the old woman —
as you think of the duration of words, as you go
out of time, out of the portal of the poem.

*

A man smiles by himself in the dark,
perhaps because he can see in the dark,
perhaps because he can see the dark.

*

Leave off explanations — what are they worth? — rather to the
      contrary, they tend
to confuse things more — since you already know that poetry,
naked, modest and arrogant, is nothing
more than the wonderful achievement of the inexplicable.

*

The girl cut off a willow twig, threw it away
and smelled her fingers — this movement of hers
was the projection of time into the interior of fragrances.

*

Behind the large sunflowers was the wall,
behind the wall, the road—it couldn't be seen at all.
Then houses, trees, hills, crimes. At noon
the workers at the lumber yard would go there to piss.
At night the dead would emerge to whitewash the wall.

*

Don't beat about the bush, speak bluntly, although in gasps,
(the beautiful implications, the omissions—he would say— are for
    the accomodated)—
perhaps even the shattering of the poem will give birth to the
    poem.

*

Always leave the spear in the corner of the room,
leave the shield upside down in the garden to fill with water
so the birds may come to drink as you look through the
    windowpanes,
as you watch the rabbits chewing the vineyard leaves
with that creaking of a paper kite's tail as it plunges in the blue.

*

The significance of art—he said—may be found perhaps
in what is omitted, willingly or unwillingly, like
that glittering knife entirely concealed in the basket
under the red, golden, purple grapes.

*

Whatever you pile up in your trunk goes the way of death.
Whatever you give away goes the way of life. The old blind man
recognizes the counterfeit coins by touch. He fingers

everything before his eyes, names them one by one,
no matter how much you hide in the corner or behind the
  curtain.

*

They grow further apart, the one from the other; they no longer
  believe in innocence; they no longer believe
in ideas, in words, in roses. As they separate,
each appears to carry his own mountain on his back.

*

Don't ask how long it will last—it won't; others make the
  decisions.
Turn the table upside down; extinguish the lamp. The mirror
is full of bullet holes. Don't look inside.
I shall look—the other answered—through these holes.
Each time I see my stolen face again, intact.

*

The ship left. The lights faded away. On the wharf
the sacks filled with dynamite remained stacked in rows.
In the public square, the statue held the matches.

*

For some time now he has exhausted the words. Nevertheless,
with his lamp lit, he is always waiting
lest he come across the poem in the middle of the night.

*

He would always observe the thermometer on the wall.
According to the degrees, he would grow hot or cold.
When the thermometer broke one day, he became confused—

he no longer knew when to warm himself or grow cold.
The drops of mercury flowed on the floor below
with a dispersed, inadmissable, dreadful freedom.

*

He wants to make the memorial statue of a small frog —
not the frog itself — it is the softness he wants,
the complex mechanism of hereditary leaps
in the watered garden at night under the two Bears
the moment when Helen was undressing behind the glass door.

*

I will leave — he says — the voices of the market place, the
        refrigerators, the baskets,
the miscellaneous, stale produce and the new advertisements;
I will go into the house, close the door, sit in my own chair,
shave the point of my pencil politely, carefully, and cry.

*

A slice of red watermelon on the plate.
The book you loaned me was beautiful.
I am thinking now about writing a poem.
In it, only the birds will converse.

*

Each belief — he says — is either naiveté or cowardice or a cunning
        subterfuge. I
smoke my cigarette calmly under the very nose of death;
button or unbutton my shirt; leave first
before they can tell me to leave or drive me away.
At night I sit dead center in the void, cross my hands,
pretend to be my corpse in front of the mirror and go to sleep.

*

For days on end his hand in his pocket gropes
at the angular cheek bones of the void. Then suddenly
he draws out a blind doll, to which he adds eyes,
and gives it to the daughter of the secondhand dealer. She
strips it naked with interest, and takes out its eyes again.

*

It was poetry again this night with conjectures of miraculous
    probabilities. It was the steps
of the beautiful sinning woman hugging the wall,
the rustling of her dress over the large thorns in the field of dogs;
the odor of her armpits suddenly lit up by the streetlamp in the
    town square
at the moment when, exactly behind this streetlamp, the hand of
    death was hiding.

*

No matter how much alone one is in his fear and pain,
with seaweed and windowpanes, with unknown shadows on the
    low ceiling,
the red line of your fire from the crack under the door
tells us of life's alphabet again, the uniting, the excellence, the
    pride,
the beautiful moment when you leave the house and meet a tree,
when you become a leaf among leaves, in the same song,
O you who emerge from statues and tall cypress trees.

*

In the deserted field at night we would burn our shadows.
The fire flared. Amid the flames
an enormous crutch rose to the heavens
like the star of Judgement.
                    Down that stair
the burnt Angel descended, holding his wings over his heart like
    two dead girls.

*

They were asked for their last wish.
"Paper bags," they said. These were brought to them.
They blew them up, turned,
burst them against the wall, and fell.

*

Since he knows they are watching him from the window,
how can he move so simply, so beautifully?
I want to learn the mechanism of this simplicity.
I close the shutters, look at myself in the mirror.
A hole in my forehead blocks me.

May–October, 1970   (K.F.)

ىل

from

THE CARETAKER'S DESK
(1971)

Translated by Kimon Friar

KNOWN CONSEQUENCES

For years and years he fretted; he undressed
before small or large mirrors,
before any pane of glass; he tried out carefully
first one and then another position in order to choose, to discover
the one most his, the one most natural, that he might become
his own finished statue — although he knew
that statues were most often prepared
for the dead, and even more often
for certain unknown, nonexistent gods.

Athens, March 17, 1971   *(K.F.)*

NOCTURNAL EPISODE

He hammered a nail on the wall. He had nothing
to hang. He sat on an old chair
and stared, facing it. There was nothing
he could think of or remember. He got up
and covered the nail with his handkerchief. Suddenly
he saw that his hand had turned blue, dyed
by the moon standing by the window. The murderer
had lain down on his bed. His feet,
naked, strong, with faultless toenails, with a corn
on the small toe, protruded from the blanket,
and the hairs curled erotically. This is how

statues always sleep, with their eyes open,
nor need you fear whatever dream, whatever word;
now you have the trustworthy witness you needed,
the most accurate and discrete; because you know
that statues never betray, but only reveal.

Athens, March 30, 1971   (K.F.)

WELLS AND PEOPLE

We had our wells within our houses.
We drank well water, washed,
kept a certain order, a cleanliness. One night
someone got up and emptied his cup of poison
into the well. After that, each got up
in turn, one by one, and emptied out
his cup of poison. When day broke,
no one would drink water. Until, finally,
the stairs sank into the well. The inhabitants
went up on the roof and remained there motionless
for hours with open mouths in hopes that a drop
of rain might fall. The itinerant photographer
passed by on the street below. He did not see them.
He was looking at the death notices stuck on the pillars*
and on the large doors of the shuttered shops.

Athens, February 3, 1971   (K.F.)

---

*In Greece it is still a relatively common practice to have death notices printed
and to affix them to walls, kiosks, telephone poles, *et al.*

FORGED PASSPORT

The woman shakes a blanket from the window.
The blanket slips from her hands, spreads out on the air
quietly, steadily, horizontally. The woman looks at it, smiles,
then leaps on the blanket from the window. The blanket sags,
closes like a sack, hovers, stops. This very sack
is carried peacefully by a man as he ascends
the sky with slow strides. He knows, nevertheless,
that he has lied. This is why he has turned his back
on the large door of the printer's shop from which
three newspaper boys emerge, weeping, without newspapers.

Athens, April 14, 1971   (K.F.)

STRANGE TIMES

The three messengers arrived. They went up the stairs.
The heralds left by the back door. A dog
passed by, hugging the wall. The scent of lilacs
entered the room of the slain man. The soldiers, outside,
were taking off their swords and helmets and placing them
on the stones heated by the sun.
                                    Has the murderer perhaps
passed the river? Has he crossed it? And was it he
perhaps? Why have human doubles recently multiplied?
Is it because of habit, the similiar injunctions, the epidemic —
when one looked at others, he had the impression
he was looking into many mirrors. This alleviated matters
to a degree — a general guilt or forgiveness,
and at times a general indifference.
                                    But now
no one wanted to take upon himself such responsibility,
and one by one they ceased to resemble each other. Then, across the
    street,

before the gate, between the two tall columns,
the murderer stood erect, holding with reverence
the largest wreath of all made of white and red lilies.

Athens, April 16, 1971   (K.F.)

DETERIORATION

Deep in the inner space denuded of trees,
yet suggesting, nevertheless, the trees that had now become
stools, tables, chests. On the trunk
sits the silent woman covering her feet
and looking at the caterpillar crawling on the floor —
a green, greasy caterpillar that has veered from its path,
the one that had devoured the forest and has come now to eat the
    house,
the picture frames on the wall and the rope hanging from the
    ceiling.

Athens, April 24, 1971   (K.F.)

THE UNCOMPROMISING

Streets, avenues, signs, names, doors,
dust, smoke, a tree, self-interests. It was I
who threw the ring into the plate. Every night the beer pubs
open and close with calculated noise. The windows
are opaque with golden letters. The waiters have gone
to the toilets for a smoke. The other man is tired,
gazes at the floor or the wall, avoids seeing,
avoids showing, avoids naming. Every word
is a betrayal. On the billboard table

the flabby woman is lying naked, hiding
her eaten face in her scant hair
as large flies with cut wings walk on her breasts.

Athens, April 27, 1971   (K.F.)

HONESTY

In the month of May, when the sun turns, it strikes the house
on its western side. The sunsets grow longer. A ribbon,
almost golden, engraves the middle wall vertically. Men
find themselves on the brink of a deep revelation.
The small tables of a confectionary shop have been brought out on
   the sidewalk.
The red lilies can be discerned behind the glass pane. On the tall
   house
across the street the windows have been opened. The emptiness of a
   room recently vacated can be seen.
                        And perhaps—who knows—
perhaps it is you who gives the order, even before night falls,
to light the green globes in the church courtyard,
for this is a time of difficult contraries.
                        Yes, you,
who have been authorized (by whom?) to put in the poem openly
the wooden horses, the keys of old lost valises,
and those rubber imitations of three or more frogs
so they may leap softly in the watered nonexistent garden.

Athens, May 17, 1971   (K.F.)

REVERENTIAL COMPARISON

Close to each other, the coffeehouse, the drug store, the candy shop,
and a little before, the small flower shop. People don't stop.
Women look at themselves in the shop windows before night falls.
    Behind
the half-built wall, in the plot overrun by mallows,
everyone throws what he wants — paper plates,
medicine bottles, broken cups, glasses,
rotted flowers.
                    There the old women and their dogs gather
to search among the heaps carefully, absentmindedly — they do not
    see
the golden sunset; they search like poets for the poem,
the most bitter and forsaken crones, so happy
with a dry orange peel, with a piece of mirror,
with a blue tube from the drug store on which
the white tracks of the homeless snail remain,
and in the tube's cavity the sound of the train from Lárisa.

Athens, May 8, 1971   (K.F.)

THE OTHER PRECISION

Measure everything well, calculate with precision
the frontiers, the distances; for thus by stopping, by laying out
your ruler on the earth, by thus dedicating yourself to number,
you may — who knows? — forget the frontiers; you may
reveal the great precision, single and self-sufficient,
as, purely by chance, your finger on the earth touches the buckle
from Helen's belt — the one she wore one evening
on the walls, above the disputes of the Achaeans and the Trojans,
while behind her, following ecstatically like fate,
with her eyes half closed, came the black pregnant bitch.

Athens, May 10, 1971   (K.F.)

ENCOUNTER

Nothing, of course, comes entirely by itself.
You too must search in order to find. In the morning
the sun comes in from the window to the east and discolors
the two crimson armchairs; it stays a while, then withdraws,
leaving behind it but an idea of mildness — that
quiet effacement.
                              And the carpet flowers,
previously stepped on, have their justification, have
their ear glued to the floor, listening
to the rhythmical galloping of underground horses. Then
the unspeaking woman enters; and you see
how she takes care not to step on the flowers.

Perhaps the inconceivable can be endured by two together,
although it never reveals itself to more than one.

Athens, May 11, 1971   (K.F.)

THE RELATION OF THE UNRELATED

Why should we speak? — he said — What's the use of many
      explanations
when, as you are hurrying to arrive in time
for friends awaiting you to discuss a matter
of much importance, which has to do with you and many others,
you suddenly stop in the middle of the street to look
at that bird serenely walking on the asphalt,
with its head raised ecstatically, more informed than you,
with a bus ticket in its long beak?

Athens, May 12, 1971   (K.F.)

313

from

SIDESTREET
(1971–1972)

Translated by Kostas Myrsiades

THE LAUGH

He saw the clouds from the park bench.
He tore out his coat lining,
removed his hat band,
wrapped the kidnapped infant
and pitched it in the well. Standing with his feet apart,
he pissed, smiling before you did.
I'm speaking about this smile, about night's spectacles
about the moon's spectacles. The infant,
no, it wasn't kidnapped. Nor did there exist
a well or an infant. Only the clouds.

Samos, December 19, 1971   *(K.M.)*

IN THE RAIN

He walks in the rain. He's in no hurry at all.
The drenched railing glistens. The trees
are black with a hidden red. An old
bus tire is discarded in the sheepfold.
The blue house is significantly bluer.
So that's how nothingness is lessened. Rocks fall.
Hands clench. An unused envelope
floats in the river. Perhaps
your name is written on the other side.

Samos, December 21, 1971   *(K.M.)*

MULTIDIMENSIONAL

He ate his bread. He drank water. He didn't eat
the iron; he placed it in the fire, melted it,
and forged two birds; for eyes he used
his four coat buttons. The birds
were laid at the Charioteer's feet. Then
he suddenly noticed he didn't have hands . . . His hands
had stuck to the iron.

Samos, December 21, 1971   (K.M.)

ETHOGRAPHY

Large shark roam our shore—he said.
At night they're red like fire. Our children's
teeth show even through closed mouths. Then
the old woman took the oar; she pitched it underneath the ikons;
she didn't cross herself; she remained standing. Outside,
the men could be heard sharpening their knives.
The four women could not keep awake.
They stayed at the window; they yawned. Ah—they said—
seeing the mailman in the galaxy.

Athens, January 3, 1972   (K.M.)

CONDENSATION

He placed the fish on the chair.
The woman fell asleep in the mirror.
The fresh butter is in the refrigerator. The salt

is in a small plastic bag. My children—he said—
(he said it turned to the wall from which all the pictures
had been removed). My children, my children—he repeated—
the best are the dead; I am not;
I stash myself naked in my hollow wooden horse;
I sit cramped; I light a cigarette; I put it out; I fear
lest the smoke escape through the horse's eyes and it betray me.

Athens, January 7, 1972   *(K.M.)*

SIMPLE HONESTY

If—he says—I placed the bird in the green cage,
and if I placed the bird on the statue's head,
it was this, only this; just like
my nails are attached evenly on my fingers
and every moment without my noticing they grow.
Could you call it resistance to death? Call it that.
Ask for nothing else. I don't know. I don't know.

Athens, February 2, 1972   *(K.M.)*

BELFRY
(1972)

Translated by Kimon Filar and Kostas Myrsiades

Then mute days came sprawled on the sidewalks
above hidden sewers with warped shoes;
in a corner of the room, stilts covered with a bedsheet —
these were what the nightmare wore at night up to the curtain
    frame,
and hunger strikers with a cut lemon in their fists,
waiting, waiting, shutting their eyes more and more tightly;
"Are they dead?" he asked. He was wearing large dark glasses;
the other approached him, removed the glasses, stared him in the
    eye,
replaced the glasses, stepped back to leave — on his back
a large piece of paper was pinned with the number 11;
and the children never stopping, not even in their sleep,
silently questioning over and over again from the beginning,
with fixed eyes; a cuckold's bastards; plug up their ears with wax,
    pretend
you've heard nothing, you've seen nothing;
look in the well where the stone fell,
where the stone hit the sky's eyeball;
the hole remained deeper still under the water under the glitter,
because the water always closes over it;
the hole remains on the bottom and shouts at night; the women
    fall silent,
may that hour be cursed, a groove between the eyebrows, they
    clutch their depleted keys;
the aroma of warm bread rises from the bakery without asking,
trips over the cables, splits in the middle,
half is not enough;
              well then, they fall silent
to find time, perhaps, and come to a decision; they stare
at the bullet that struck the wall next to Sotíri's ear;
a bit of plaster falls to the ground; they take a broom, sweep,
raise a cloud of dust lest the sentries opposite

see that their dresses and chins are black. It doesn't mean
    anything—they say to themselves—
the light cannot be executed—they say—just try cutting it
with a penknife or a butcher's knife; just try.
                                    They preoccupy
    themselves
with some such matters in prisons from afternoon to nightfall
    when the shepherd's star peeks
above the few olive trees on the hill and a little above the pine
    trees
with large caterpillars wrapped in cotton,
and the rifle hidden under the roof—a deep anxiety—
the red cross in the stable under the dead horse's hay;
from the terrace the small summer boats could be seen as they
    swerved round the breakwater;
the grasshopper perched on the water glass, a copper foot lifted on
    a copper generation.
                        We were always forgetting,
because indeed we had to sleep, wake up, go to work, give birth;
many alarm clocks were needed on the table, on the chair;
the cicadas still had something to do with the centuries,
the marble ruins, although they were mutilated, were white,
a touch of red had remained on the breast's nipple;
the severed clay hand was hollow,
you wore it on your hand like a rigid glove,
delighted in the fit, in the fist's disguise—
these gloves, you know, are warped by machine oil, by gasoline,
    by the steering wheel,
embalmed in a driving position, they smack the wind. False
    heroics—he said
cardboard suburbs decked out in flags;
pimping, a wine glass crushed in the palm,
blood on your best suit;
                        and Pétros,
his mouth stuck with saliva,
trying to say *freedom* or *sky* or *tomorrow*,
while the woman's hand, washing the windows of the beer joints,
was almost absorbed by the light,
with her damp cloth outside time.
Damn the hour—Vangélis would repeat,
half in water and half in sun—finally, at the end,

in one way or another, the cypress trees; on them rest
a lame sparrow, a cloud, Anésti's cap,
the silver palms of votive offerings,
Artemis' cut braids—
                                Alas!
what paths are not opened by hope—said the old woman—
men—their only pride is to have nothing,
the children drenched with wild-pear vinegar. I can do without
     it—
said Katína, shaking her shoe. The others
remained on the high mountains, kept awake by the gunblasts
     from the galaxy;
when they saw the cat in the bushes, they realized they'd been
     betrayed,
their testicles shrunk by morning frost into black hairs,
their ears, their penises were burned by cigarettes, they didn't
     utter a word.

Hey, the valiant lads of honor with a nation of a few smattering
     letters,
untrained in heroics, political organization, sociology,
and the night with a moon-knife nailed upright to the door,
the lads, locked out,
the others locked in,
gazing through narrow windows at the sea,
climbing the spiral staircase of the lighthouse—a large marble
     stairway,
the exact same steps going downwards,
well on well closed below, explosives and fuses;
bang, nothing was heard;
night, the bear, lumbering through the woods, knocking down
     trees,
history, the bear. What dreams we had—
dreams by the bushel. What bodies fell—

All the bitten apples strewn about the ground of the huge
     detention camps,
a half hour's stroll, with permission, behind barbed wire,
you trip over the apples, guard yourself against broken bones;

do you guard yourself? — wrong; do you break your bones? —
    wrong;
do you guard yourself against wrong? are you imprisoned? aren't
    you imprisoned? — wrong;
oh come now, what with your wrongs, their wrongs, our wrongs —
are we to be stuck here, for God's sake!

Where's the drum, the drum made of Electra's flayed skin?

*

House with a garden, with red shirts on the washline,
house with a balcony, with plaster statues,
house without a balcony — itinerant knife-grinders piss in the
    corner,
house with a lank Crucifixion outside the door, with the paralyzed
    woman on the bed;
hooks in the basement, mouse traps, instruments of torture,
the afternoon is a star thumbtacked on the wall.

There's no rationalizing the fact that we'll all die — he used to
    say —
let's live at least — he used to say — as long as we live.

The second star fluid in the bucket on the well's rim,
inside the well the three outlaws and the other three and the
    sixteen
without a deck of cards and cigarettes;
they lit the lamp later under the water,
the matches on the kitchen rack were damp; Mrs. Evlambía
    couldn't get the fire going in order to boil
two chicken eggs — Captain Vangélis had laid the third
in the middle of the bed; Mrs. Persephóni found it —

Just think of it, chickens now laying eggs in beds! And Captain
    Vangélis
left with his pipe between his teeth
for the 11:05 boat, clucking and clearing his throat
so much that the elevator filled with eggshells and panes of glass,

together with those colored pieces from St. Pelayía's West
    window.

There the saints kept vigil one by one; in the morning
the leanest with the thick black mustache
waved the large white sheet, the shroud of Jesus,
beckoning to the cabin boy skimming by the sea's edge in his
    small motorboat;
just as he rounded the pier, he pissed calmly into the sea;

but the other, the more corpulent saints, weren't idle either,
one brandished his dirty handkerchief
the second his suspenders
the third the bull's three ribbons
the fourth the belt from the painters' waists
the fifth the knight's chastity belt
or an edge of his yellow blouse
or the year-before-last's newspaper
or the nylon crown of thorns
or the real barbed wire of Yiáros or Parthénis
because the nun in the adjacent cell was called Parthenía
while the water in the coffeepot boiled unattended—

This was not for boiling the eggs, because the eggs
had already hatched into chicks that were pecking the grass
between the stone slabs of the prison yard, those big white slabs
on which the blue bird walked secretly on one leg—

such things were also to be found in the countryside, in the month
    of July or August
with a full moon or starlight, guitars, boatrides,
while dogs barked in the vineyards;
rocks tumbled down from the hill to the seashore,
small dry burs stuck to the Virgin's hair,
the walls of the inns smelled of dried sun in the night's coolness,
wheels of unknown wine-presses spun, or wristwatches
on the hands of girls who left them (the watches) on the pebbles
    before diving into the sea,
blue, lemon, cyclamen-hued pebbles,
watches sent them by their brothers who had emigrated—

So it was on these white stone slabs on which at daybreak
the Twelve barefoot Apostles paced
or Blok's Twelve
or half of the Twenty-Four Hour Period
or the Twelve Months of Leap Year,
and the footprints were very wide;
the woodshop's apprentice measured them centimeter by
    centimeter
with that wooden rule from his pocket;
he was late in getting to work, his boss yelled at him,
and threatened to toss him out on the street;

he would give him the list with precise measurements;
the footprints were very long and wide,
they didn't fit the Apostle's feet
the way Electra's feet fit into Orestes' footprints
there on the humid soil of Mycenae
most likely wet with blood than with yesterday's rain
drained through the mouths of stone lions
and the oval holes of gold masks — no;

the feet of the Twelve clumsy privates fitted much better
(ah my brother Alexandhros)
with lice on their undershirts and knapsacks, in spite of so much
    snow,
or the feet of the imprisoned proletariat throughout the world
because all the feet of prisoners contain an indispensable equality
and all the imprisoned were proletariats
because on all their shoulders hung
the ropes of God or of death or of professional hangmen,
(we said on their shoulders to avoid saying around their necks)
and their footprints on the sand were identical with the boatmen's
except that these were not wet from the sea
and their little toes were swollen with corns
because they were forced to move in a cramped space
while fleets threshed the seas with telescopes and torpedoes.

At any rate, this is not what it's all about,
we were talking about the water boiling in the coffeepot —
it was neither for rice pudding nor for eggs

but simply that Sister Parthenía might make her coffee,
and she forgot it on the alcohol burner,
feeding and talking to the red pig—the one
slated for the Easter holidays. Always of course
the Crucifixion is followed by the Resurrection; and so it was quite
    convenient
to mourn in other clothes, knowing beforehand that fasting
lasts forty days (and optional at that) until Easter Sunday,
written in much larger letters on the calendar. And so

all things are accommodated—what can we say?—they're
    accommodated,
everyone is accommodated—what can we do? we're
    accommodated,
the nettles in the keyhole, the ball on the playing field,
the hanged man on his rope, voices at their highest pitch—
—scat, scat, you suckers, spoon-and-knife slingers!

                              *

And then Gárgaros rose from the rock
and struck the trash can, straining to listen in the wells
above the rotted stairs and the dark corridors
where kepis and helmets hung in rows;
he struck it a second and a third time,
he shouted
there is no time for postponement
this is no place for procrastination
this is not the moment for a folk dance
with a knife between your teeth
with a knife in your ribs
with a knife in your navel—

those who await the resurrection are dead
policemen reside in the statues
the melon peel slippery
the orange peel peppery
salt is spread on the asphalt
and flour on the sea
there is only half a wheel—

All those living
come now, get up,
all those living — he shouted —
all those living — Gárgaros howled. And the cargo ships were by
    the pier
lifting copper crates high into the heavens with windlasses,
large coffins for three or four drowned,
stacks of surveillance files,
windows of old houses, clay Caryatids;

women wore their nylon hose over their faces,
they prepared to walk single-footed on their heads,
their shoes piled mountain high on the barges,
they were more beautiful this way with socks over their faces
concealing the wrinkles, the sins, the concessions,
shopping at stores with rose or yellow shopping nets;

they bought mirrors mostly,
stood in front of them,
parted their thighs, and waited,
they waited, and gazed at themselves;
one mirror was cracked at the knees
the second had a hole at the temple
(from which kitchen vapors issued, the smell of cauliflower)
the third was covered up to the top by empty hat boxes and
    X-rays;

outside the mirrors were the other women,
the ones below the cellars, the others inside the storage jars,
    others
held three apples, bread, garlic wrapped in towels,
five cigarettes folded in a piece of paper,
a small bottle of gasoline
two aspirins in another piece of paper;
they travelled to the prisons, the concentration camps, staying up
    all night and day
before large doors with guards and bayonets;
bobby pins fell from their hair,
they picked them up from the ground, placed them in their
    pockets,

their hair fell over their eyes, their mouths;
they chewed their hair, they stammered,
their teeth were not false—

the only sturdy part left me is my teeth
Madam Konstandína used to say;
I can crack an almond, a walnut, a stone
and, with any luck at all, a whole rock—she used to say. Ah,

ah my wretched mothers (Gárgaros again)
with any luck at all, with the revolution, my little old ladies
who sat in the afternoon on the half-moon's edge,
with your skirts gathered about your knees,
with your shoes hidden beneath your skirts,
poor, withered, obstinate ladies with clenched jaws,
with whitewashed mid-brows, with mulish heads,
chattering for hours with illiterate shadows,
with small wooden crucifixes threaded on a string
inside the shirt of a gallant youth who renounced his faith in God
but did not renounce his faith in the land;
and you know this, brainless mothers,
better than your late husband's balls,
better than the old gramaphone record in Mr. Vasílis' tavern at
    dusk
outside the windows with the basil plant, dear mother;
and crabs stroll on the pier,
and the sea-urchin within—you called it fear,
it *is* fear, stings with a thousand thorns even in your sleep.

A wretched life, you said it many times and as many more,
don't expect to get by with begging your way, locking yourself up
    at home,
the nail needs the hammer
and a great straightforward cry,
a thundering mountain,
throwing the informer down the stairs,
knifing the torturer,
the agent, the loan shark, the parasite,
the deaf-mute loneliness
the shortsighted sitonyoureggs

the blind Godwillprovide
with the Acropolisa CIA hangout
with microphonic ears on the roof-beams
or under the bed where you are fucking your wife;
in your nostrils, that smell the future
in your ears with their two eardrums of sky—

Alack, alas, brave youths who fell asleep with your nose between
    knees,
alack, alas, my student with your bloodstained shirt,
alack, alas my country raped by dictators,
cast dice into the air, O woman baptized in the wind,
play with your flags and the small mandolin of Makriyánnis;

scoundrels piss in Kolokotrónis' helmet;
I told you, I can't bear it,
I'm not wearing glasses
I'm not a diplomat
I can't take all that hemming and hawing
I'm neither a starlight pianist nor St. Sotíra's candlelighter.

Alas, my murdered bloodbrothers, let's avenge your murders;
vengeance—I shouted at midnight—vengeance,
not forgiving and forgetting and shitted words,
vengeance, I shouted
fire and the hatchet
fire
hang the gallows
fire and the hatchet and Che and the hatchet and Che Guevara;

with rubber boots as high as one's head
it took me five weeks to pass through the sewer plugged up for
    five years
with its severed hands, with severed feet
with corsets of obesity
with military buttons, with plaster masks
with long cutlery and clotted bandages
with big balustrades and beds.
                              I ascended
I stood before secret agents

I threw away my rubber boots
I shouted, down with the tyrants,
they shot at me
they killed me

and I remained here ten meters above the Hilton
observing the tourists and the avenue traffic,
the likenesses of Judas in the brilliantly-lit shop windows
and I hovering high, slain among the slain,
with the two wings of the beheaded Victory on my shoulder
    blades,
many-storied electric wings operated by batteries
guaranteed to last three thousand years or more—

Here I remain
here I return
I call to you
with my wings singed along the edges
by the passing of B-52s on their way back from Viet Nam,
I parcel out my wings and whatever years I have not lived
a tuft of down in each worker's pocket
along with the crushed cigarette, the crippled wages, the hammer;
it was I who placed this tuft of down there
because I am Gárgaros the Gárgarogagárgaros,
son of the people and Mrs. Penelope who finally broke her loom;
I who have youth and smokestacks on my side;
with my fist I break a watermelon on my knees,
with my teeth I crack black seeds and spit them out—

Come now my lads, my summer lads,
Enough now.
Enough.

Then the great silence formed that had always existed.
And he struck the bell. We're agreed.
We set our hands on this sound again and took the vow.

Athens, Karlóvasi, February-August 1972.   *(K.F. & K.M.)*

329

* * *

NOTES

Page 321 — "a nation of a few smattering letters": The Greek word for "Greece" consists of five triangular letters (ΕΛΛΑΣ).

Page 323 — "Yiáros or Parthénis": Military prison camps where Yannis Ritsos spent several years during the Papadópoulos regime (1967–1974).

Page 323 — "Blok's Twelve": A poem by the Russian poet Alexander Blok (1880–1921) which Ritsos translated into Greek in 1957.

Page 325 — "Gárgaros": In a letter to the translators dated May 27, 1977, Ritsos writes, "Gárgaros (Γκάργαρος) is a personal name (it is used often in *Belfry* and must remain in this form or in its English transliteration, Gárgaros). Naturally in Greek it takes on a special meaning because it is similar acoustically to the adjective (γάργαρυς) which means purling, brawling, murmuring, limpid, transparent, clear and is derived (onomatopoetically) from the sound of gurgling, flowing water—(γάρ), (γάρ), (γάρ). In this way the word Gárgaros symbolizes the pure democrat, the pure citizen-fighter, the pure contemporary proletariat. But beyond these (and many other) parallelisms concerning meaning, that which concerns me is: the two bass vowels (a), the two liquid consonants (r), and the harsh double consonant at the beginning of the name (g)."

Page 325 — "folk dance": Zeibékiko — the dance of the Zeibéks who lived around Izmir. It is essentially a war dance of a slow, heavy-footed nature.

Page 328 — "Makriyánnis": Yánnis Makriyánnis (1797–1864), an outstanding commander of irregulars in the Greek War of Independence and a notable politician thereafter in the reign of King Othon.

Page 328 — "Kolokotrónis": Theódoros Kolokotrónis (1770–1843), supreme commander of the Greek forces during the Greek War of Independence.

from

SCRIPTURE OF THE BLIND
(1972–1973)

Translated by Kimon Friar and Kostas Myrsiades

ULTIMATE INNOCENCE

He put on his shoes, his gloves, his cap.
Underclothing and clothing — none. And he went out into the
    street.
The plumber, the coal dealer, the butcher, the policeman,
the old dog with its tail cut, two flags,
the large red woman on the wall. Approaching her,
he removed his right glove with his other hand,
he detected that ancestral ring lost years ago,
and at the same time saw himself naked under
the red woman's gaze. Nothing was left him any more.
He then removed both shoes also, placed his gloves
in one of them, his cap in the other. And thus, alone,
smiling in an ultimate innocence, he proffered
his naked hands to the handcuffs.

Athens, September 28, 1972   *(K.F. & K.M.)*

WITHOUT A MIRROR NOW

Her hair fallen over her eyes, her mouth,
she chews at her hair; her saliva whitens.
A great shadow on the curtain. The water glasses on the floor.
Shout it until the end; turn it about, hide it.
Hide what? Hide yourself where? "Death!" she shouted.
"Old age, death!" she shouted. I'll run away. Hold me back.

A hill strewn with shell fragments. And there,
amid bones, a comb, a red piece of string,
to comb yourself without a mirror now, to bind your hair
that it might not fall over your eyes, that it might not hide from you
    the white worm
that slimily, serenely, sluggishly crawls up the table.

Athens, September 29, 1972   (K.F. & K.M.)

NAKED FACE

Cut the lemon and let two drops fall into the glass;
look there, the knives beside the fish on the table—
the fish are red, the knives are black.
All with a knife between their teeth or up their sleeves, thrust in their
    boots or their breeches.
The two women have gone crazy, they want to eat the men,
they have large black fingernails, they comb their unwashed hair
high up, high up like towers, from which the five boys
plunge down one by one. Afterward they come down the stairs,
draw water from the well, wash themselves, spread out their thighs,
thrust in pine cones, thrust in stones. And we
nod our heads with a "yes" and a "yes"—we look down
at an ant, a locust, or on the statue of Victory—
pine tree caterpillars saunter on her wings.
The lack of holiness—someone said—is the final, the worst kind of
    knowledge;
it's exactly such knowledge that now remains to be called holy.

Athens, September 30, 1972   (K.F. & K.M.)

WISDOM

What was a mountain and afterward air and later a star;
and he who said "Thank you"—said it softly so that
neither the two nor the third might hear it, because they were very
    angry;
they were throwing their shoes out of the window, their flower pots,
their gramophone records, their water glasses and their napkins
that we might get angry too, that we might shout at them "Don't!"
and thus give them an excuse for what they'd already done.
In the room next door, with its large iron bed,
we can hear the old man coughing; on his blanket
he has placed a small frog, and for days and nights now,
calm, fasting, ecstatic, he stares at and studies
the soft mechanisms of the frog's leaping.
Afterward he stops coughing. We hear him jumping on the bed.
On the third day we encased him completely in plaster,
leaving only his toothless grin showing.

Athens, October 2, 1972   (K.F. & K.M.)

LACK OF WILL POWER

Just as he was falling asleep, standing upright in the garden with his
    back against a tree,
(within himself he could already hear the distant roar of the
    sunlight)
at the moment he was about to touch serenity with one of his
    fingers,
they drenched him through and through with a long rubber hose.
    He felt
he should smile or become angry. But he couldn't. He closed his eyes
    again.

They picked him up by his armpits and his feet. They flung him into
    the well. And he
heard the thump on the water below, and from above cast down a
    stone.

Athens, October 4, 1972   *(K.F. & K.M.)*

UNCERTAIN OBLIGATIONS

This morning reluctance — you gaze on the street below;
people are in a hurry, they can't see five feet before them —
half in the air, half inside themselves or inside the wall;
wall bumps against wall — not a sound emerges.
A dust rag caught in a tree. I lost — he says —
all five of my keys. The other man looks at the cyclist.
The third enters the shoe shine parlor. The fourth will fall
before the cheap furniture store. The fifth
wrapped himself in three newspapers. You must gather them up;
you must take care of the coffins; you must find
their real name — one name — otherwise what will remain
from your large sign, ambitious architect —
white, with red letters, hanging high up
on the seventh floor of the new glass apartment building?
And what will remain of you who, with an ancient pair of scissors, cut
    off
your five fingers that all may believe in the indivisible, and that you
    may believe?

Kálamos, October 8, 1972   *(K.F. & K.M.)*

AT THE HARBOR'S EDGE

The deaf-mute was waving his hands—he didn't hide his fear—
and pointing somewhere high up in the night. No one paid him any
     attention. But he,
only he, had heard the croak of the wild bird
above the coal bins. When they carried the five coffins
out of the ship, the deaf-mute put his hands down, fished out
a piece of string from his pocket, and tied the bird by one of its feet.

(With such obscurities—he says—I seek to escape the dark.)

Athens, October 9, 1972   *(K.F. & K.M.)*

MIDNIGHT STROLL

In the end, afraid of the poems and the many cigarettes,
he went out at midnight to the suburb—a simple, quiet
walk along closed fruit stores, among
good things with their true, vague dimensions.
Having caught a cold from the moon, he wiped his nose
now and then with a paper napkin. He lingered
there before the pungent odor of fresh brick,
before the invisible horse tied to a cypress tree,
before the granary's padlock. Ah, like this—he said—
among things that demand nothing of you—
and a small balcony shifting in the air
with a solitary chair. On the chair
the dead woman's guitar has been left upside down;
on the guitar's back moisture sparkles secretly—
it is sparks such as these that prevent the world from dying.

Athens, October 12, 1972   *(K.F. & K.M.)*

LITURGICAL

He placed the paper box on the table quietly
as though it were a closed, uninhabited monastery. For a while
he was gone in the other room. We could hear the faucet running —
perhaps he was washing his hands with soap. On returning,
he opened the box with great care and placed
his left hand within it. Then with his right hand
he grasped his left by the wrist, took it out,
raised it up high, and showed it to us.

Athens, October 13, 1972   *(K.F. & K.M.)*

EYEWITNESS

I saw them — he said — the two burglars behind the grilles
forcing the door open opposite —. I didn't shout at all;
there was a moon, and I could see their passkeys clearly,
even the plaster ornaments on the wall. I waited
for the others next door to shout first. No one cried out.
I left the window, sat on a chair, leaned
my forehead on the marble table, and believe
I fell asleep close by the poor ink-stained hand
of the child who did not pass in school. In my sleep
I caught a headache from the moon. At daybreak
they knocked on my door. It was the two burglars
holding two beautiful bouquets of flowers. I went into the kitchen
to put the flowers in some water. When I returned
with a vase in each hand, they had gone.

Athens, October 13, 1972   *(K.F. & K.M.)*

TRANSPOSITION

With that same imprecise smile in his eyes
he approaches, eager to show us from the window
the trees, the well, the flower-beds, the statues in the garden,
and even the five wet benches. And yet, the moment
the younger gardener appeared before the chrysanthemums,
bare-chested, with a sack of seed, he then
immediately closed the curtains and showed us a large
rusted nail on the wall from which the picture no longer hung,
with its two naked women, the guard, and the gallows.

Kálamos, Athens, October 14, 1972   *(K.F. & K.M.)*

REAL HANDS

He who disappeared inexplicably one afternoon (perhaps
they came and took him) had left on the kitchen table
his woolen mittens like two severed hands,
bloodless, uncomplaining, serene, or rather
exactly like his own hands, a bit swollen, filled
with the tepid air of a very ancient endurance. There,
between the slack woolen fingers,
we would place from time to time a slice of bread, a flower,
or our own wineglass, in the calm knowledge
that gloves, at least, can't be handcuffed.

Kálamos, October 15, 1972   *(K.F. & K.M.)*

337

STAGES OF IGNORANCE

What he dreamt of as a support had day by day removed
all his supports. Behind the windowpanes he watched
to distinguish all he had abandoned — the garden chair,
the old sooty chimney-stack he had once
called a headless statue, and they had both agreed
with that simple agreement between two saddened strangers
who had no mutual pretensions or rivalries. A little later,
    nevertheless,
as he was climbing the stairs, disguised as a blind man,
the real blind man, hidden in a niche within the wall,
suddenly snatched away his dark glasses, and he was then
compelled to close his eyes (perhaps forever)
lest he betray or refute his previous life,
even though he didn't at all know what his life was, or even life in
    general.

Athens, October 17, 1972   (K.F. & K.M.)

THE MEANING OF ART

To Hubert Juin

For hours he gazed at the statue's severed hand — only one hand
stopped in a quiet gesture toward the reconstruction
of its entire body. Perhaps in this way he had learned
the deep secret not even he must reveal. And besides,
who would be able to reveal it, and how? Poetry — he said —
always begins before the words or after the words. It was then
we saw the bird as it emerged out of the severed hand and sat on a
    loaf of bread.

Athens, October 18, 1972   (K.F. & K.M.)

338

THE UNDRESSING OF THE HANGED MAN

I saw him — he said — with my own eyes; he was hanging one meter
    high
entirely from his smile, as though from a hook
held in his teeth. His eyelids were not blinking. I approached,
loosened his belt, took off his trousers, his shorts, and looked at
    him.
He half-closed one of his eyes, nodding. (Oh, this is what he had
    been waiting for,
with how much despairing civility, how much cunning. He had
    never dared
assume the responsibility himself.) In the pockets
of his coat and trousers I found nothing, only
five broken toothpicks. I left him, and went away. In the evening,
when I passed by again out of curiosity, he was not there.

Athens, October 19, 1972   *(K.F. & K.M.)*

AFTER A SETTLEMENT OF DEBTS

He had nothing to say. He fed the mutes, wrote on his empty
    cigarette box
what he wanted ordered, and left it on the table
for the five deaf-mutes in the other room. He leaned the wooden leg
upright in a corner of the bathroom, then went out to the field next
    door,
to the dog house, and changed the water there — but he didn't pat
    the dog. In the evening,
he returned earlier than usual. Traffic cops were leaving the streets
with a sense of a dampness forever unknown on their white bands
and their white gloves. What possible punishment is he preparing

in his compassion, what retaliation? When the moon came out,
the small bench in the town square shone with moisture, utterly
     alone,
as though God were going to sit there and take off His shoes.

Athens, October 20 1972   *(K.F. & K.M.)*

THE OTHER MAN

We had a guitar, a knife, three unmatched chairs,
and were peeling boiled potatoes on a newspaper.
The woman with a candle was descending the stairs. From above
the lame man was striking the floor with his crutches. The other man,
     alone,
sat in a corner apart. He wasn't eating. He was looking at his nails,
trying to achieve an enlargement, a positive disfigurement,
a resemblance at least, to break away from our words, to penetrate
into rhythm or into the surface of rhythm, undulating
like the cut and squeezed lemon floating on the river
together with the half moon, beside the wooden likeness of the
     drowned man,
while on the riverbanks men were gesticulating, shouting,
     running —
men who were amassing great debts to pay off smaller debts
and spending both these and those without paying off any.

Athens, October 23, 1972   *(K.F. & K.M.)*

340

COMMON MIRACLES

They took out the candelabra into the open air under the trees
and scrubbed the church. From the large door
a dark humidity spread out over the steps
and over the white sunwashed tiles. The beadle
kicked a limping dog that had drawn near
to drink water from the bucket. Then, from the beautiful altar door,
the Archangel with his large red wings came out,
stooped to the dog, and gave it to drink out of his cupped hands.
And so the next day the five paralytics walked.

Athens, October 23, 1972   (K.F. & K.M.)

LIKE A PRAYER

Permit them one more day with their small words,
their small peripatetic deaths, in the month of November
under the few gold-glimmering trees. The old ship
moors behind the rocks in the secret bay,
discharging its silent sick, its somber gendarmes,
to be locked up in the leper house. Dear God, how alone they are,
what strangers to one another — so alike, grasping one another by the
    shoulders
and dancing to that sluggish and forgotten song:
my black cypress tree, black clouds, my black bread and salt.

Athens, October 25, 1972   (K.F. & K.M.)

HUES OF A CLOUD

Alone that afternoon also. O red cloud — he said —
you who dyed my hands red, I've not learned who's to blame;
perhaps no one, perhaps only I. It was I who saw
the mute's small boy vanishing in the dust of the street,
himself a mute — the one who used to sell small paper flags
of each soccer team, raising one finger
to point out the price of one drachma, and perhaps pointing out
something much higher which I could not see. Then two on
    motorcycles
approached him, placed him in the middle, tied his hands together,
threw away his little flags, which the air scattered till I grabbed one
without paying for it. It was then I understood
the price he was pointing out with his raised finger. O cloud,
red cloud who dyed my hands red, you
who turned toward the violet sunset with two golden wings.

Athens, October 25, 1972   (K.F. & K.M.)

EXTINCTION

A tranquil sea behind the windowpanes. A poem expected.
White bare branches of the fig tree with long fibers
of an unraveled nautical sweater. Two passed by.
One with his eye bandaged. The other hesitating
with the fear of repetition. Should he leave? Should he remain?
A forgotten smell together with a yellow dust
drifts out the door of the sawmill. And the words — he said —
our slightest ones, without weight now, like down
falling on a mute river after a hunter's gunblast.

Kálamos, October 28, 1972   (K.F. & K.M.)

GRADUALLY STRIPPED BARE

A plow thrust into the earth. A large smoke-blackened pot
thrown overturned on the dry grass. A dog barks. Hens
scatter behind the wire netting. In the dark waters of the cistern,
a child's red plastic automobile floats. And the swan? — he asked.
What swan? — said the other. I didn't see any. The swan — he
     said — the swan.
O Lord, you cannot deceive me — not me, at least. I've
deceived so many dead — I've brought them back. Under the stones
I found a table spread, and in its middle, on a large plate,
the swan naked, Lord. With its delicate down I've stuffed
my two pillows. And here are its six largest feathers,
arrogant in the wind, passed through the hat of the mad woman.

Kálamos, October 29, 1972   (K.F. & K.M.)

BLOODLETTING

His behavior was all one gesture to drive away the big fly
that doggedly kept returning to the same spot, to his temple,
to his cheek, to his nose. At last he stood still. The fly
also stood still on his cheek, where it sucked his blood and grew
     larger.
In his place only the fly remained, it too wrapped around
by the spider's cobweb, where droplets of moisture glittered.

Athens, November 1, 1972   (K.F. & K.M.)

IMITATION OF AN IMITATION

He spoke with a studied indifference, gazing at his fingernails. Night
    after night — he said —
we are transferred from the loneliness of one person to that other
    loneliness
of the many — and the choice is not ours. I hold
the soldier's empty canteen, the animal tamer's whip, Cassandra's
black stocking full of holes, Agamemnon's false beard;
I throw the overcoat over my head, I darken, breathe
very quietly so that my pockets won't hear me; in a little while
I half open a crack in the two folds of my overcoat, catch sight
of one of my eyes in the mirror, begin a secret friendship with it,
grow heated, cast off my clothing, and remain stark naked
beside my naked statue. Suddenly three women come in
with their vegetables in three nylon net bags. I now
have nothing more to do than to remain clumsily motionless,
playing the part as well as I can of my statue's statue.

Athens, November 1, 1972   *(K.F. & K.M.)*

INDICATIONS

The light is refracted at regular intervals on the wall
like the carotid artery of the sick woman. Nevertheless, the vague
warm sensation of some object floats in the air,
very firm, very green, almost square, hidden
under the army camp bed with the shoes of the adulterer.
Perhaps this is why we look so intensely in a lit shop window
completely yellow with two black lions. Perhaps this is why
the mouths of the masks always gape open,
that the other within them may speak with greater candor.

Athens, November 4, 1972   *(K.F. & K.M.)*

WITNESSES EVERYWHERE

The statue has no preferences, not even any objections.
It doesn't judge your gesture. Completely naked, unconcerned
in its arrogant submission. You cannot
penetrate into the stone. You remain
outside the statue. You take off the rope from your neck
and pass it carefully around its neck. A little further off,
between the statues or amid the statues, someone
is watching you, the museum guard, perhaps
the carpenter's son, or your death. You're not in time.
Your sperm spurts on the white, glistening tiles.

Athens, November 11, 1972   *(K.F. & K.M.)*

THE EARTH'S ATTRACTION

A moon glued to the windowpane like a canceled postage stamp
on a letter undelivered. The closed furniture shop filled
with tables, armchairs, mirrors. A lone dog frightened by its own
    shadow
barks alone amid the avenue lights. No matter
how high you may sling objects, they will not remain in the air,
they will not sprout wings; they will fall with a thud on the earth
in almost the same place, like the coins of chance,
revealing exactly that side you did not want to appear.

Athens, November 13, 1972   *(K.F. & K.M.)*

THERE

Shouts, lottery vendors, florists, cardplayers, death.
Other shouts from the house, from the curtains, from the furniture,
from the forefather's forgotten portraits. The woman stooped
and with her right hand held her dress to her knees
as though fearing the noise might sweep it away. Her hair
leans to one side, blown there by remembrance. And suddenly,
around her neck, she feels her necklace, almost weightless,
in an intangible position of studied silence — there
where poetry always waits to be discovered.

Athens, November 17, 1972   *(K.F. & K.M.)*

EXONERATED

The whole length of the seashore was strewn with dried fish.
The approaching ship was painted red with a white stripe.
Under the overturned boat drawn up on shore, still
sleeping in the sunlight, were two burglars
together with a pederast, a mute, a necrophile. How strange — he
      said —
to realize suddenly that no one is to blame.

Athens, November 17, 1972   *(K.F. & K.M.)*

THE STATUE IN THE CAFE

No one knows how this naked statue came to be found on the
      mezzanine floor
of the popular café — probably from the auctioned wretched remains

of some unknown sculptor; thus naked, covered with dust, somewhat classical in style,
yet beautiful for all that, with the air of an adolescent's simple shyness,
as though it wanted to urinate and then withdraw into that corner where old men,
failed actors with dyed hair and painted eyes, spent their days and nights
waiting for a call forever. All have given to their friends and acquaintances
(even though the failed and poor do not have friends) the same telephone number, that is to say,
the number of this café. No one has ever called them. Now
when the telephone rings, they no longer turn their heads. Slowly they sip their coffee,
sketching, on their cigarette boxes, swords, laurel wreaths, tragic masks,
and at times, meditatively, almost erotically, trying out on this plaster statue
the linen tunics of roles they've never played, forgetting time thus,
believing this statue depicts their true selves in their true age.

Kálamos, Athens, November 19–20, 1972   *(K.F. & K.M.)*

1972

Nights with guns firing and walls. Afterwards, quiet.
Scrubbed floors. The chair legs, straight.
Behind the door, a second door and a third; between them
insulating cotton of the kind used to stuff the mouths
of the hungry or the dead. The heroes—he said—
have grown white, dear God, they've grown fat and small.

Athens, November 25, 1972   *(K.F. & K.M.)*

THE EYES OF THE STATUE

That which you make you become — he used to say. And the
    unalterable — said the other.
Oh, you justify the indolent, the thoroughly dead — he said —
and went out the door. We did not see him again. Perhaps they
    killed him. He was
a man of medium height, and suddenly how did he become
a towering statue erected in our own house
above the staircase, in the mirror? It gazes at us
with its large white eyes. It doesn't permit us for a moment
to sleep or to powder our faces secretly
with that dazzling golddust. What enormous eyes,
white, pure white, blind (we call them blind); we turn
our backs, facing the wall, sucking like babies
the thumb of its right hand wrapped in cotton.

Athens, January 1, 1973   *(K.F. & K.M.)*

ج

from

PAPER POEMS I

Put the flower pots
all around the well
in lovely order
like poems
around nothing.
No matter that
they're empty—
this is our first courtesy
and the last.

*

He whitewashed the house
the sidewalk the tree.
He whitewashed her face
in the mirror.
The dead enter
through the back of it
and scratch at the whitewash.

*

White on white
sheep on snow
you can't pick them out.
The same with our choicest
        words
on paper.

*

You can't count
beyond your fingers.
Count your fingers.
Something's wrong.
Ten are missing.

*

Glory
is the second child
of loneliness.

*

Better this way.
Always: better this way.
Keep us from worse, Lord.
Give me some breathing space
between two coffees
and three wars.

(N.C.G.)

*

The wall is yellow
the nails are black.
You remove the nails.
The holes are red.

(G.M. & N.T.)

*

Words have another shell
further inside
like almonds
and patience.

October–November, 1970   *(N.C.G)*

*

from
PAPER POEMS II

The word had me
found me
spoke me.
And I
just "Thanks."
A word
to a word.
The world.

(N.C.G.)

*

Look at it from this side.
The second cloud.
In one of its corners
seven little crosses.
One for each of your knees
for each of your palms
for your breasts.
The seventh
on my forehead.

(G.M. & N.T.)

Nothing particular
except that feeling
in sleep:
apart from sleep
on the old top stair
a bottle of ice-cold milk
the milkman passing
quite unheard.
On those stairs — remember? —
the three of us used to dash up
years ago
into the future.

You who seek the truth
seek the wall.
The stone, the other stone, the other.
Lean your back or your forehead
against the wall
upright in the night
with the small coins in your pocket
noiseless
gold or silver
unrefunded.
And dreams.

Body
thin as a matchstick
white
from one end of the horizon
to the other.
A slain bird
on one shoe.
In the navel

a one-eyed Christ
weeping.

                    ⸭

The hammering of the nails
on the back side of the mirror
leaving cracks
in the saint's yellow mask.
From these cracks
his real tears exude
the vapor of sweat
the blood
the uncomitted crime.

                    *

This severed
marble hand
(from your statue?)—
you still hold in your arms
like a dead baby—
it weighs you down
this severed hand
which pointed with its outstretched
        forefinger
up, up, ever higher
perhaps to the kite
to the cloud
or to you.

                    *

Wicked old women with candles
        and sheets
in huge uninhabited rooms
the framed portraits of ancestors in
        the corridor
their glass cracked
tangled strings hung on nails

from one wall to another.
The guard
tossed his pants onto the table
his shoes on the moon.
The mice went up the stairs.

*

Ah cock, cock of treachery
my brother, my distorter, my witness
one of your feathers, the gold one,
       in my hat
the other in my pocket, the black
       one.

*

Now you're caressing
that knife planted
in your breast by an opposing hand
slicing up
the rest of your fingers.
Is this why your face is shining?
Afterwards
you stomped vigorously on the floor,
the wild geese flew up from the
       window
one of which
got entangled in the curtain
and lay on the carpet
like a dead bride.

January–June, 1973   *(G.M. & N.T.)*

*

from

PAPER POEMS III

How to prove
the necessary
the grand
under the whips
under the jeers
of the uniformed guards
you naked
with your genitals
totally vanished
into fear
and over there the kite
stuck in the tree
its six ripped wings
beating in the twilight.

*

I saw the water flow
and stop in the cistern
and the leaf halt in the water
and an insect on the leaf
one of its wings azure
and the other gold—
The miracle is in my fingernails
I threw a stone into the river
I shouted: I'm me
I shouted: I'm you
I shouted: I'm the world—
the miracle is the world—
I keep the curled hair from your
　　armpit
tucked away in a matchbox.

*

That same night
a little while after the fire

355

the enormous hollow
wooden horse
without the hoplites in its guts
opened its toothless
jaws
and spoke:
Was it the Trojans you deceived
or conceivably yourselves?
The blood flowed right down to
    the shore.

June 1973–May 1974   *(G.M.& N.T.)*

SLUGGISHLY

We measured the place, flung the dead in lime,
then climbed into the rowboats under the waning moon;
the fourth man held the iron box on his knees
wholly withdrawn in himself as if being warmed
by some secret private fire of his own. The smoke
stood low over the water; it would not rise.

(K.M.)

DESCENT

"Eurydice," he called. Hurriedly he descended the stairs.
The caretaker's desk was unlit. He searched the mirror with his
    hands.
In the distance the woman holding the yellow parasol was leaving.
The second woman in the cellar called out to him: "She's dead."
The three aviators came out of the elevator with a large suitcase —
in it were her two severed hands and my manuscripts.

(K.M.)

SMALL DIALOGUE

The sky burned desolately behind the houses.
Why are you crying? — he asked, buckling his belt.
The world is beautiful — she replied —
so beautiful and such a headache; and the bed
is a silent, savage beast preparing to flee.

(K.M.)

ALMOST COMPLETE

You know, death does not exist — he told her.
I know it, yes, now that I am dead — she replied.
Your two shirts are pressed and folded in the drawer;
I'm missing only one small rose.

(K.M.)

EXHIBITS

The woman was still lying in bed. He
took out his glass eye, set it on the table,
took one step, stopped. Do you believe me now? — he asked her.
She picked up the glass eye, raised it to her eye and looked at him.

(K.M.)

THANKSGIVING

You heard your voice saying: *thanks*
(such a sudden, mute naturalness)—you were certain now:
a large piece of eternity belongs to you.

(K.M.)

STRIDING OVER

The drunk ones lay down; they fell asleep immediately. He
looked over the accounts, turned off the light, went out into the
    garden.
He felt under his shoe the round softness of a bud.
O distant, you who are forgotten, unfenced; O divination,
a drop from a secret moon-fountain on a single leaf. And suddenly
all seven windows lit up behind the trees. The drunk ones,
standing on their beds, were showing each other their erections.

(E.K.)

THE MORE SUFFICIENT

You can accomplish it rather easily—it's enough
not to want to persuade or deceive. Alone and alone
the birds, the children, the music, the couch, the curtains.
The sick woman is ironing. A last fly
almost ready to die wanders along the warm sheet.
And there are secret sequences with mild deaths
beyond our common death, beyond its statues
polite and laudatory within that fleeting miracle,
within the light of this mirror that knows how to copy
(however false and fragmentary) the glory of two naked bodies.

(E.K.)

359

THE STATUES IN THE CEMETERIES

The statues naked under the trees in the cemeteries
besieged by the passionate voices of the night birds
when the last of the procession retires. The statues
faithfully imitate death, sensual love, calm,
with a small iron lamp in hand, with a marble lily,
with stone swords, with stone wings, stone flags,
from far to near to elsewhere; windows lit; beds,
night dance in the garden. Leave, leave, Petros yelled;
the custodian has my keys on his belt; his dog
is following me — it's my rejection of him. The statues
don't copy us; they are alone too; they suffer; they contradict
    nonexistence,
they get excited, blush; their central vein swells with blood.
That's why the birds cry out so: to cover the defeat of serene death.

(E.K.)

THE DISTANT

O distant, distant; deep unapproachable; receive always
the silent ones in their absence, in the absence of the others
when the danger from the near ones, from the near itself, burdens
during nights of promise with many-colored lights in the gardens,
when the half-closed eyes of lions and tigers scintillate
with flashing green omissions in their cages
and the old jester in front of the dark mirror
washes off his painted tears so that he can weep —
O quiet ungrantable, you with the long, damp hand,
quiet invisible, without borrowing and lending, without obligations,
nailing nails on the air, shoring up the world
in that deep inaction where music reigns.

January–February, 1975   (E.K.)

MONOVASIA
(1974–1976)

Translated by Kimon Friar and Kostas Myrsiades

I. MONOVASIA

Rock. Nothing else. The wild fig tree and the ironstone.
An armed sea. No room at all for genuflection. Outside the
  Elkoménos Church gate
a crimson crimson in the black. The old women with their cauldrons
bleaching the longest woven cloth in history suspended on rings
from the forty-four Byzantine arcades. The sun
a merciless friend with his lance on the walls opposite
and death disinherited within this vast illumination
where the dead interrupt their sleep now and then
with cannon fire and rusty lampposts, going up and down
on step after step carved in the rock. They strike their tinder boxes
against the edge of their palms until the sparks fly. I — he said —
will climb higher, above the soft continuation, stepping
on the dome of the large submarine church with its lit candelabra. I
with the blue bone, the red wing and the pure white teeth.

Monovasiá, September 28, 1974   *(K.F. & K.M.)*

IV. THE DEAD

We found them again under the rock, in the rock. Silent
but not angry because we had forgotten them; no, not at all, but not
  at all
angry, because they too had forgotten us. Their silence now
is their voice — they have nothing to proclaim;
a mute understanding with the prickly pears in the ruins,
mute encounters beside the sea or in the moon —
there is no need for them to hide now or to disclose their papers

in the infinite transparency of nowhere or of nothing, here
where the trees can be seen naked, the mountains, the undisputed
    boundaries
of all separations and of all centuries, here where the frontiers of the
    ages,
together with the birds, the persistent pomegranate trees, and the
    stones
are abolished in the clarity of the pellucid forever.

Monovasiá, July 12, 1975   *(K.F. & K.M.)*

VII. REMEMBRANCES

Your boyhood years waited for you in forgotten corners,
in demolished buildings, in Byzantine arcades —
the barber shop had been there, and there the shoemaker's; over
    there
must have been the fish market — the low stone wall seems familiar.
    The woman
with the very long hair — the mailman had abducted her;
afterwards she died. It was raining. The four children
had locked themselves in the other room. They held
the old sea-blue chest. We didn't have much time —
events one on top of the other, wars and wars, expatriations, books,
half-completed recollections, loves, the closed well;
the parish priest missed a few names — who remembers them? Later
the same child, during leap years, lugging water in a basket,
and the ordeal of the great desolation on the shattered watchtowers.

Xifiás, July 14, 1975   *(K.F. & K.M.)*

IX. DECEPTIVE DISCOVERIES

What more can we say? What can we do? We found the old again
reconstructed the ruins, put a roof over our heads. On every eve
    before death
we discovered our origins. Conscientious men,
we fought the good fight, won our just laurels. Now,
day by day, night by night, the color of stone
changes from ash to brown. And rust at its work
on the iron fortress door, on the locks, on the words
and in the depths of silence. He who greeted us was a stranger.
Later they turned on the lights. In Matoúla's old restaurant
the smell of fish soup once more glorified the narrow flagstone
    place.
The most common history is dazzling in the eternity of its
    repetition.

Monovasiá, July 14, 1975   (K.F. & K.M.)

XII. GEOGRAPHIC ORIGINS

Precipitous rock—all day long drinking the scorching sun,
holding it in its entrails as it faces the sea,
and you with your back leaning against the rock, with your breast
bared to the sea—half fire, half coolness,
cut vertically, double, in a struggle only
to unite water with stone. Already on your hair
the fern has sprouted, burned by the sun. A bird
stood there—it said something ambiguous. On your nipples
the large cool hand of the sea. Ah, the voluptuousness
of two and of one, insufficient self-sufficiency. Among the nettles
I found my childhood's sling and the Argonaut's oar.

And then the night, the largest night, sanctified by stars.

Karlóvasi, July 27, 1975   (K.F. & K.M.)

XIII. INSIDE THE RUST

It was the privation, the thorns, the stones, the well,
the water salty—nor could thirst be quenched. The brine
indicating the depths of thirst, indicating, measuring
the immeasurability of the sea—windows, balconies,
handkerchiefs of departure for the large encounters
of the other time, a little beyond death, much beyond. On the
    square
the ancient cannon eaten away by time and salt;
the same for the bolts and keys of the temples. Rust
has its great share. From this place the handsome boy
with the cage and the lantern had leapt out with one
dogtooth protruding in an expression of perplexity,
or probably even of sarcasm. His gaze always fixed
(even when looking elsewhere) on the winged lion carved
on the rim of the reservoir and on the gate. This boy
who is preparing to make the great Resurrection come true.

Karlóvasi, July 27, 1975   *(K.F. & K.M.)*

XVI. COINS

He stopped at the bend of the cobbled road under the extinguished
    lamplight
and counted the gold, the silver, the copper coins; at the end
he counted those made of bone (they gleamed white in the night).
"With these," he thought, "you can buy
most things, the most profound." Below on the bastioned town
    square
the first cannon shot thundered. You waited for the second, the
    third.
Nothing. Nothing. Only the large brilliantly lit ship
could be seen sinking on its side in the dark moon.

Karlóvasi, August 18, 1975   *(K.F. & K.M.)*

364

XX. ITEMS OF IDENTIFICATION

The date of my birth is probably 903 B.C. — but also quite probably
903 A.D. I studied the history of the past and the future at the
   contemporary School of Struggle. My profession:
words piled on words — what could I do? Ragpicker they called me.
   And it was true.
I collected a whole heap of ostrich feathers from the hats of the
   subterrestrial Maiden,
buttons from military duffel coats, one helmet and two worn-out
   sandals;
further, I collected two matchboxes and the tobacco pouch
of the Great Blind Man. At the Registry these last years they gave me
the most improbable date of my birth: 1909.
I adjusted to this and stayed put. Finally
in 3909 I sat on my stool to smoke a cigarette. Then
the flatterers arrived; they bowed down before me and on my fingers
placed glittering rings. But these ignoramuses did not know
I had myself made them from their empty cartridges left on the hills.
Because of this exactly, because of their lovely ignorance, I rewarded
   them richly
with genuine precious stones and double doses of flattery. At any
   rate,
the only certain item is the place of my birth: Ákra Minóa.

Karlóvasi, August 18, 1975   (K.F. & K.M.)

XXI. TIME

Tanneries, wine factories, cotton mills — what celebrated silks,
what leather and what aromatic wines in great demand both in the
   East and the West. This region
betrays nothing of its ancient magnificence. Rusty lampposts,
houses riddled with thousands of holes, time-eaten balustrades,
   fallen balconies,
a carved window frame, a large wardrobe in a demolished cellar,
limestone anthemions, scratched icon paintings, arches —

the nobility of Byzantine architecture thoughtfully supplemented
with prickly pears and tall yellow thorns. How many wars,
sieges, pillages, slaughtered priests, stolen icons,
boiling oil, catapults, cannons. In the end
they surrendered the keys and received in return crimson cloth
    trimmed with gold
and beautiful battle steeds—one white, two red, two black. Now
only a few fishermen remain and, of course, the dead. In the
    evenings
we see them leaning over the moon's lintel shaking
a velvety worn-out mantle. One morning
we found their violet glass buttons amid the withered daisies,
and now and then a red sandal beside two bones and a truck's inner
    tube.

Karlóvasi, August 28, 1975   *(K.F. & K.M.)*

XXVIII. WHITE

I was looking at the prickly pears. The beautiful aged woman
was peeling stones with her nails. I am gathering dandelion
    greens—she said;
I boil fish in very little water. To tell the truth,
I shall die just as spring starts. I prefer to be outside
of this we call marble or showcase or well.
On top of the trunk sits the cat. Inside the trunk
the old alarm clock will be found wrapped in my bridal gown.
Call it complicity—I too saw the seagull's egg. I know white.
I can shout it. I do not shout it. I shut my door early,
I can't shut my eyes. The luster of the huge open sea
disembowels the night like a fish and leaves me to the mercy of the
    mendacious stars.

Karlóvasi, September 5, 1975   *(K.F. & K.M.)*

XXXV. FINISHING TOUCH

They are tranquil now. They can sit on the pier to smoke,
to remember, to forget, to sleep, or even not to exist. We gave them
the silent word, the noiseless stride which, for all that, goes further.
    Now
neither the void nor the stone has any weight. The hand
that lights the match, and then the large candle, is full of air,
placid air like that in the middle distance between the smallest stars;
placid also is the hand like the yellow glove fallen on the marble
    stair—
it may get up, wave, knock on the windowpane from the inside,
or remain there, stepped on by the feet of the night watchmen;
or, long past midnight, with equal devotion, it may write in a fine
    script
the word *here* or *there* the word *beginning*, or even the word *end*.

Monovasiá, October 18, 1976   *(K.F. & K.M.)*

XXXVI. LEAVING MONOVASIA

Very ancient olive trees, hollow twisted trunks;
the wretched color of ash; the smoked yellow;
shadows of clouds on the opposite hills.
The distant comes obediently, looks at you sideways;
you forget what you wanted to ask it; your hand
absentmindedly walks on the soft back of the animal.
Was it that? And what was it? Time reversed?
The old women wrap their feet in newspapers,
tie them with strings. Precautions, precautions—
O silent duration; we are sitting on the ground
with a basket of prickly pears, with one of the sprinter's shoes—
and this persistent woman, all skin and bone, savage,
under the tree in the obdurate brightness
holding in both her hands the inconsolable infant.

It was precisely then we learned that nothing had been lost.

Athens, October 19, 1976   *(K.F. & K.M.)*

* * *

NOTES

I. MONOVASIÁ.   Monovasiá, as it is called by the demoticists, and Monemvasia by the purists, is a town and island promontory on the Argolic Bay some four hundred meters from land on the southeastern Peloponnesos, in the prefecture of Laconia. The promontory was called Ákra Minóa in ancient times, which indicates that it may have been a Minoan port of call. Elkoménos Church: "Christ Dragged," the largest church in Laconia, and the seat of the metropolitan of Monovasiá.

VII. REMEMBRANCE.   Xifiás: A region outside of Monovasiá on the coast, good for swimming and fishing.

XII. GEOGRAPHIC ORIGINS.   Karlóvasi: A town on the island of Samos where Ritsos spends every July and August with his wife and daughter.

XX. ITEMS OF IDENTIFICATION.   Subterranean maiden: Persephone, who lived for half of every year with Pluto, god of the underworld. Great Blind Man: Homer. Ákra Minóa: See I. Monovasiá.

ﻼ

from

SO?

(1976)

Translated by Kostas Myrsiades

6. Somewhere
   there should be an elephant
   hidden in the night
   its wound
   was on the moon.

12. He
    sits on the bridge
    smoking
    below
    the river passes by—
    he too will hunger.

    Athens, June 10, 1976

15. He changes shirts
    he changes clothes
    he does not change his body
    in the yard he dug a grave
    and buried his hat
    how handsome he is
    the wind rumpled his hair.

21. A tangled ball of yarn
    which he unwinds and winds
    but he does not undo the knots
    he hangs
    dead children's
    small baptismal crosses.

    Athens, June 11, 1976

25. Red sunset
    I hammered a nail in the wall
    I hung up the towel
    it fell
    a colorless descent
    the naked body collapsed
    on the red carpet.

32. In the morning
    he wakes up dead
    at night
    he lights two candles
    ties his two hands
    and proceeds to the corridor
    before the guard.

    Kálamos, June 13, 1976

40. He cracked almonds
    ate them
    undressed
    the shells on the floor

the waterglass on the chair
the most handsome
unsuspecting man
in my mirror.

46. Illustrious tree
small mirrors in its branches
silver bells
echoed
above the sealed well—
attendant poetry
—whom did you ask for?

60. The dog barked
beside the river
in the garden
then it stopped
in its teeth it held
the maimed doll
which I had buried years before
behind the rosemary
both looked at me
through green eyes.

Athens, June 14, 1976   *(K.M.)*

THE WORLD IS ONE
(1978–1980)

Translated by Kostas Myrsiades

DOUBTFUL ENCOUNTERS

Those who met by chance in the street, strangers, did not speak;
they neither beckoned with their hands nor with their gaze. In this
they seemed in harmony with the moonlight finding its way through
    the grille
of a closed country house; in harmony with the rustle
of a dress shirt falling on the floor—Greeks perhaps. They had
a scar on their brow—an intimate mark—once red,
it has turned whitish; it illuminates their face. They did not speak.

Only on September evenings they look indifferently
at the gardens of the old people's home, the service stations, the
    kiosks,
a blue electric lamp under the trees, the customhouse clock
and little by little their hands lengthen, they become fish,
those which discovered the monstrous submersed voices and keep
    silent now.

Montello, September 16, 1978   *(K.M.)*

MORNING IN SALERNO, IV

In spite of a Sunday idleness, selling and buying continued
at the wooden barracks. Large motionless fish
shimmered in wide baskets. The salt dried sparkling
on their rosy, grey scales.
                  One of those

winked at me for a moment; its eye opened again; it stared at me
    gaping;
I rejoiced in the guile of the dead, especially in their apparent
    preference
for me—a private affinity perhaps,
perhaps they expected their resurrection from me.
                                  The customs' official
stood austerely at the door. I pretended not to notice him.

Hands are certainly rapacious animals—they speak with a greater
    sincerity than lips.

Salerno, September 17, 1978   *(K.M.)*

IMMOBILIZING THE BOUNDLESS

Nicóla—he would shout—drive a bit more slowly. I want to see
this face, this body, that rock,
this half-naked girl with water dripping from her breasts,
this pedlar with a basketful of silver lemons,
this blooming sonorous tree. Take your foot off the gas pedal. Stop.

Take my picture; not with this old tourist woman
made up like a harlequin with a spotted bikini; no, no;
rather with this statue—I'll lean on its shoulder lovingly,
handsomely, imposingly, a Greek, and behind my back
the whole incandescent sea—my azure mother,
boundless and limitless—the azure mother who embraces without
    holding.

Pozitano, September 17, 1978   *(K.M.)*

ENCOUNTERS

Handsome, sea-born lads on gravel roads
across the shimmering sea sell tourists
hazelnuts, pistachios, walnuts, lemons, and large braids
of red peppers.
         This red more than anything else complements
their underhandedness and their black hair. We wrapped the
    peppers
in two morning papers headlining in large letters
the five brutal homicides and the three unexplained suicides.

Sorento, September 17, 1978   *(K.M.)*

VATICAN MUSEUM

Da Vinci, Raphael, Michelangelo—they committed
the loftiest heavens to the human face, the human form,
toenails and fingernails, leaves and stars, nipples, dreams, lips—
red and blue; the tangible and the elusive. Perhaps,
when these two fingers touched, the world was reborn. The space
between these two fingers measures with exactness
the attraction of the earth and its permanence.

                                      I cannot endure—he said—
so much beauty and so much sinful holiness. I'll step out on the
    white balcony
to chain-smoke fifteen cigarettes, admiring the Roman view
from above, watching the big buses below
unload groups of tourists on the Museum portico,
snapping with my two fingers in my pant's pocket
bunches of stolen toothpicks as if cracking
all the wooden crosses on which were crucified human aspirations.

Rome, September, 18, 1978   *(K.M.)*

cʌ

from

EROTICA
(1980–1981)

Translated by Kimon Filar

CARNAL WORD

I

Erotic sleep, after the act of love. Sweaty bedsheets
hanging from the bed to the floor. In my sleep I hear
the strong river. In a lingering rhythm. The trunks of huge trees
roll with it. In their branches a thousand birds
sit motionless, voyaging with a prolonged song
of water and leaves, interrupted by stars. I pass
my hand underneath your neck lightly, fearful
of stopping the birds' song in your sleep. Tomorrow at ten,
when you open the window shutters, and the sun rushes into the
        rooms,
the bite on your lower lip will be seen more clearly in the mirror
and the house will turn a bright red, all spotted
with golden down and far-off unfinished verses.

II

You returned from the market, laughing, laden
with bread, fruit, and a mass of flowers. The wind, I see,
has passed its fingers through your hair. I tell you once more:
I do not love the wind. What do you want with so many flowers?
        Which of these
have been thrown in by the florist? And perhaps your image
has remained in his mirror, lighted sideways

with a blue stain on your chin. I do not love flowers. On your breast
lies a blossom as huge as an entire day. Well then, sit opposite me;
I want to look at the slope of your knees by myself, alone, as I smoke
until the night falls secretly and an underworld moon, magnetized,
    stands fixed above our beds,
a Saturday night moon with a violin, a clarinet, and a santoúri.

III

I am still sleeping. I hear you brushing your teeth in the bathroom.
    In this sound
are rivers, trees, a mountain with a small white chapel,
and a flock of sheep in the grass (I hear the bells), two red horses,
a flag on the tower terrace, a bird on the chimney;
a honeybee is buzzing in a rose — the rose trembles —
Ah, how long you are taking! and don't start combing your hair
    now,
for I am sleeping, I tell you, waiting for your mouth. I don't want
the odor of mint on your saliva. As soon as I awaken
I shall throw down the skylight all your combs, hairpins, and your
    toothbrushes.

IV

The poems I lived on your body in silence
will ask me one day for their voices, when you have gone.
But I will no longer have a voice to speak to them. Because you have
    always been in the habit
of walking barefoot through the rooms, then huddling in the bed,
a tangle of down, silk, and savage flame. You would cross your
    hands

around your knees, permitting the rosy dusty soles of your feet
to stretch out provocatively. Remember me—you would say—like
    this;
like this remember me, with my soiled feet, with my hair
falling over my eyes—because in this way I see you more deeply.
    Well then,
how can I possibly have a voice? Never has poetry walked like this
under the pure-white blossoming apple trees of any Paradise.

V

When you are not here, I don't know where I am. The house empties.
    The curtains
flutter outside the windows. Keys on the table. On the floor,
open suitcases from old journeys, with the curious costumes
of a theatrical troupe that was once triumphant and later dispersed;
one night the beautiful leading lady committed suicide on the stage.
    When you are not here,
soldiers run in the streets outside, women scream;
the heavy vehicles rumble; the sirens whistle;
ambulances go by and stop; nurses in white
gather up the wounded from the asphalt, gather me also,
take me to an immaculately white hospital without beds;
I shut my eyes like a child besieged by the dangerous white. A nurse
has remained in the garden by the fountain; she stoops and gathers
some white flowers the wind has shaken from the acacia trees. And
    there—the door opens,
and you enter with a basket—the ripe pears smell sweet.
Are you sleeping?—I hear your voice saying. Are you sleeping alone?
    Aren't you waiting for me?
I open my eyes. And here is the house. And here am I. And the two
    armchairs.
Red armchairs. And matches on the table.
O pure white light, O red blood, love, love.

VI

In the morning I am always more tired than you,
perhaps even happier. You get up noiselessly;
the bedsheets rustle a little; you go off on bare feet. I
still go on sleeping in the warmth your naked body
left on the bed. I sleep in the shape
of your body, sunk in a whitish darkness. I hear
you washing, making the coffee, waiting.
I hear you standing above me, undecided. Your smile
traverses my entire body, softens my fingernails. I sleep.
Pure white sails flash by motionlessly. A red blanket
hangs on the washline. The red weighs on my eyelashes.
Naked women in the river. Naked men in the trees.
Majestic horses (not sad) saunter in the sea's shallow waters. One of
     them has an erection,
his black penis barely touches the water. A girl is weeping.
With his jacknife a boy carves the number 99 on a mulberry tree,
then adds one more 9. I sleep more profoundly, more within.
A sparrow perches on the mane of a white lion. *Tir, tir*—it cries. The
     world
is fresh and light and thick sperm. Good morning love, good
     morning.

VII

You've taken all of me. Death will no longer have anything to take.
Within your body I breathe. I have sown a thousand boys in your
     sweating field;
a thousand horses gallop on the mountain, dragging behind them
     uprooted fir trees;
they descend to the outskirts of the town, lift their heads,
gaze with their black almond eyes at the Akropolis, the tall
     lamplights,
open and close their short eyelashes. The green and red traffic lights
     bring them

to a disagreeable perplexity. And this traffic policeman
moves his hands as though cutting an invisible fruit from the night
or grasping a star by its tail. They turn their backs
as though defeated in a battle never fought. Then suddenly
they shake their manes again and gallop toward the sea. On the
    whitest
of them all you are mounted, naked. I shout to you. Encircling
your breasts crosswise are two sprigs of ivy. A snail
lies motionless on your hair. I shout to you, love. Three gamblers, up
    all night,
go into the neighborhood milkshop. The day is breaking.
The lights of the city go out. The vast pale hue pours smoothly
over your skin. I am within you. I shout from inside you. I shout to
    you
here where the rivers converge tumultuously and the sky rolls
in the human body, lifting with it
mortal creatures and things—wild ducks, windows, buffaloes,
your summer sandals, one of your bracelets, a sea-urchin, two
    doves—
to the open grounds of an inexplicable and unsought-for
    immortality.

VIII

I don't want you ascending the marble stairs of hospitals. I don't
    want you standing
before the half-shut door of the operating room—torn flesh, blood—
it's not your 27-day period, although this too makes me withdraw,
    impedes me, enchants me. Blood is made
to flow invisibly in the veins, to be heard in the night,
heart to heart, like music on the floor below where another couple
is preparing to deepen their love with music. I don't want you
wandering in these corridors that smell
of iodoform, camphor and death. I don't want you to be
anyone's nurse, not even my own nurse. I don't want you taking care
    of
cripples, amputated statues and turtle-dove

whose right wing has been shattered by buckshot. I don't want your smile
falling on murdered naked bodies, even though they are my comrades. It becomes you
to remain motionless in your youth, or with a few movements
to govern the waves before the bed, or at most combing
my wet hair with lovely, joyful patterns of your own, or even
bringing the large tray with tea every morning as though you were bringing
a harp, without any intention of playing, since the harp
plays by itself as I raise my eyes toward you. Because, you know,
on the fiery jewel of the ring you gave me shines
a city lit up with green lanterns. On its avenues
small dancers are swirling with crimson paper lanterns and daisies,
and from the balcony a young man sprinkles their hair with my torn poems.
This is why I turn the ring's jewel around, to squeeze it
against my palm so that a stranger's envious or innocent eye
might not bewitch this inexhaustible happiness within time, outside time,
that on the next morning we might not find in the elevator the three deer killed.

IX

How beautiful you are. Your beauty terrifies me. I hunger for you. I thirst for you.
I implore you, hide yourself; become invisible to all, visible only to me, covered
from head to toe with a dark, diaphanous veil
spotted with the silver sighs of spring moons. Your pores emit
vowels, yearning consonants; secret words are uttered,
rosy explosions from the act of love. Your veil swells up, shines
above the benighted city with its half-lit bars, its sailors' hangouts;
green spotlights illuminate the night pharmacies, a glass globe
swirls swiftly showing the landscape of the earth's sphere. The drunken man staggers

in a storm blown from your body's breathing. Do not go. Do not go.
So palpable, so elusive. A stone bull
leaps from the pediment onto the dry grass. A naked woman ascends
      the wooden stairs
holding a basin of hot water. The steam hides her face. High in the
      air
a reconnoitering helicopter buzzes random spots. Take care.
It's you they seek. Hide yourself more deeply in my hands. The fur
of the red blanket that covers us is constantly growing until
the blanket becomes a pregnant bear. Underneath the red bear
we make love endlessly, beyond time and even beyond death,
in a solitary, universal union. How beautiful you are. Your beauty
      terrifies me.
And I hunger for you. And I thirst for you. And I implore you: hide
      yourself.

                          X

All the bodies I've touched, I've seen, I've taken, I've dreamed of,
      all,
are condensed into your body. O carnal Diotíma
in the great symposium of the Greeks. The flute players have gone,
the poets and philosophers have gone. The handsome young men are
      already sleeping
far away in the bedrooms of the moon. You are alone
in my lifted supplication. A white sandal
with long white thongs is tied to the chair leg. You are absolute
      oblivion,
you are absolute memory. You are uncracked fragility. Day is
      breaking.
Fleshy prickly pears sprout from the rocks. A rosy sun
lies motionless above the Sea of Monovasía. Our double shadow
is dissolved by the light on the marble floor with its many trodden
      cigarettes,
with its small posies of jasmine pinned on pine needles. O carnal
      Diotíma,

you who gave birth to me and to whom I have given birth, it's time for us
to give birth to acts and poems, to go out into the world. And in truth, don't forget
when you go to the market place, buy a heap of apples,
not the golden ones of the Hesperídes, but those large red ones, for when you bite
into their crusty flesh with your flashing teeth, your vital smile remains
fixed like an eternity above the books.

XI

I want to describe your body. Your body is limitless. Your body
is a delicate rose petal in a glass of clear water. Your body
is a wild forest with forty black woodcutters. Your body
is deep humid valleys before the sun rises. Your body
is two nights with bell towers, with shooting stars and derailed trains. Your body
is a half-lit bar with drunken sailors and tobacco merchants; they snap their fingers in dance,
break glass, spit, blaspheme. Your body
is an entire navy — submarines, battleships, gunboats; clanging
anchors are raised; water floods the decks; a ship's boy
jumps from a mast into the sea. Your body
is a polyphonic silence torn by five knives, three bayonets, one sword. Your body
is a translucent lake — in its depths can be seen the white sunken city. Your body
is a monstrous fierce octopus with bleeding tentacles in the glass bowl of the moon
above the illuminated avenues where in the afternoon
the funeral of the last emperor passed by with slow dignity. Many trodden flowers
drenched with gasoline remain on the asphalt. Your body
is an old bordello on Suburbia Street with old whores painted
with greasy cheap lipstick; they wear false eyelashes;

there is also an inexperienced young whore — she enjoys herself with
    all the clients,
leaves her money on the night-table, forgets to count it. Your body
is a rosy little girl; she sits under the apple tree eating
a slice of fresh bread and a red salted tomato; now and again
she thrusts an apple blossom between her breasts. Your body
is a cricket in the ear of the grape harvester — it casts a violet shadow
    on his sunburnt neck
and by itself sings all that grapes together cannot say. Your body
is a lookout, a large threshing floor on the summit of a hill —
eleven snow-white horses thresh through the sheaves of the
    Scriptures; the golden straws
pin small mirrors on your hair, and the three rivers glitter
where large black cows with adamantine crowns stoop,
drink water, and weep. Your body is limitless.
Your body is indescribable. And I want to describe it,
to hold it tightly against my body, to contain it and be contained.

XII

The day is mad. Mad is the house. Mad the bedsheets.
You also are mad; you dance with the white curtain in your arms;
you beat on a saucepan above my papers as on a tambourine;
the poems run through the rooms; the burnt milk smells;
a crystal horse looks out of the window. Wait — I say —
we've forgotten Phymonóis' tripod in the woodcutters' guild hall;
the oracles are turned upside down. We've forgotten yesterday's
    bleeding moon,
the newdug earth. A carriage passes by laden with oleanders.
Your fingernails are rose petals. Do not justify yourself. In your closet
    you have placed
tulle bags filled with lavender. The sun's umbrellas have gone mad,
they've become entangled with the wings of angels. You wave your
    handkerchief;
whom are you greeting? What people are you greeting? — The whole
    world.
A brown water-turtle has comfortably settled on your knees;

wet seaweed stirs on its sculptured shell. And you dance.
A hoop from a barrel of olden times rolls down the hill,
falls into the stream, tossing off drops that wet your feet,
and also wet your chin. Stop that I may wipe you.
But in your dancing, you do not hear me. Well then, duration
is a whirlwind, life is cyclical, it has no ending. Last night
the horsemen passed by. Naked girls on the horses' rumps;
perhaps this is why the wild geese were screaming in the bell tower.
    We did not hear them
as the horses' hoofs sank in our sleep. Today before your door
you found a silver horseshoe. You hung it above the lintel. My
    luck — you shout —
my luck — you shout, and dance. Beside you the tall mirror is also
    dancing,
glittering with a thousand bodies and the statue of Hippólytos
    crowned with poppies.
My parrot has gone — you say as you dance — and no one imitates my
    voice any more; aye, aye —
this voice from within me comes out of the forest of Dodóna.
Clear lakes rise in the air with all their white waterlilies,
with all their underwater vegetation. We cut reeds,
build a golden hut. You clamber up the roof.
I grasp you by the ankles with both hands. You don't come down.
You fly. You fly into the blue. You drag me with you
as I hold you by the ankles. From your shoulder
the large blue towel falls on the water; for a while it floats
and then with wide folds sinks, leaving on the surface
a trembling pentagram. Don't go higher — I shout — . No higher.
    And suddenly
with a mute thump we both land on the mythical bed. And listen —
in the street below strikers are passing by with placards and flags.
Do you hear? We're late. Take the handkerchief you dance with, too.
    Let's go. Thank you, my love.

Athens, February 15–18, 1981   (K.F.)

சு

3 × 111 TRISTYCHS
(1982)

Translated by Kostas Myrsiades

---

from

FIRST SERIES

3. A Sunday moon.
    Consumed
    in a blue glass.

5. Doors to the left and right. A woman appeared in the corridor,
    naked. She did not see the big clock. Her hair wrapped
    in a huge, fluffy, white towel.

6. In the fog, lemon trees hang their lanterns.
    Two horses—one white, the other red—before the door.
    The white one is for you. The red one will kill me.

9. Monday, Tuesday: thorns. Thursday: iron.
    Saturday: the glass's shadow on the table.
    Sunday: a small tattered flag.

10. You punched a hole in the paper;
    the wind entered
    and brought the poem.

12. The oranges fell to the ground.
    The old women gathered them.
    And I the sun.

17. The small moon
    sat on my knees
    combing my mustache.

26. Long summer nights.
    Lumberjacks make love
    to severed trees.

37. Parades, heroes, wreaths —
    mourning: to remind us once again
    how unremembered the dead can be.

64. A dark rainy night.
    An old man searches for the matches
    he holds in his hand.

80. Barefoot. Big feet.
    He might walk
    on the sea.

84. From a beautiful mouth
    even a great curse
    a hymn.

92. Kisses and poetry you endured;
    Death then has nothing
    to take from you.

1982   *(K.M.)*

from

SECOND SERIES

14. In the white egg,
    a yellow chick
    a blue song.

26. The new moon
    hides up its sleeve — you saw it? —
    a knife.

52. Naked, astride an elephant,
    the moon crosses the river.
    Dewdrops shimmering at its feet

61. Guatemala, Nicaragua, Salvador.
    Where did so many bodies go? On a tree, wind-swept,
    a pair of worn gray trousers.

63. Where is the time to light a cigarette,
    to look at a star, to speak with a turtle,
    to scratch your nose, and fart?

80. Seek not, want not, be not.
    I bite—he says—a bitter apple.
    Freedom.

104. They tagged you an illiterate, those idle bureaucrats.
    Unaware how on arid islands you memorized
    the twelve Gospels of the Struggle.

from

THIRD SERIES

101. Corpses below wooden crosses. At night
    we hear their crosses, worn as wings, flying
    above the castigated city.

    1982   (K.M.)

from

CORRESPONDENCES
(1985)

Translated by Kostas Myrsiades

THOSE YEARS

There was a great frost those years.
They wrapped themselves up in the nation's
    shabby mantle
and fixed their gaze. They vanished
among rocks and large thorn.
Behind them soared the wind ripping
acorns, flags, mountains of rock.
And we, here, still wait.

(K.M.)

HEARING

Amidst great clamor,
fissures of silence. We clearly hear
the silent depth. Time expands.
Old men with canes cross the bridge.
Two cyclists on the hill's horizon.
Large birds appear.

(K.M.)

IT EXISTS

You who always gaze horizontally should know
there exists yet a heaven below. From there
soar leaves with small spiders,
from there six winged fish,
little women with mottled parasols
and my nine sad children.

(K.M.)

AN ACROBAT

Night acrobats laid down in a dark carriage. In
    the morning
one arose barefoot lest the others awake,
carrying his worn out boots. He placed
both hands in his pockets and kept going,
smiling in his smuggled complacency. We
watched from behind the window panes;
will he come toward us? will he knock on the door?
will he enter the flower shop and buy gladioli?
or will he hide behind the two frozen sharks
delivered to the market by the enormous semi?

(K.M.)

THEY

These men look askance, always suspicious.
Their hands locked in their pockets.
They have much to say. They say nothing.
The sky extends within them.
That's why you often see them under the moon,
smiling alone before some closed door.

(K.M.)

BITTER KNOWLEDGE

An idle man. Sometimes he feels like crying
without knowing why, without cause. Perhaps he's aging,
perhaps it's music from somewhere. He knows it:
house repairs are not improved by phony contrivances;
rain falls; his knees get wet;
his books, his papers get drenched. At the train station
a blind violinist stands in the rain
and when he draws his wet bow
instead of notes he gets raindrops.

March 16–September 27, 1985   (K.M.)

from

SLOWLY, VERY SLOWLY IN THE NIGHT
(1988)

Translated by Kostas Myrsiades

INERTIA

In the bedroom, the woman with the black dog.
The old manservant passed by the corridor with a lantern.
Without a stir of air, the curtain moved.
We no longer waited for their return. Their clothes
hanging in the wardrobes grew old. During the night
we heard the messenger stop before the door.
He didn't ring the doorbell. He didn't speak. The next day
we found his gold stamped cigarette buts in the garden.

Kálamos, January 6, 1988   *(K.M.)*

SAME AS ALWAYS

Houses and trees are bare. Birds
don't know where to perch. All day long
pedlars pass us by. We know them.
Cheap fabrics, cheap jewelry.
In the evening they leave, their wares unsold. And yet,
outside on the coastal road, after the lights are lit,
large packs of wild stray dogs
still fight over a single bone.

Kálamos, January 6, 1988   *(K.M.)*

CARDPLAYERS

I heard the ship pass by. You were late.
I was trying to remember a white bird
on top of a rusty anchor. But,
looking through the pane of the low-lying window,
I saw in the half-lit room,
the men playing cards—one
with a sailor's hat, the other bareheaded, the third,
a black patch over his right eye, the fourth
handsome, young, a Greek. I understood nothing.
Jack, spade, five, nine, queen of spades,
and the *zero* card hidden up my sleeve.

Kálamos, January 6, 1988   *(K.M.)*

SNOWY WEATHER

Winter has arrived. Frozen sparrows
perch on the window frames,
looking with their small sad eyes
inside the houses; pecking the windowpanes. No one lets them in.
Vendors have gathered their baskets from the street.
Ship schedules have been cancelled.
The time has come for the wide white snow. The cellar key
has been forgotten at the foot of the equestrian statue.

Kálamos, January 6, 1988   *(K.M.)*

"PERHAPS"

Perhaps they have some value,
the things we left behind;
perhaps the twelve glasses will glisten

396

on the long narrow formal table;
perhaps some day they'll lend our name
to a village, a mountain, a street.
Perhaps. Perhaps. But for now
even this "perhaps" on your lips
has paled and aged.

Kálamos, January 7, 1988   (K.M.)

THE NAILS

This too is excessive, and that, and that.
The dog died. The horse died.
The empty pail is under the stairs.
Itinerant fishermen cry out in the street.
The house drones its absence, and in the mirror
a pale Christ on the Cross avariciously
clasps the two nails in his palms.

Kálamos, January 9, 1988   (K.M.)

UNJUSTLY

Weary faces, weary hands.
A weary memory. And this
vacuous silence. Evening.
The children have grown. They've left.
You no longer wait for an answer. And besides
you have no requests. Unjustly,
for so many years you strove to place
an approving smile
on this paper mask. Close your eyes.

Athens, January 16, 1988   (K.M.)

DISTINCT MOTION

His eyes are always turned inward.
Outwardly he sees nothing. And when, at times,
he is caught redhanded,
he scratches his ear or his nose. Nevertheless,
he eats his meals. He wipes his lips
with the white ironed napkin, but perhaps,
from behind this napkin, he secretly hands his bread
to his unseen younger brother, Christ.

Athens, January 16, 1988   (K.M.)

ALTERATIONS

The ones who left were ours. We felt their loss.
The ones who returned are total strangers.
Before, they didn't wear glasses. Now they do.
One can't tell whether there are eyes behind their glasses.
We'll have to look at them asleep,
when their open suitcases in the hallway
inhale the alien air of new underwear,
during that hour when the big street lamp outside is lit,
illuminating the closed doors of stores,
and the impenetrable becomes accessible, because you no longer
have anything to buy or sell.

Athens, January 23, 1988   (K.M.)

THE BLACK BOAT

The old man sits on the doorsill. Evening. Alone.
He holds an apple in his hand. Others
left their lives under the auspices of the stars.
What can you say to them? Night is night.
Nor do we know what is to follow. The moon
seems a little playful,
endlessly shimmering on the sea. Nevertheless,
within this radiance can be clearly seen
the black double-oared boat with its dark boatman drawing near.

Athens, May 4, 1988   *(K.M.)*

࿂

THE TRANSLATORS

ATHAN ANAGNOSTOPOULOS (*A. A.*) is Director of the Greek Institute in Cambridge, Massachusetts. His translations include George Seferis' *A Poet's Journal* and Odysseus Elytis' *Maria Nephele*.

PETER BIEN (*P. B.*) is the celebrated translator of Nikos Kazantzakis' *The Last Temptation of Christ, Saint Francis,* and *Report to Greco*. His other work includes a critical study of Kazantzakis and an edition of Kazantzakis' letters. He is Professor of English at Dartmouth College.

ANDONIS DECAVALLES (*A. D.*), Emeritus Professor of Comparative Literature at Farleigh Dickinson University, is a poet and translator. In 1988 he was awarded the Poetry Prize of the Academy of Athens for his fourth volume of Greek verse, and a collection of his selected poems, *Ransoms to Time*, translated by Kimon Friar, was published in the United States in 1984.

KIMON FRIAR (*K. F.*) is the translator of many books of Greek poetry, including the comprehensive anthology, *Modern Greek Poetry*, Nobel Laureate Odysseus Elytis' *The Sovereign Sun*, and Nikos Kazantzakis' modern classic, *The Odyssey: A Modern Sequel*.

N. C. GERMANACOS (*N. C. G.*) was born in Cyprus, raised in Wales and England, and has lived in Greece since 1965. In 1976 his translation of Yannis Ritsos' *Corridor and Stair* was published in Ireland. He is also President of ITHAKA, Cultural Study Programs in Greece, with offices in Greece and in Boston, Massachusetts.

GEORGE GIANNARIS (*G. G.*) is a translator, a poet (the author of six volumes of poetry), and a cultural observer whose work includes *Mykis Theodorakis: Music and Social Change*. He is also Professor of Modern Greek Literature at the University of the Aegean in Greece.

KARELISA HARTIGAN (*K. H.*) is Associate Professor of Classics at the University of Florida, where she is also a Distinguished Alumni Professor.

Her other publications include critical studies of Greek tragedy and essays in comparative literature.

EDMUND KEELEY (*E. K.*) is the author of five novels, four books of non-fiction, and fourteen volumes of translation. His *Ritsos in Parentheses* won the Landon Translation Award and his *Yannis Ritsos: Exile and Return* won the first European Prize for Translation of Poetry. He teaches Creative Writing and Hellenic Studies at Princeton University.

THANASIS MASKALERIS (*T. M.*) is Professor of Comparative Literature and Creative Writing, as well as Director of the Center for Modern Greek Studies at San Francisco State University. His publications include many translations of contemporary Greek poetry and prose, as well as *Kostas Palamas*, a critical-biographical study.

GWENDOLYN MacEWEN (*G. M.*), a native of Canada, published ten volumes of poetry, several books of fiction, and was twice the recipient of the prestigeous Governor General's Award before her untimely death. She also wrote poetic dramas for the CBC and translated both classic Greek tragedies and the work of modern Greek poets.

MARTIN McKINSEY (*M. M.*) has had translations from Modern Greek poetry appear in many places. He is currently a Fellow in Creative Writing at Syracuse University.

KOSTAS MYRSIADES (*K. M.*) is Professor of English and Comparative Literature, as well as Chairperson of the Department of English at West Chester University. In addition to critical studies of Greek literature, his books of translation include Yannis Ritsos' *Monemvasia and The Women of Monemvasia* and *Scripture of the Blind* (both with Kimon Friar).

PHILIP PASTRAS (*P. P.*) teaches English and Greek at Pasadena City College. With George Pilitsis he has translated Yannis Ritsos' six dramatic monologues to be published as *The New Oresteia*.

GEORGE PILITSIS (*G. P.*) is Associate Professor of Classics and of Modern Greek at the Hellenic College in Brookline, Massachusetts. With Philip Pastras he has translated Yannis Ritsos's six dramatic monologues, two of which, *Agamemnon* and *Orestes*, appear in this volume.

MINAS SAVVAS (*M. S.*) is Professor of English and Comparative Literature at San Diego University. He has published a wide variety of critical essays and reviews and two volumes of his translations of Ritsos' poetry, *Chronicles of Exile* and *The Subterranean Horses*.

JOHN STATHATOS (*J. S.*) is a Greek artist and writer based in London. His anthology, *Six Modern Greek Poets*, was published in England in 1975.

NIKOS TSINGOS (*N. T.*) was born in Greece in 1937 and is a musician and song-writer living in Toronto. He has translated classic and modern Greek poetry with his former wife Gwendolyn MacEwen.

❧

YANNIS RITSOS:

A BIOGRAPHICAL NOTE

The youngest of four children and the son of a land-owner ruined by gambling, Yannis Ritsos was born on May 1, 1909, in Monemvasiá (in the district of Laconia, on the southeastern tip of the Peloponnesos). Having begun to paint, to play the piano and to write poetry when he was eight years old, at the age of 80 Ritsos is now one of Greece's most popular poets, as well as one of the greatest and most prolific living poets in the world.

Since the publication of his first book of poems, *Tractor*, in 1934, Yannis Ritsos has published 93 collections of poetry, 3 dramatic works, 9 books of fiction, a collection of essays and 11 volumes of translations. As of 1989, his more popular and important collections of poetry include such long poems as *Epitaphios* (1936), *Moonlight Sonata* (1956) and *Romiosini* (1966), dramatic monologues like *Orestes* (1966) and *Helen* (1972) and the 4 volumes of his collected poetry, *Poems: Volume I* (1961), *Poems: Volume II* (1961), *Poems: Volume III* (1964) and *Poems: Volume IV* (1975), which include more than 40 smaller collections, long poems and sequences, several of them previously unpublished by Ritsos in Greece.

Yannis Ritsos is also one of the most distinguished poets of modern Europe who has been celebrated throughout the world. Among the many honors accorded him, in addition to the Greek State Prize for poetry, are the Great International Prize in Poetry of the Biennial Knokkele-Zoute (Belgium, 1972), the Alfred de Vigny Award (France, 1975) and the Lenin Prize (U.S.S.R., 1977). His poetry has been translated into at least 44 languages, and since 1970 more than 15 books have appeared that are devoted to his poetry in English translation alone, including *Erotica*, translated by Kimon Friar, as well as *Scripture of the Blind* and *Monovasia and The Women of Monemvasia*, both translated by Kimon Friar and Kostas Myrsiades.

His personal life, on the contrary, has been replete with tragedy. At the age of twelve he lost his older brother, Dimitri, to tuberculosis. Within three months, his 42-year old mother died of the same disease; five years later, Ritsos himself was stricken with tuberculosis and his father was interned in the asylum of Daphni for the mentally insane near Athens. His sister, Loula, also suffered mental problems and was institutionalized in 1936.

From 1927 to 1938, Ritsos found himself in and out of sanatoriums, working in the interim as a professional actor, dancer and poet. With the outbreak of World War II in 1941, he joined EAM (the socialists' Greek Democratic Left) and followed its guerilla arm (ELAS) as it retreated before the British troops to Northern Greece, where in 1945 he oversaw the Popular Theatre of Macedonia which extolled the actions of the partisans. From 1948 to 1953, during the Greek civil wars, he was interned as a prisoner in a number of concentration camps (Kontopóli, Makrónisos and Ághios Efstrátios) because of his continuing political association with the socialists; but from 1953 to 1967 he was at last provided fifteen years of respite during which he produced about half of his poetic output.

The coup of Papadopoulos on April 21, 1967 and the junta of the colonels, which once again stifled freedom in Greece, led to Ritsos' further arrest, imprisonment and exile on various Greek islands (including Léros and Yáros). During four years of that junta, he also spent considerable time in military hospitals because of his recurring bout with tuberculosis. And he was subsequently under house arrest until the revolt of the students at the polytechnical institute in Athens brought about the fall of the junta in 1974.

Yannis Ritsos continues to be an ardent and prolific artist; and he now divides his time largely between his home in Athens and his other home in Karlóvasi, on the island of Samos, where his wife practices medicine. Whether in Athens or on Samos, Ritsos spends virtually every waking hour working, a habit he developed in concentration camps as a means of preserving both his art and his sanity, writing or painting on whatever material he finds at hand — pads of paper, canvas, cigarette boxes, glass, stones, bits of wood, bone.

∽

THE SHORT POEMS
OF
YANNIS RITSOS

Kimon Friar

Before writing *Notes on the Margins of Time* (1938—1941),
Yannis Ritsos had published six books, the first three in meter and
rhyme, and the last three in a free verse which, with increasing
mastery and a variety of line lengths, has become the staple of his
poetry ever since. The first two books, *Tractor* (1930—1934) and
Pyramids (1930—1935), had been composed primarily of poems of
normal length ranging from about one to five pages, but the last
poem of *Pyramids* spread over twenty-four pages in several sections, a
precursor of things to come, for his subsequent four poems were of
book length. Although he continued throughout his career to write
poems of medium length, these are few in comparison to the prepon-
derance in his work of book-length poems and the short poems of
which *Notes on the Margins of Time* is the first example.

From now there is to be a seeming dichotomy in Ritsos between
short poems and those long poems in which he can ruminate at
leisure on large themes involving characterization, motivation, the
political scene, or whatever he felt needed long and subtle elabora-
tion. But as he wrote these poems, or perhaps because he was writing
them, he felt impelled, often shortly after, to jot down laconic
impressions sparked off and ignited when the imagination is
stretched to its boldest endeavors on a large canvas. The short poems
are flames that flickered off from the larger conflagrations, planets or
satellites around the generic sun, but all containing the same bio-
chemical or atomic composition. Although "notes," they are written
"on the margins of time," microcosms reflecting macrocosms, and
thus contain a quality of mysterious suggestivity, of something larger
than their finite boundaries enclose, of evocative and varied distinc-
tions that were to increase in density as Ritsos continued to write
them under changing conditions. Some may be associated in mood,
tone and theme with the long poems he was writing at about the
same time. As I stated in my anthology, *Modern Greek Poetry: From
Caváfis to Elytis* (N.Y.: Simon & Schuster, 1973), many poets have

written some of their best, their densest, their most original poems as offshoots of longer poems on which they were engaged, like those Pound wrote when he was composing the *Cantos*, Eliot *The Waste Land*, Yeats his epical-lyrical prose poem *A Vision*, or Elytis his *Áxion Estí*.

It might be the place here to note briefly that we may group the early short poems under several categories: those written during years of freedom, those written during the German-Italian Occupation and the Civil Wars that followed, and those written during seven years of incarceration in detention camps for political prisoners, or under confinement. A distinction might also be made among poems loosely grouped under some theme, style or point of view, and those grouped specifically around some central subject, as the *Twelve Poems for Caváfy, Monovasía,* or *Erotica*. The individual poems range in line length from the one-line verses of *Monochords* (1979) to those which ordinarily take up a third of a page or more and rarely range beyond a page. They are almost always written in unrhymed free verse and in long lines that usually run over. But there is another category: poems written in short, staccato line lengths, often of book size under a central theme, and composed of rather short, untitled stanzas, such as *Hints, Paper Poems,* and *Exile's Journals*. All these, of course, are simply categories of convenience that make possible a more coherent analysis, but should not be taken too rigidly. I shall concern myself with all but the last category, and in chronological order.

The thirty-eight poems of *Notes on the Margins of Time* (1938–1941) were written in the three-year period flanking Mussolini's invasion of Greece on October 28, 1940. In many ways they are notes or summaries of many of the styles, themes, images and points of view which the poet was to deepen and expand in subsequent poems of this series. Indeed, the first two poems may well serve as examples of his method.

DOXOLOGY

He was standing at the far end of the street
like a bare and dusty tree
like a tree burnt by the sun
glorifying the sun that cannot be burned.

Like most of the poems in the first part of this series, this poem is simple on the surface, presents a clear image, and is capable of several interpretations. Man in his isolation stands naked, dusty and weary, having suffered the blows life has given him, nevertheless glorifying what has given him birth and yet torments him, knowing that this is his destiny and the meaning of suffering. The sun is the source of light, of heat, but also of destruction: life and death in one interchangeable process. We are burned by what creates us. The sun symbolizes any of those dual essences, such as love, that both hurt and revive us. Although there is no great complexity in the poem, it cannot be taken simply as a surface image.

This is also true of the second poem:

HOUR OF SONG

Beside the jug of wine
beside the baskets of fruit
we forgot to sing.

On the evening of our separation
under the approbation of the evening star
we sang by ourselves.

Again, what impresses is the simplicity of the images combined with the ambiguity of interpretation. The "we" might refer to only two persons, perhaps lovers, but it might also refer to a group. Ordinarily when two or more people share wine and fruit together they may be inclined to sing, but the people in this poem have forgotten to sing, implying that when one has had enough to eat and drink, when one has everything one wants, song is dispensable. It is when we suffer the loneliness or solitude of separation, when we are alone with the world that true creativity arises, often under the laws and thence the approbation of nature. No theme is stated implicitly, much is left to be inferred, several interpretations are possible. There is always an "Exchange" (the title of another poem) between dualities, one aspect intensifying the other. Stars are luminous keyholes to answers for which we must find the key. It is in these poems that the catalogue of common everyday objects begins to appear, insignificant in themselves, but taking on infinite reverberations when juxtaposed in a long series of combinations. In "Assistance," after images of wind, furniture, olive trees, a field, cicadas, a drizzle, the moon, a plough-man, and the back of a chair that still keeps the warmth of a man's broad shoulderblades, the poet concludes:

> About these insignificant things—I don't know—
> I want to write a small song that will show I don't know
> anything about any of them—only that they are as they are,
> alone, completely alone, and neither do they ask for any mediation
> between themselves and someone else.

"It is possible," writes Joseph Campbell in *Creative Mythology* (N.Y.: Viking Press, 1970) "to view an object not in terms of its relationship to the well-being of the viewer, the subject, but in its own being, in and for itself. The object then is seen with the eye not of a temporal individual but on an uncommitted consciousness: the world eye, as Schopenhauer calls it—without desire, without fear, absolutely disso-ciated from the vicissitudes of mortality in space and time and those laws of cause and effect which operate in this field. . . . Or, as James Joyce formulates the same insight in his discussion (in *A Portrait of the Artist as a Young Man*) of the moment of aesthetic arrest in the contemplation of an object: 'You see that it is that thing which it is and no other thing. . . . . The mind in that mysterious instant Shelley likened to a fading coal.' "

Man has the need and longing to see the thing-in-itself-as-it-really-is, but he knows full well that he is forever interpreting accord-ing to the limitations of his individual senses, that he can only "read" it as he reads a passage from Chaucer or Bach. Indeed, man suspects that even between themselves so-called insensate objects have an interdependent relationship. If at times he insists on the autonomous integrity of things, this is because he knows well that, like sensate human beings, each is an enclosed world all its own and yet, at the same time, sensitively receives messages from the groping antennae of other objects, of other worlds. This is not a paradox but involves the duality inherent in every monad. There is an impregnable secrecy in the heart of things which the poet is forever trying to breach, a message so secret indeed that in "A Small Invitation" the poet says: "And I have something to tell you/which not even I must hear."

The twenty-one poems of *Parentheses I* were written in a one-year period, 1946–1947, during the Civil War when the poet was 35–36, and published in Ritsos's collected *Poems* Vol. II, 1961; a second part was written in an eleven-year period, 1950–1961, when the poet was 41–52, but which have not yet been published in Greece. As the title suggests, these are poems in which many parenthetical remarks occur (whether in parentheses or not) and which the reader is inclined to take as keys to the meaning intended, although the true meaning may lurk elsewhere. They are like those asides in Elizabethen drama which, while pretending to inform and alert the audience to what is going on, cunningly succeed in diverting their attention from the real action—a death, perhaps, or a stolen kiss behind the arras. The reader must be careful, for these lines often deliberately mislead, shunting him off into another direction that opens up unexpected vistas, or into another dimension which, he may be surprised to discover, penetrates more deeply or more essentially into the poem. In other words, the misleading cue may be the real cue after all, but the reader is never quite certain. The straightforward in Ritsos must also be confronted with reserve (especially if he insists upon it), for its apparent visibility may be a ruse to draw away the attention from another, more secret revelation, or by its very clarity obscure as clearly as a bright sun blurs objects on which it shines too intensely. "Tell the truth," says Emily Dickinson, "but tell it slant," and Ritsos often leaves us in doubt as to whether the highway or the byway leads to the desired destination. One answer might be that both lead, in their own way, to the same desired end; but another answer might be that both lead to different endings, each equally valid, and perhaps interrelated. Such hide-and-seek, such misleadings, such doubling on tracks already doubled on, are part and parcel not only of the technique but also of the multiple vision with which Ritsos views the world, especially in his later phase.

The first poem of this group is cunningly entitled:

THE MEANING OF SIMPLICITY

I hide behind simple things that you may find me;
if you don't find me, you'll find the things,
you'll touch what my hand touches,
the imprints of our hands will merge.

The August moon glitters in the kitchen
like a pewter pot (it becomes like this because of what I tell
    you)

it lights up the empty house and the kneeling silence of the
   house —
always the silence remains kneeling.

Every word is a way out
for an encounter often canceled,
and it's then a word is true, when it insists on the encounter.

The poet informs us (parenthetically) that if the moon is glittering in
the empty house like a pewter pot, this is because he has chosen to
tell us so, thus warning us that the poem we are reading and its
themes exist only in the words he has chosen; that we are entering a
world peculiarly his own; and that we who enter here must abandon
hope of ever again living in a world we once knew. "Every word," he
tells us, "is a way out/for an encounter often canceled," and in so
telling us leaves us in doubt as to whether the "way out" is an
opening toward that meeting or an escape from a meeting that,
anyway, has been canceled. But having once heeded the poet's paren-
thetical warning that we are entering a private house of words (where
silence remains forever kneeling), where no two seemingly similar
words for inhabitant and visitor ever denote or connote the same
things or meanings, we must not be misled by the impasse of this
encounter, because it is exactly the words themselves which are not
only a bridge between each other, and so between ourselves, but also
a bridge between ourselves and whatever they symbolize, whether
things of the world inside each of us or outside us all. The imprints of
our hands *will* merge, though not completely, for no two imprints are
exactly alike, but sufficiently enough for an over-all pattern to be
discerned. The miracle is that communication is at all possible, and
to the extent it is. The meaning of simplicity is complex.
   Such communication must necessarily take place between person
and person, as well as between person and things, and if the poet
hides behind things, this is because he has no choice but to hide,
since words, which are his medium, are, after all, but masks; and
things, or the words for things, are his only signals. There *is* a point of
contact, no matter how blurred. Indeed, the blurring, the diffused
meeting, the ambiguities, are ultimately not only to be preferred but
to be prized, for the poet knows that words are in themselves inade-
quate mediums for what he wants to communicate. Only through
hints, allusions, and indications between words, things and himself
can he possibly hope to allude to what is even to himself not clear

because so vastly beyond his or any man's comprehension. This is the secret of ambiguity in poetry, and the meaning of simplicity; the two are intertwined. It is only by a charged ambiguity that the poet can ever hope to communicate the incommunicable, not only in regard to complex matters, but also in regard to the simplest object or event.

The images or objects that Ritsos most often uses, as we shall see, are almost always the ordinary objects in daily life we encounter in house, city or countryside, but set side by side in such evocative juxtaposition that the reader is ill-advised to seek any *one* precise meaning. The images, the words, are impelling, even insistent, leading, the reader feels, to an actual meeting. In Ritsos' poems the insistence is always there, the urgency, but the actual encounter rarely takes place. What the reader often receives is not the firm handshake but the multiple impression of one: "you'll touch what my hand touches, / the imprints of our hands will merge." The poet can only trust his own revelation, though blurred and unclear, and hope that somewhere along the way his vision and that of others will somehow meet in the poem or outside the poem (the poem used as springboard), as in the conclusion of "Maybe, Someday":

But I'm going to insist on seeing and showing you, he said,
because if you too don't see, it will be as if I hadn't—
I'll insist at least on not seeing with your eyes—
and maybe someday, from a different direction, we'll meet.

It is often as difficult for the poet to find his own true voice as for the reader to encompass the penumbras of the poet's vision, and no "Final Agreement" may be possible. When in the fields on a sharp sunny day the poet shouts, not knowing what he is shouting, but shouting only in the exuberance of the day, unhesitant and unimpeded, then he may acknowledge that this may be his true voice "in agreement with all the unsuspecting voices that filled the air." But this agreement is often fortuitous or fortunate. The poet may seem serene or disciplined, kind or indifferent, showing an outward restraint, but only he knows what blows he must sustain "under the dreadful hammer" of life in an attempt to forge a poem so that "from the formless you pass toward form." Whether he shouts or whether he remains silent, he and his work are under constant "Reformation."

In 1941, during the German-Italian Occupation, Ritsos had joined the educational branch of the communist-led National Liberation Front (EAM) as part of the resistance movement. After the

Germans were driven out of Greece in 1944, two civil wars erupted that lasted from 1945 to 1949. With the intervention of British troops and the defeat of the Greek People's Liberation Army (ELAS) in December 1944, Ritsos accompanied the withdrawal of ELAS into the mountains of Macedonia as part of a troupe of actors and writers; but when, on the promise of amnesty, ELAS was induced to lay down its arms on the signing of the Várkisa Agreement of February 12, 1945, the poet returned with others to Athens. However, within a month thousands had been arrested, Ritsos was fired from his position with the Greek National Theater, the second civil war erupted, and on July 1948 he was himself arrested and was to spend the next four years in various detention camps for political prisoners on several islands. Between 1948–1949 he was incarcerated in Kondoúpoli on the island of Límnos, where he wrote *Exile's Journals I*, from October 27 to November 23, 1948, and *Exile's Journals II*, from November 24, 1948 to January 31, 1949. He was then transferred to the dreaded island of Makrónisos in May 1949, where he remained until July 1950, and where he wrote *Petrified Time* during August and September of 1949, and *Exile's Journals III* between January 18 and June 1 of 1950. Of these, the twenty-four poems of *Petrified Time* fall into the category of the poems we are considering. First published in Greek in Bucharest in July 1957, and mistakenly entitled *Makrónisos* (because the title page had been lost en route), these poems were later extensively revised and published in Athens in 1974.

Other than one heavily censored letter per month, the prisoners were not permitted to write. But whenever he could evade the surveillance of the guards, Ritsos managed to write his poems on scraps of paper saved from cigarette boxes, or on toilet paper, and to hide these poems in bottles and to bury them in the earth, from which they were later retrieved. Some were smuggled out in the hollow wooden edges of cardboard valises the prisoners made for themselves. In these poems the poet confronts his tormentors who tried to force him to renounce his political ideals, to deny himself, to sign a renunciation or "confession" that he might go free. Indeed, these years of detention had the contrary effect on Ritsos than that intended by his captors. It was during these years of trial that he overcame initial depression and became more deeply committed to his political faith. It was then he learned the love of comrades, and the love of solitude as opposed to the loneliness of confinement. It was then also he learned those habits of daily creative work that have obsessively ruled him ever since. When he was finally released, he left not only with secreted poems but also with five hundred water colors he had been permitted to paint.

In *Petrified Time* the struggle between the strident attack of tyrannical rule and the silent resistance of the individual takes on the terrible hardness of stone, savage, naked and speechless. The island of Makrónisos, known to the prisoners as the "Island of the Devil," is itself one barren, treeless stone where even time itself becomes petrified. In "Recognition," the sun has turned to stone. In "Ready," "The bed we sleep in is of stone, / stone the bread that sharpens our teeth, / stone the hand that cups the chin of night." "While the prisoners are working the stone all day long" in forced labor, they discover that even "the shadow doesn't hide the stone's hardness" ("The Roots of the World"). But stone must oppose stone, and in defence the old men stare seaward "like lions of stone at the gateway of night." They prepare themselves in the "silence that falls before the first stroke of thunder" ("Our Old Men"), as they "throw their hearts like an illegal proclamation / under the closed door of the world" ("Recognition"). These four years lived so inhumanly in various detention camps when he was in the prime of life, between the ages of thirty-nine and forty-three, were to mark all of Ritsos' subsequent life and poetry deeply. He was to have fifteen years of freedom, from 1953 to 1967, before he was again incarcerated on the first day of the colonels' military coup on April 21, 1967.

The one hundred and sixty-three poems in *Exercises* were written between 1950–1960 and published in 1964 in the third volume of Ristos' collected *Poems*. Culled over a ten year period, they are given a modest title because the poet wants to indicate that they are but studies in the techniques of his craft, exercises in how the invisible may in part be apprehended and "from the formless pass into form." The depth and pulse measurement of each word is taken, then related to the work that precedes and the word that follows, because each word, like a two-sided mirror, encloses the treasure trove of its own historical origin and development and like a chameleon changes hue and nuance according to what reflections it receives and emits in any one particular juxtaposition. Thus by mutual reflection the various emphases, stresses or impressions are sparked off by many crossings, encounters or concurrences that reverberate with allusions, meanings or suggestions. One of the poems in *Exercises* is entitled

THE USEFULNESS OF ART

It was not only those that came of themselves,
those that were, the inevitable, but also the others,
those he himself added, those he wanted or the others
    wanted,
those he chose, and the manner in which they multiplied or
    were added.

And perhaps these last were particularly his,
that continued as arrested or diffused things,
presenting a story or a face to the immobile, like a
    transparent windowpane
that suddenly thickens when darkness comes and turns into a
    mirror,
presenting noble performances out of unsuspecting events,
presenting their forms and their phantoms, presenting
the interior of nocturnal rooms illuminated by lamps or by a
    bouquet of flowers,
or by anger or privation or poverty. Presenting
things known and unknown, known in another way,
in a sequence, even though constrained in a value at least
    interchangeable.

This poem may be taken as a description of the poet's method. Although neither he nor any other poet can preclude "inspiration," he does not wait upon "those that came of themselves," but deliberately chooses words or objects which he feels to be particularly his, with which he has many associations, and places them in some kind of sequence, some coherence, in such a way that they are forced to reveal their inner, phantom or invisible natures, to present "noble performances out of unsuspecting events." In this manner both known and unknown objects or events, interpreted or seen anew by the juxtapositions or sequences in which they have been impelled by the poet to take, are thus forced to interchange their values and present a new, complex value.

   Such interchangeability between things is the subject of

INTERCHANGES

They took the plough into the field,
they brought the field into the house —
an endless interchange shaped
the meaning of things.

The woman changed places with the swallow,
she sat in the swallow's nest on the roof and warbled.
The swallow sat at the woman's loom and wove
stars, birds, flowers, fishing boats, and fish.

Field and house, woman and swallow are interchanged, and the
weavings by both woman and swallow gather into their warp and
woof elements of their wider environment: "star, birds, flowers, fish-
ing boats and fish." Thus far, but for the transposition of objects not
ordinarily associated with one another, the poem contains the sim-
plicity and directness that, on one plane, is one of Ritsos' chief char-
acteristics, but the concluding couplet extends the mystery and com-
plexity of the poem:

If only you knew how beautiful your mouth is
you would kiss me on the eyes that I might not see.

In the wonder of this interchangeability between things, in this par-
taking by one thing of the integrity and mystery of the other (as one
partakes of divinity in the wine or the wafer), the poet becomes so
charged with the mystical significance of such relationship that it
becomes unbearable. He turns to another equally distracting beauty
and longs for the one to cancel out the other. In the same manner
Gerard Manley Hopkins contemplated in concealed excitement the
various attributes of the windhover and the big wind with which it
contended, and in admiration of the various seemingly opposed ele-
ments invoked by this image, exclaimed:

Brute beauty and valour and act, oh, air, pride, plume here
Buckle! AND the fire that breaks from thee then, a billion
Times told lovelier, more dangerous, O my chevalier!

The various nuances set off by such juxtaposition are not really defin-
able and must vary from reader to reader; but it is the couplet in

Ritsos' poem that is the fuse to the explosions set off in the reader's imagination.

The poems in *Exercises* have a cohesion and clarity of exposition that revolve around a cluster of interrelated images whose interconnections are not too difficult to follow. They are small dramatic scenes that imply more than they state. The poet is fascinated by the infinite variety of each separate event or object. Each in itself is so beautiful in what it is, so evocative, that the eye is forced to focus upon it, to rivet itself there; and yet the poet knows that there is some invisible connection, some coherance between them as though they were parallel lights emitted from the same center. It is this ever-shifting center that is invoked in poem after poem, as in the medieval concept that God is a circle whose center is everywhere. Whether the poet is obsessively observing "the sound of water/falling in winter from an overbrimming drainpipe," or the way in which the knees of his beloved form an angle on the bedsheet, he confesses that these are all inexplicable experiences which he has sought again and again to explain to himself and to the reader. But he confesses finally that even he does not know the meaning of what he is describing, knowing only that he is drawn to them not only because of the wonder and beauty they contain in simply being what they are, but also because together, one against the other or in sequence, they partake of and invoke implications which it is the agonized privilege of the poet to attempt to capture:

NECESSARY EXPLANATION

There are certain stanzas — sometimes entire poems —
whose meaning not even I know. It's what I do not know
that holds me still. You were right to ask me. But don't ask
   me.
I don't know, I tell you.
                 The parallel lights
from the same center. The sound of water
falling in winter from an overbrimming drain pipe,
or the sound of a waterdrop as it falls
from a rose in a watered garden
slowly, slowly on a spring evening
like a bird's sobbing. I don't know
what this sound means; even so, I acknowledge it.

I've explained to you whatever else I know. I've not been
     neglectful.
But even these add to our lives. I would notice,
as she slept, how her knees formed an angle on the
     bedsheet —
It was not only a matter of love. This corner
was a ridge of tenderness, and the fragrance
of the bedsheet, of cleanliness, and of spring supplemented
that inexplicable thing I sought — in vain again — to explain to
     you.

Ritsos entitles "Wonder" a poem that simply depicts a man
placing his wrist watch under his pillow as he falls asleep while the
wind is blowing outside: "You/who know the wondrous succession of
the slightest movements,/you will understand. A man, his watch,
the wind. Nothing more." For Ritsos the most routine, the most
common, the most insignificant movements are a "wondrous succes-
sion." In "Question," he places side by side a man dwindling at the
far end of a street, the round mirrors of parked bicycles throwing
their reflections on an empty public square, a woman contemplating
by a dark window, an older woman fetching water from a well as a
tiny spider perches on her jug. The entire sketch has the still-life
illumination and mystery of a painting by Edward Hopper or de
Chirico. "Explain to me," says the poet, "What do they all want?"
Ritsos has spent a lifetime obessively observing the common details of
such enigmas, sometimes attempting to give direct answers, but more
often than not simply hinting at several possible interpretations,
some his own, some deliberately set to entrap and involve the reader,
all possible. At times a common moment of living is set against the
backdrop of eternity, as in the middle plays of Tennessee Williams.
In "Moment," a downtrodden sailor's quarter in a harbor town, the
light gloves, the shabby beer pubs, the dark streets, "the pure white
laughter of a young man" from one of the pubs, are all heightened in
their poignant and transitory passage through life by being depicted
against "the endless, uniform, unconquerable sea."
     By this time the short poems Ritsos had been writing began to
be formulated in his mind under the general title *Testimonies*, for he
had begun to see that, no matter what their theme, or whether they
dealt with good or evil, they were all his epiphanies, his witnesses to
revelations for which he had sworn, as poet, to testify. The eighty
poems of the First Series were written during 1957–1963 and pub-

lished in 1963; the one hundred and ten poems of the Second Series were written during 1964–1965 and published in 1966; the Third Series, written during 1966–1967, have not as yet been published. We are fortunate in having about this time, in 1962, one of two brief essays Ritsos has written about his short poems, entitled "By Way of Introduction to *Testimonies*," in which he summarizes the kind and intent not only of these specific poems but of all his shorter poems of which they are prototypes. He writes in part:

> I cannot say exactly *how* or *why* I, who from inclination and preference have worked primarily with long, compositional poems, have occupied myself with particular persistence and love for so many years continuously and continue, even now, concomitantly with my other work, to occupy myself with undiminished interest with *Testimonies*, attributing indeed a special significance to these by continuing to write *laconic* and frequently epigrammatic poems. This is so perhaps because I am by origin from Laconía (and this is not simply a play on words); perhaps from a proclivity to prove to myself and others that I am able to express myself in a concise and dense language; perhaps from a disposition to rest after the sleepless tensions of long creative periods; perhaps from the need of exercising myself in the perfecting and preparing of my craft so that I might, with immediacy and as faultlessly as possible, give value in art to life experiences constantly renewed; perhaps from an attempt to condense expression in reaction to the dangers of verbosity and rhetoric that often lurk in ambush behind long poems; perhaps from the need to respond instantaneously to the grave and urgent problems of our times; perhaps even from the desire to detach and pin down *a moment* of time that would permit a microscopic examination of it in depth and thus to discover all those elements of time that probably would have scattered to the winds in a limitless horizon — that is to say, to conceive of the indivisible by what is divisible, to conceive of everlasting motion by what is immobile.

Ritsos takes the things themselves, unencumbered as they seem by man's manifold problems, and entrusts to them a leading role in the drama. He calls them "those small accumulators of useful human energy, those small everyday myths which participate involuntarily and together with us play leading roles in a drama which does not concern them. They are called upon to play the role of *nothing is happening* when precisely everything is happening." As for the large element of mystery, perhaps even mystification, that exists in his work, Ritsos writes, in part: "A personal objectivity suffices — the only one, I believe. I am simply explaining, as much as it is possible and permitted me to do so, some gestures of the verses not completely irrelevant to the poem (and thus not completely without purpose), knowing nevertheless that they remain incomprehensible. (Can it be perhaps that this which remains utterly incomprehensible, even for the creator himself, is precisely what belongs to poetry and which perhaps impels the reader toward creation — that is to say, toward his own discovery, or at least toward inquiry)?" The poet believes that he has the right to be forgiven for being so conscious of the "ambiguity, complexity, incomprehensibility, inexplicability and unaccountability of life." "Perhaps," he says toward the end of his essay, "the final flavor of *Testimonies* is a silent gratitude toward human life, acts, thought and art in spite of all tribulations and death — indeed perhaps because of these."

In this same essay Ritsos also points out how often, indeed how obsessively, he uses the conjunction "or" and the adverb "perhaps" to emphasize the many and often contradictory dimensions in life and art, the infinite choices that occur among many options, the essential ambiguity of life as it oscillates between antitheses. Indeed, in *Repetitions*, (1968–1969), in a poem entitled "The Conjunction 'Or'," he points out that "accuracy does not exist (and this is why / the pompous tone of certainty is unforgivable — may God help us)." He then apostrophizes that ambivalent connective:

> "Or," conjunction, humble consequence of the mystery of ambiguity,
> deep correlation among the multiplicity of essences and phenomena,
> it is with you we adjust to the difficulties of life and dream,
> to the many nuances and versions between black to invisible white.

In a long poem he wrote in 1942 on a painting by El Greco, "The Tomb of Orgath," Ritsos demonstrates how man is forever doomed never to know things as they really are, because between him and all phenomena must always intervene the collective consciousness not only of all mankind but also of each man's individual percep-

tions. For man, the word by which he designates a thing, the image
he forms of a thing, must necessarily be the thing itself:

> And images are no longer representations of things, he said,
> they are the things themselves. And words
> are not the meanings and the name of things
> but the things themselves, as they are before we think of
>   them
> and after we have touched them and thought of them deeply,
>   until finally we no longer think of them,
> the things simply, self-sufficient in their solitude and in their
>   endless relationships,
> a table hovering in the sky and on which you lean your
>   elbows
> cheek to cheek with the night cloud,
> and the ashtray with the cigarette stubs side by side with
>   stars,
> and this samovar still lukewarm (or perhaps the moon?),
> a moon-samovar. I look and marvel
> at you, at me, at the stars. My only pride, he said,
> is this humility of mine: to know, to not know, to fall silent
> and to speak things in their primary silence. And he fell
>   silent like one guilty.

Ritsos thus is always exploring that mysterious middle-ground
between man and things of which words and images are the bridges
or the identification tags, and through that void he tries to find some
connection with the absolute, the invisible, the ultimate, the inex-
pressible. As recent scientific photographs have shown, there is a
penumbra of radiant energy pulsing around a man's body and
around all things animate or inanimate, a wordless, invisible commu-
nication. Experiments have been conducted in which the leaves of
plants shrivel when in their midst live shrimps are cast into a pot of
boiling water. In "Knowledge of the Ambiguous," when a woman
takes off her shoes under the table, the man beside her not only
knows how weary she is from the "tempered glow" of one of the five
glasses on the table, but also that her weariness is "wonderful, proud,
deathless." In "Conformity," there is no dichotomy between the ani-
mate and the inanimate, for the horseman of an equestrian bronze
statue himself dismounts and directs the dismantling of his own
statue. In "For Greater Accuracy," the slightest interval of a breath

intervenes when a man tries to convince himself that two and two make four, knowing uneasily that such addition is as ambiguous as "a star behind a light veil of mist at that quivering hour,/so very beautiful, between dusk and night." In "Silent Agreement," a transposition of roles takes place between the three men, a window and a wall map, and the poem concludes: "Then the three agreed without any discussion/on the significance of music and metamorphosis." In "Under Oblivion," "the firing wall with four bullet holes" still remains imprinted on the coat of the slain man hung up in a closet and long forgotten. Poets, like the masons in "Builders," build better than they know. Some may build (or write) "out of instinct," some "professionally," some "to avenge themselves against death," and some "consciously, with resolution." Suffering as they create, but exactly because of their struggle, their building "proceeds much beyond their purpose." The ultimate aim of the builder is to mix in with his plaster, with his words, that strife and those tears which may cause his work to invoke more than it seems to connote. "Because of this," the poem concludes, "all builders dream at night/of that unknown, that invisible 'beyond,'/and every morning they build the 'here' a bit better."

We depart from our chronological survey in order to say a few words about *Testimonies II*. Since they have the same epicenter as the poems in *Testimonies I*, any analysis of these poems would simply repeat, in a new context, what has already been written. However, there are about a dozen poems in this group that indicate a new and very important departure for Ritsos: the use of ancient Greek mythology or incidents. We have in recent years associated such use almost exclusively with Cavafy, but he simply transformed into a constant method a form used by Greek poets since ancient times, and later even by poets and prose writers throughout the world. Cavafy concerned himself primarily with the Hellenistic, Greco-Roman and Byzantine periods, but Ritsos did so almost exclusively with the classical or preclassical periods. Ritsos was later to concern himself more extensively with these themes, primarily in his long monologues and in *Repetitions* (1968–1969), where such poems may more carefully be examined, especially in regard to their contemporary implications. Many of the poems in *Testimonies II* deal with Homeric themes, not so much to match them with modern parallels as to take some one incident, primarily from the *Iliad* or the *Odyssey*, important or seemingly insignificant, and to invent some detail around it that may reveal some aspect of destiny or character. In "The First Sensual Delight," the poet draws an imaginary depiction of that moment when Achilles stoops to tie his sandal and feels a particular sensual delight, compounded in part by the sensuous summer landscape about him and in part by premonitions of his destiny as his fingers busy themselves near his vulnerable heel; he feels the sensual langor of death. In the poems revolving around Odysseus, we are given new descriptions, interpretations, or ruminations about actual events that would not have occurred to the objectively-minded Homer but which the more introspective sensibilities of a modern poet bring into play. The poems remain primarily in their own period, but seen with modern, sophisticated eyes. In "The Peacocks of Perilampes," the poet reminds us that the Greeks of the classical period not only had an Apollonian love of form and clarity but also a Dionysian delight in the love of color, in the exotic and luxurious.

In 1963, when he was fifty-four, Ritsos wrote and published his tribute to a poet from whom he had learned much, his *Twelve Poems for Cavâfis*. He admired in Cavâfy the absence of rhetoric or pomposity, his use of lean, concrete words and sentiments, his ability to find an exact measure between sensual passion and spiritual impressions, his use of the chill and warm colors of words in such a way that chill did not freeze passion or passion explode the form of the poem. Such balance takes on a social, moral as well as aesthetic "Evaluation" (Poem XII), for Cavâfy has left us "an excellent standard by which to measure ourselves and, above all, to measure/our neighbor." Thus Cavâfy stood as a teacher and forerunner of techniques to many later poets. In addition, Ritsos was moved by the personal drama of the poet, how he struggled to find a technique and masks by which to give his particular, often sexual, drama dimensions that might take on universal proportions. In this way Cavâfy enlivened incidents he took from history by injecting into them intense living experiences of his own in such a way that history might take on new life and at the same time might be used as a superb mask behind which, by hiding, he could reveal more than he could openly declare. Cavâfy never placed marks of ommission in his poetry because this would call attention to the lacunae, whereas much of his poetry was, according to Ritsos, an omission of things he preferred to leave unsaid; this was his manner of "silencing his silence."

In the first poem, "The Poet's Space," Ritsos describes Cavâfy sitting with his back to the light, flooding his young admirers with illumination "while he himself remains hidden behind his words,/ behind history, behind persons of his own creation, distant and invulnerable." He is "cunning, voracious, carnal, the great innocent,"

424

but in "Final Hour" (Poem X) Ritsos shows how he had come to reconciliation and redemption in his maturity when contradictions met in "the supreme union of poetry." Realising that he is leaving on his final journey, alone, having "never wanted/to delude anyone," the poet began to weep, "knowing/his innocence for the first time with such certainty." He knows now that we are all victims of our time and circumstances, that to be a poet basically means to mold confusion into form, to give shape and meaning to life, and in this sense there is always a deep innocence in every poet no matter how much his hands are dyed with the materials he has used. The poet must make the void tangible, turn the invisible into art, give both endurance and durability against time, In a fine image, Ritsos makes of Caváfy's glasses a balancing scale on which Caváfy weighs the ultimate void of our annihilation, for on their polished surfaces is reflected a procession of "his inner and outer visions in a balanced unity/so material, so incorruptible, that it refutes the entire void" (Poem V; "His Glasses"). Ultimately, for Caváfy, as for Ritsos, art is the bridge of passage from visible to invisible, from formless to form, and it is a poet's only hope of redemption. "If poetry cannot absolve us," Caváfy whispers to himself in the first of these poems, thus setting the tone of all twelve, "then let's not expect mercy from anywhere." From Caváfy Ritsos has learned many of the techniques, attitudes and masks which he has utilized in his short poems.

The 105 poems of *Summer Preparatory School*, written during 1953–1964 and published in 1975 in the fourth volume of the collected edition, are the poet's celebration of the almost notorious beauty of the Greek sun and light which so impresses millions of visitors every year and which is never taken for granted by the Greek himself. They are a paean to endless Greek summer days with their thousands of yellow eyes when stones, cornfields and bodies blaze in an expanse of endless erotic desires. Unlike the lush, green, flowering summers of more northern countries, the Greek summer extends into limitless azure seas and skies under a dry desolation that deepens into the sensation of nothingness, of "inexplicable, immaculate absence" ("Absence"). In this luster poetry grows blind and, in seeking to create a shade, glows, becomes more luminous than before in its attempt to reconcile opposites in a landscape where there is no chiaroscuro, where light and shade intensify each other and interchange essences. Sights and sounds become vibrant with moments of unbearable beauty: a pail falling as though of its own volition into a well on a hot August evening; or the glowing beauty of youthful sunburnt bodies rising from the sea, as in their thick hair or in the pores of their skin glitter small cubes of salt. The beholder is stricken, fearing that no poet will ever observe a detail of such unbearable beauty and give it its inevitable place in a poem. In these poems Ritsos has painted aquarelles in hot, primary colors as intensified by a Greek summer day. In "Probabilities," the sight of a white caique pulsating against six red boats in the dusk arouses inexplicable stirrings, emotions, impressions, and so stuns the senses that only later, in Wordsworth's "emotion recollected in tranquillity," can the beholder begin to understand what he has experienced. It may be, the poet concludes, that beauty is "the silent, inexplicable certainty of a postponed happiness." It is such stirring, half-apprehended moments which Ritsos seeks to capture in these poems: in "Adolescent," the unfathomable beauty of a white shirt abandoned on a rock by a young man who had undressed to swim, while "the shirt shone like a small marble wing/ on the shoulder blades of the golden noon." It is of such epiphanies that these poems are composed. They are the idle yet deep lessons learned in summer's preparatory school with which to withstand the haze of autumnal transition and the oncoming of freezing winter, for as the poet reminds us in "Accented Colors," it is in that infinitesimal distance between a bird and a leaf that death sits waiting.

The sixty poems of *Small Dedication*, written during 1960–1965 and published in 1975 in the fourth volume of the collected edition, were written for and dedicated to his wife Folítsa and to his daughter Éri, then barely of school age. Most of them were written in his home on Karlóvasi on the island of Sámos where his wife is a practicing physician and where Ritsos spends almost all of his summers. Composed far from the noise, pollution and crowds of Athens, they are saturated with the calm and quiet atmosphere of family life. They are imbued with thankfulness and tenderness, silent contacts and relationships with the house, the rooms, the bedsheets, the tables, the windows and with what lies beyond the windows—the sea, a tree in bloom, a leaf on a tree, the water in the well, a butterfly, the secret life of nature and creation. Many of the poems addressed to his daughter, some of them in rhyme, try to make her aware of the infinite variety of things, to name them, to differentiate them in shape, color, smell or taste, or enlarge her spirit and enrich her language. They are a secret conversation with the still unwinged soul of his child and thus with all children throughout the world. They are among the most peaceful poems Ritsos was to write before catastrophe fell.

On April 21, 1967, some months after the resignation of George Papandréou as prime minister, the provisional government was overthrown by a military coup of the colonels, and Greece was to live under a dictatorship for seven years. Warned by friends who begged him to go into hiding, Ritsos calmly packed a valise and waited. At 6 A.M. that morning the police arrested him, nine days before his fifty-eighth birthday, then after three days transferred him to the Hippodrome at New Fáliron with thousands of other political prisoners. From there, at the end of April, they were taken on battleships to the island of Yáros, bare rock, where 6,500 were crammed, under deplorable conditions, mostly in tents and a few abandoned buildings. After pressure was exerted by the International Red Cross, they were transferred, in September, to the island of Léros, where two detention camps had been prepared, Lakkí and Parthéni. More humane conditions prevailed in Parthéni, for here Ritsos was permitted to write a poem or two a day in his notebooks. His health, however, had greatly deteriorated, and after an international outcry, he was sent, under guard, in August 1968, to an anticancer clinic in Athens, was returned to Léros after a month, and finally, in December 1968, with his poems and two large sacks of pebbles and stones covered with his ink sketches, he was permitted to return to his home in Karlóvasi, Sámos. His movements, however, were restricted and always shadowed by spies, mail was forbidden him, and no persons other than those of his immediate family were allowed to approach him or to speak to him, not even his neighbors or townspeople. In January 1970, he was permitted to go to Athens for an operation, but was sent back to Sámos in April, where he remained until the fall of the dictatorship. At the beginning of 1970 the junta relaxed censorship; authors could now publish but at their peril and were liable to sudden arrest and military trial if their writings were in any way judged to be censorious of the regime. After the courageous uprising of the students at the Polytechnical Institute in November 1973, and the debacle in regard to Cyprus in July 1974, the junta fell on the twenty-third of that month, and Karamanlís was called from Paris to form a transitional government.

The fifty-six poems of the first part of *The Wall in the Mirror* were written between November 1967 and January 1968 at Parthéni, and the seventy-seven poems of the second part were written between March and October 1971 under restricted arrest in Karlóvasi and Athens. They were first published in French translation in Paris in 1973 and in Greek in Athens in 1974. When Hamlet instructs the players how to interpret their roles, he advises them "To hold, as it were, the mirror up to nature." This has been Rítsos's practice all his life. His mirror registers not only nature herself but all that man has made of nature and himself, particularly the sufferings of the Greek people during dark or tragic political conditions. But now that his country was once more oppressed by dictatorship and he himself again incarcerated, the mirror of expression reflects the barrier of a repressive wall. This second incarceration, after fifteen years of freedom, was for Ritsos far worse than the first, and forced him for the first time into expressions of despair. "He sits alone,/looks at his hands, his fingernails—they are alien" ("Exultation"). It is all he can do to prevent himself from breaking the mirror, for all have turned nauseous: colors, light, bread, water. The colonels had brazenly used as their symbol the phoenix rising out of her own flames, and the slogan "Greece of Christian Greeks." In "Unfamiliar Instrument," Ritsos speaks of the protagonist as one who "no longer loved things, words, or birds that had become/slogans or symbols." He comes to the despairing conclusion, in a poem significantly entitled "Need to Express," that "With time and fatigue . . . words die too./Nothing is left him to express nothingness. His fingers/have grown very thin. His ring slips off . . . Desolation." At times it seems that "Not Even" poetry is possible, that from the seventh floor it normally occupies it has been lowered in a basket with all the instruments of the profession—a shaving machine, bread, shoes, a little mirror, a mute canary—and little by little is smothered with nettles. But "nevertheless/you still keep the rope tied to your bed rails," and one day you will draw it up again.

We will find a brooding despair occurring often in poems during these years, but alternating with an ultimate hope and belief in mankind's regeneration. Exterior walls do not entirely block up his mirrors but are reflected in them like any other object, and indeed become in time battlements behind which to fight or hide the explosive truth of poetry. Once again, in the transforming strength of his art, Ritsos begins to alter negative into positive, once more he reaches toward an affirmation of life. He now begins to write with the cunning devices that censorship imposes on the inventiveness and craft of all poets: "And if he spoke,/he always took care to change the place, the names, the dates,/hiding all of them, and hiding himself too behind the hidden/(or was he by chance revealing, on the contrary, the unknown they had in common?)" ("Mutual Concessions").

Even in detention camps there is some saving grace—a bit of sea glimpsed through barbed wire, the blue mountains in the distance, olive trees on a hill, a pregnant cow scratching her back on the outstretched hand of a statue. As in much of modern Greek poetry, statues play a significant role in Ritsos' poetry where they primarily represent the human condition turned into art, into form, into poetry. In these particular poems, statues rise out cautiously from wells to climb trees; they weep heavy stone tears; they stand with a noose around their necks or walk with cracked marble knees patched together with cement. The artist has become a blindfolded tightrope walker on electric wires high above the parade. After initial numbness and despair, Ritsos need hardly tell us that "he still insisted on thinking and observing," that he had once more discovered his own center to be the center of the universe, that nothing can destroy the human spirit, that on the statistical number stamped on his back there is "the most secret, the most white bird sitting" ("Invention of the Center"). The wall in the mirror is not an impassable barrier. Behind it the poet continues to function with the cunning and sleight-of-hand tricks of a conjuror.

Stones, *Repetitions* and *Barriers* were first published in one volume in a bilingual French and Greek edition in Paris in 1971. With seventeen poems added to *Stones*, ten to *Repetitions*, and nineteen to *Barriers*, they were published in Greek, again in one volume, in Athens in 1972. The thirty-two poems in *Stones* were written from May 15, 1968 to October 21, 1968; the fifty-two poems of *Repetitions* from March 17, 1968 to June 27, 1969, both in Parthéni; and the fifty-four poems of *Barriers* from November 7, 1968 to June 3, 1969 in Karlóvasi.

In *Stones*, the poems are harsh, hard implements by which men are stoned and with which in turn they stone the enemy; at times "the first stone/was cast by his friends" ("The Unacceptable Man"). The word is a refrain that recurs throughout many of these poems: "Only the stones have remained. It is with these we must make do now;/with these, with these, he keeps repeating" ("With These Stones"). The poet watches the birds flying in their freedom above him, but below there are only stones, thorns in the fields; and although he struggles to keep his creativity alive, he finds that "The poem is slow in coming. Emptiness./The word is marked by what it must pass over in silence" ("Unaccomplished"). He discovers that the body, on which the spirit depends, endures, although it is tortured, beaten, exiled; that there is another body within the body with an unknown, gluttonous mouth which must be fed. Although one body dies, the other flourishes; this is a time when one's pride must not depend on the errors of others but on one's own virtues. And although the next to the last poem is entitled "Epilogue" and consists of one verse only, "Life — a wound in non-existence," it is followed by a poem entitled "Night" in which the poet, hearing the leaping of fishes in shallow water, ends with the line: "Ecstatic large orphange — freedom."

Continuing and expanding a method he had first used in *Testimonies II*, Ritsos in *Repetitions* has gathered together poems whose incidents are taken from ancient Greek mythology and history, with frequent references to the *Iliad* and the *Odyssey*. Although at times, as in *Testimonies II*, he uses such incidents to probe into nuances of the general human condition, he now most often uses this method to speak symbolically about contemporary events in order to escape or bypass the censorship of the dictatorship. Just as the actors of ancient Greek tragedy used masks with which to hide their faces, so Ritsos covers his own tormented face during this period with an equally tragic mask to depict a tragedy common to all. He was to expand this method into the long monologue in which he uses the mask of ancient Greek heroes and heroines.

Ritsos finds it pertinent to use ancient myths and symbols to represent contemporary events because, he discovers, history is forever repeating itself under different disguises. His poem "Talos" begins: "Repetitions — he says — repetitions without end; — what fatigue, my God;/the entire change in tints only — Jason, Odysseus, Colchis, Troy,/ Minotaur, Talos — and in these very tints/all the deception and the beauty too — a work that's ours." "After the Defeat" may be taken as typical of the poet's method. Although the speaker is a soldier in an ancient Greek concentration camp, it is obvious that what he describes parallels the events of the colonels' dictatorship, as the date of composition makes even clearer, March 21, 1968, eleven months exactly after the military coup of April 21, 1967. The soldier tells how after the final defeat of the Athenians by the Spartans at Aegospotámi that ended the Peloponnesian War, "our free discussions ceased. Then the Periclean glory also ceased,/ the flowering of the Arts, the Gymnasiums, the Symposia of our wise men. Now/there is heavy silence and gloom in the Agora, and the license of the Thirty Tyrants./ . . . Our papers and our books are in the fire,/and the honor of our fatherland in the trashbin." [Ritsos's own "Epitaphios" (1931) was burnt before the columns of the Temple of Olympian Zeus in Athens by the previous Metaxás dictatorship]. A symbol bridging the centuries and underlining similarities is the anachronistic reference to "barbed wire" in this poem, or the "gramophone" in "Achilles after Death." The final outlook, however, is one of hope, for the imprisoned soldier in "After the Defeat" discovers that it's "good to be here — we may even acquire a new contact with nature,/looking from behind the barbed wire at a little bit of sea, some rocks, plants,/or some cloud in the sunset, deep, violet, moved." In "The Golden Fleece," the poet asks whether the pursuit of that fleece was worth the murders, the trials, the torments suffered, for its possession became a further target for danger. The poem ends: "Nevertheless, what would our life be without this golden (as we say) torment?" And in "Philomel" the poet reminds us that without her suffering, without her severed tongue, Philomel would never have woven her beautiful tunic, nor would she have been metamorphosed into a nightingale. Ritsos knows that the only recourse of the poet is to turn suffering into art. And thus in "The Flute Player," the instrumentalist must distort his face, puff out his cheeks, narrow his eyes, grow physically ugly in order to play with spiritual grace.

The poems in *Barriers* were written, as we have seen, when Ritsos was under restricted arrest in his home in Karlóvasi, Sámos. As in all the poems he wrote under detention and tyranny during this period, these too alternate between despair and the stubborn belief that freedom will triumph and art redeem. Under the bars and barriers of confinement, powers of resistance have been clipped, but the poet can deepen his inner creative sources of resistance that have always helped man withstand submission and permit him, alone, unaided and in isolation, to hold his head high in dignity and thus aid his fellow men from submitting completely to despair. The poet becomes a conjuror, a tight-rope walker, a magician who takes the skulls he finds about him stripped "almost beyond pain," sticks them with hair, glues on ears and noses, inserts colored glass for eyes, paints on cheeks and mouths, then puts his patchwork art on display for passersby to recognize as "Peter" or "Mary." This is all an artist can do during such destructive times: patch things together, give them a resemblance of life and perhaps — on a high, aesthetic plane — the integrity of art. "Ah," he realizes, "What I need myself, I want to give to others too" ("Tricks").

Whenever the artist feels exhausted, as though everything within and without him were sinking, he remembers to utter the word "statue," for throughout his works statues for Ritsos symbolize primarily the creative act itself, the poem, a form of silent testimony and resistance that speaks to those who know how to decipher, even though what may be left at times is only the "serene and inexhaustible/gesture of a severed, marble forearm" ("One Word"). In "The Craftsman," after the sculptor molds a clay statue, he "blows his breath into the clay mouth—/a taste of earth remains on his lips;/ afterwards he takes his hat, walks out into the street/with a guilty smile of secret happiness/as though he were playing the part of a deaf mute, which in fact he is." In "News Report," the victimized dead are hidden in storerooms together with a catalogue of their names so that they may be remembered in the future; the headless statue of a stone angel is also kept so that this Unknown Angel may in time commemorate these dead, like the Unknown Soldier. In "Roughly Square," the poet feigns "the immobility of statues," perhaps their detachment, their bid for immortality.

Ritsos knows in his isolation that his sufferings and the sufferings of his nation have united him all the more indestructibly with all others in the world and have made them blood brothers. In "Blood," a red spot appears at first as only a simple stain, but it spreads until it covers the entire world; and only then, when all the universe has been inundated, can one begin to feel a sense of comradeship, a common fate, and can become ennobled in an enterprise beyond the petty concerns of the self: "And only when we perceived its size, could we feel again/beautiful, simple, back in place, absolved." These poems, as we have seen, alternate between outer despair and inner rebirth. There is always present "The Ready Man," playing dead, but wearing his best suit, his toothbrush in his vest pocket, ready to rise up at the least sign of hope. Ritsos deliberately ends the collection *Barriers* with a poem depicting the Greek land as a ruined garden gone to seed but sprouting miraculously again, if only one person has the courage to water the flowers (the poet to tend to his poetry). The gardner, Greece herself, is caught up in an Assumption that scatters the cool dew of hope to all about her:

RENAISSANCE

No one had taken care of the garden for years. And yet
this year—May, June—it had burst into bloom again by itself,
and all of it blazed up to the fence—a thousand roses,
a thousand carnations, a thousand geraniums, a thousand
    sweetpeas—

colors, color-wings—so that the woman once more appeared
with her old watering can to care for them—beautiful once
    more,
serene, with a vague good faith. And the garden
hid her up to her shoulders, embraced her, won all of her,
and raised her in its arms. And then we saw, on the drop of
    noon,
that the garden and the woman with her watering can were
    taken up into the heavens—
and as we raised our heads high, a few drops from the watering
    can
fell softly on our cheeks, our chins, our lips.

The eighty-seven poems of *Gestures* were written under the
same conditions as the previous poems, in Karlóvasi between Sep-
tember 1969 and May 1970, and were published in 1972. The silent
person, the mute, is used more and more during this period by Ritsos
to indicate that when poets are forbidden freedom of thought and
speech under dictatorships, they are still capable of gestures, move-
ments of the hands, which are at times more eloquent than words,
particularly when a finger is raised high and points with precision to
tyranny. Each poem in itself becomes such a gesture. The significance
of a poem is not so much in what it says but in what it is. What the
poem is does not necessarily reside in what the poem says. The true
gestures of a poem may lie in the seeming ommissions, in the
silences, the gaps that separate image from image, for poetry is "the
few words with the long intervening pauses" ("New Pretexts"). In one
of his one-line verses in *Monochords*, Ritsos makes a sweeping ges-
ture: "You say the poem has meaning. Does it have a body?"
    Among the ninety-nine poems of *Corridor and Stairs*, written
primarily in Athens and Sámos during January to June of 1970 and
published in 1973, is a poem entitled "Corridor" and another enti-
tled "Stairs." It becomes apparent from the use of "corridor" in other
poems in this series that this "austere space," this "oblong uniform-
ity" is a symbol of our passage through life where we move like
sleepwalkers in eternity (much as in Venerable Bede's dark tunnel).
The large clock on the far wall has stopped, revealing nothing, "not
even/the relativity of time." On either side of the corridor are closed
doors, each concealing its own muffled sound as of objects falling—a
tray, perhaps, a plate, a comb, a shoe, a mirror, a treasured obol. We
can only guess; we are never certain. Behind a dim pane can be

discerned the shadow of the landlady, "mute, fleshy, bulky," but we recognize her immediately as Fate herself "spinning her keys like an iron spindle, working out/the new evictions of her tenants and the lovely Helen." But just when we think we have apprehended the poem within the normal ambiguities of images and symbols, the poem ends with a gesture by the landlady which, though clear-cut and precise, is capable of as many interpretations as there are readers: she "takes the chewing gum from her mouth and sticks it on her forehead." Some, of course, will be confident of their interpretations, some may hesitantly hazard at several, and others (among whom I am one) may be content to allow the image to reverberate with many uncertain disturbing implications. Even the poet himself may not have a specific interpretation in mind. What is certain at least, from all the poems we have read closely thus far, is that for Ritsos images in a poem must often be vague, necessarily, because the sources or inspiration from which they arise are themselves vague, having their origins in the inexplicability of life itself. In such verses, the poem does not reside in any one line or image or symbol but in an interplay between all elements that set up correspondences and congruities and connote more than they denote. Even the title is only one element of the poem and not the precise clue to its "meaning." If an analytical method is at times used, either by the reader or the poet, it is simply a method by which to approach the poet's vision, a key, a means of entrance only, after which both poet and reader are left to their own creative resources. In one of his *Hints*, Ritsos writes: "poetry . . . is nothing/more than the wonderful achievement of the inexplicable." And in another: "Perhaps even the shattering of the poem will give birth to the poem." During the dictatorship Ritsos wrote in symbolic and cryptic ways in order to avoid censorship (although his meaning was often clear to those who understand the language of poetry), but there can be no doubt that he believes life itself, and therefore poetry, which "holds the mirror up to nature," must necessarily be cryptic and ambiguous when it wants to deal with emotions or impressions of any complexity, subtlety, or sensitivity.

The corridors of houses often begin or terminate in a flight of stairs, but although the poem "Corridor" does not present an implicit appraisal of life (unless the act of the landlady is considered to be simply an act of great vulgarity, and therefore an ethical valuation) the poem "Stairs" is more in tune with the other poems in this book which, by and large, reflect Ristos' sense of despair and dislocation during the dictatorship. Life becomes a continual and meaningless ascending and descending of stairs leading nowhere; although we are under the illusion that we are traveling, we always remain rooted to the same spot, as on a revolving wheel. Around us we observe that our companions are "successfully disguised," and that we are ourselves always playing roles, uncertain who we are or what we are pretending to be, and therefore as indecipherable to ourselves as we are to others. Perhaps thousands of years ago the Sirens truly existed, truly sang songs that were enchanting and alluring, for the world then had much with which to entice us; but although we will plug up our ears to resist them, both they and their songs have ceased to exist for thousands of years, and our meaningless existence is a mockery of life's empty temptations, a futile gesture.

The poems in *Corridor and Stairs* are heavy with despair: "I cannot pretend any more — he said; / chairs, people, my children, my cigarettes, / it is death, you are death, I am death" ("Only"). The landscape is strewn with carrion, dead owls, embalmed sheep. A man stuffs his mouth with a spider, and laughs. Men have lost their sense of direction, they don't know how to behave in spaces unknown to them, or what style of walk or movement to adopt; when they spruce up and go walking, they know they have left themselves behind locked up in mirrors. It is a time when men wear shoes on their hands and gloves on their feet, a world turned topsy-turvey. Never has Ristos spoken so openly, so despairingly: "So what's the use of sorrow, what's the use of hatred, / of freedom, the absence of freedom . . . what's the use of love and of poetry?" ("What's the Use?"). Statues, symbols of the confusion of flesh turned into form, are now eaten away in gardens by creeping vines and caterpillars; they are blind; their glass eyes have fallen out; their feet lie in rotting water and earth; they have lost their sexual organs; they have become straw dummies; only their pedestals remain. Men have turned to statues, although not into the durability of form but the hardness of stone; and when they try to hide as statues, they betray themselves by "the smoke of a cigarette, a light cough, an erection" ("Shelters"). We know, of course, that such despair is not terminal in Ritsos, that it is only a far, extended swing of the pendulum to the negative, but that it will inevitably swing toward the positive: "If death always is — it is second. / Freedom is always first" (The Fundamentals"). "Nothing is lost," the old women keep repeating, as they weep ("Memorial Services").

The ninety-nine poems of *Caretaker's Desk*, written between March 15 and May 21 of 1971, were first published in a bilingual

Greek and Italian edition in Ravenna in 1975, in French during the same year in Paris, then in Greek in Athens in 1976. In almost every large apartment building in Greece there is a caretaker, a *concierge*, either man or woman or both, who with their families live in a small apartment in the basement and keep their desk in the lobby close to the elevator and stairs. The caretaker acts as doorman and janitor, informs the inhabitants of various matters, gives them their letters, their periodicals or newspapers, attends to the heating of the build-ing or the extermination of vermin, and generally sees to the welfare of the building and its occupants. No one can enter or leave the building, go up or down the stairs or the elevator without the care-taker's knowledge. In vain the occupants may try to keep their private affairs secret from him, for his knowing ears and eyes, his sensitive nose, his honed intuition know all that is going on in the corridors, on the stairs, in the elevators, in the bedrooms. He knows of the conversations, the quarrels, the orgies, the separations, the depar-tures, the returns. He is psychiatrist, doctor, clergyman, confessor. With the compassionate eye of long and tried experience, he watches the women with their babies or their lovers, the various visitors; and when trunks or valises are brought in or taken out, he knows of their hidden contents, the ironed underwear, the cosmetics, the soiled manuscripts, the secret diary. His apartment building becomes the entire world in miniature, and thus the caretaker in these poems by Ritsos, although not specifically present anywhere, makes his pres-ence felt everywhere, a peeping Tom, and keeps a secret journal of the events not only in the building but also symbolically in his city and the universe. When we recall that these poems were written at the height of the dictatorship, we understand that this universal caretaker is no other than the poet himself. Because as an honest and honorable caretaker he cannot, and must not, give away the secrets of the inhabitants he guards, he presents them in such a way that in hiding them he reveals them more deeply to knowing eyes, and through the cryptic code of his journal binds all men into a common brotherhood. His compassion is a heavy burden, for as the poet concludes in "Encounter": "Perhaps the inconceivable can be endured by two together,/although it never reveals itself to more than one."

All but one of the one hundred and twenty two poems of *Scrip-ture of the Blind* were written compulsively at white heat, sometimes two or three a day, in a concentrated two-month period between September 28 and November 28, 1972, during the height of the junta years when it seemed that tyranny, oppression, torture and degradation were to be the fate of Greece for many more years to come. The poet's nightmare landscape in these poems is pervaded by grotesque images and absurdities dislocated and malformed by inhuman times: firing squads, handcuffs, night arrests, betrayals, oppression, guards, gallows, death, exile, surgeons, rubber hoses, identity cards, desertions, revolts, confessions behind which confessions are hidden, diplomats in top hats gathering eggs from a brilliantly lit chicken coop, old women picking out shoes to fit their hands, someone cutting off the five fingers of his hand in order to "believe in the indivisibile" ("Uncertain Obligations"), a naked baby abandoned in a large army boot, the poet holding the severed head of a doll, a dead crow placed as a head on a dead woman's wedding gown.

As all dramatists know—and Ritsos is essentially a dramatic poet—the normality of life can often best be invoked by depicting the frustrated actions of abnormality. There are over sixty different kinds of living persons in these poems, and half as many dead. Those living on the margins of time better invoke normality by their very eccentricity. There are conjurors, public executioners, deserters, dwarfs, hunchbacks, clowns, refugees from insane asylums, animal trainers, burglars, pederasts, necrophiles, failed actors, money changers, murderers. The dead are firemen, warriors, women, the drowned, the slain, the hanged, the crowned, the refrigerated. In addition, there are a handful of old men and women who are in some way invalid, either rachitic, hydrocephalic, armless, sick, leprous, crippled, paralytic, disabled, and in various ways bandaged. And then, in the very heart of these abnormalities, there are a dozen or so deaf persons, mutes, deaf-mutes, and many blind persons who stand as symbols for all other invalids, physical or mental, and who by their very illness point to the health mankind must attain unless it is to commit suicide. By their particular differences, in a world turned upside down, they teach us that it is the deaf who truly hear, the mute who truly speak, the blind who truly see.

Blind men have always played the same semantic role in Ritsos' poetry which they have played in ancient Greek history and mythology. Blind Homer saw beyond the evanescent turmoil of men and gods and plunged into a reality deeper than natural law or mythical dream. Oedipus was led step by step relentlessly toward self-knowledge, and by blinding himself attained redemption at Colonos. The one who led him to such self-knowledge was blind Tiresias, who had lived as a man and woman both, and whose blindness granted him the inner vision of prophecy. Because a blind man does not scatter himself and his vision in outer forms and enterprises, he is forced to attain an inner, a deeper vision, to deal more with the general destiny of man. In addition, the blind are forced to cultivate their remaining senses, hone them to sensitivity, particularly the sense of touch. Even the auditory and abstract qualities of speech become for them palpable in the letters of Braille. With touch, an immediate contact is attained, not externally visible but internally and bodily realized. The deaf, the mute, the blind may become keys by which to enter much of Ritsos' poetry, often through a side door. We find before us many corridors, many other doors, many stairs; although much has been revealed, more has been concealed, and we are forced to try to penetrate into what he has chosen to omit (without marks of ommission) or not to say, giving thus a deeper significance to what he has said: "The word is marked by what it must pass over in silence" ("Unaccomplished," in *Stones*). There is a difference between silence and falling silent: if you have nothing to fall silent about, you have nothing to say.

We all become involved in the debasement of our own civilization, for we have become like those men "who were amassing great debts to pay off smaller debts/and spending both these and those without paying off any" ("The Other Man"). Our words no longer carry weight, "like down/falling on a mute river after a hunter's gunblast" ("Extinction"). We have learned to synchronize our steps with the dead. We begin to wear one mask after another, at first for disguise and protection against what we detest and are threatened by; but we must beware and keep alert, for we are in danger of becoming the mask we use as a shield. We proffer our disguised gloved hands to be handcuffed; but the iron clamps may pierce deeper than we know and cut into our life-veins. Thus, masks can become both a protection against others and a betrayal against ourselves. Yet at times we may use them cunningly, to speak through symbolism and innuendo what is forbidden by censorship, for "the mouths of the masks always gape open,/that the other within them may speak with greater candor" ("Indications")—as the ancient Greek dramatists well knew. All facts, all values become double-faced in such times of trial. Heroes, both recent and historic, are either quickly forgotten, dismissed with a few brief speeches, or distorted and exploited by the ruling dictators.

Perhaps as indicative of such impasse as any other poem in this collection is the one that carries for title the dictatorial year during which the poems were written:

1972

Nights with guns firing and walls. Afterwards, quiet.
Scrubbed floors. The chair legs, straight.
Behind the door, a second door and a third; between them
insulating cotton of the kind used to stuff mouths
of the hungry or the dead. The heroes — he said —
have grown white, dear God, they've grown fat and small.

After the quiet, both apalling and serene, that follows an execution by firing squad, the charwoman comes to scrub away the blood. Amid such devastation, where men and ideals go under, it would seem that even inanimate objects, drenched with blood, would also crumple and fall, but the legs of the chair remain firm and straight, a hint that there are men, like those who have been executed, who will remain upright and firm under every trial. There are endless obstacles to be overcome, one door that opens behind another to infinity, and between each of them the repressive insulating cotton used by all tyrants to prevent outcries either of the hungry or the dead. Then suddenly, we are reminded of the very antithesis that may happen amid such scenes of heroism and moral rectitude, for our heroes — either because of their own compromises, or as exploited by ourselves or our leaders, or because we have forgotten them — abruptly grow old, white-haired and pallid, grow fatter and lose their stature.

In the Greek edition of *Caretaker's Desk*, Ritsos added a prose epilogue entitled "On Rereading the Collections of Poetry *The Wall in the Mirror* and *Caretaker's Desk*" in which he made comments he thought applicable to many of his previous collections of short poems as well; and so they do, but in retrospect they are particularly applicable to the nightmare world and imagery of *Scripture of the Blind*. He felt that his poetry had tended toward a "comic" poetry, but precisely, I would say, in the dictionary definition of that term: "a drama in which the central motive of the play *triumphs over circumstances and is therefore successful*" (italics mine), for one must pass through the inferno and purgatory in order to reach paradise. Such poetry can arrive at a state of grace only after having passed through the tortures of hell, the torments of catharsis, in order to attain the triumphal overview of life Dante envisioned in his *Divine Comedy*. The poems Ritsos wrote during his detention and the dictatorship were his exercises in suffering and purgatory, which marked him, but which he would not allow to destroy him, debase him or exploit him. Redemption for the poet lies in turning this tragic material into "comedy," into a triumphal art form, and thus finding his own still center. The dominated must absorb the shock of the dominator and thereby acquire for himself the impetus of a transferred power, for only thus can the dominated dominate. But whether he wants to or not, he also acquires some of the characteristics of the power forced upon him, and his work is thus twisted awry, comes out often as a grotesque caricature, a tragic distortion which he must keep under control, at times with irony, at times with wit, at times with satire. Only in this way can the poet give meaning and direction to the existentialist absurdity of the modern age: "And almost thus my nature is subdued/To what it works is, like the dyer's hand," Shakespeare wrote hundreds of years ago.

In this manner, tragedy is played with a comic mask, and the result resembles the distorted face of our times that tries to smile but twists into a grimace. To reach such aesthetic conclusions, Ritsos had to pass through and beyond the social realism dictated by his political faith and use the very features of Western decadence with which to play out his roles. Such a dual dilemma is inevitable for a poet like Ritsos who must live out his political ideals in an environment lethally opposed to them. In many ways Ritsos must be as much of a problem to his party as Picasso, for Ritsos' distortions, his caricatures, his nightmares, his Guernicas bear a close resemblance to the painter's in their contorted metamorphoses. Both Picasso and Ritsos have interpreted and depicted their society in the imagery and aesthetics of the environment which surrounds them, and it is perhaps for this reason that poetry of this nature speaks with greater validity and impact to the so-called "decadent" countries. Concomitantly, Ritsos has reached a plane of compassion and tolerance that goes beyond the misunderstanding and misconceptions of party allegiances.

On July 23, 1974, the dictatorship of the colonels fell. Ritsos was now free to write without fear of censorship or military trial, yet the thirty-two poems of *The Distant*, written between January and February of 1975 and published in 1977, are among his most elusive and cryptic. It is now evident that the hermetic approach was not one imposed only by necessity but is part (or had become part) of the poet's aesthetic and vision of life, a counterbalance to the committed poetry of social responsibility he had written to support his political beliefs. As the title indicates, the poems revolve around a feeling of something distant, indefinite, vague, ambiguous, removed, something absent which nevertheless makes its presence sensed, tangible, manifest. What is inexplicable is life itself, the process of creating. The poems reverberate with premonitions, with a feeling that the longed-for vision will appear when we have turned the corner ahead; that behind every object, natural or man-made, is a fleeting essence we can never grasp. The poet tries to make the invisible as visible as possible by molding words over an indefinite shape that it might become palpable, a statue, a poem where through the crevices between words (for they can never be matched or aligned with perfect jointure) a glimpse of the mystery may be caught.

These poems are replete with enigmatic situations presented either without comment or by hints designed to mislead and, by misleading, enlighten. In "Almost Complete" (for nothing is ever complete), the man tells the woman: "You know, death does not exist," and she replies, "I know it, yes, now that I am dead." In "Exhibits" the man takes out his glass eye and asks the woman if she believes him now. She picks up his glass eye and looks at him through it — as though to suggest, perhaps, that the real and the unreal are somehow related. In "Descent," the poet may be Orpheus searching for Eurydice, but his only reward is a large suitcase in which he finds his manuscripts and her two severed hands. We might take a more extended look at "Striding Over," where a man is shown pouring over his accounts, an act which might represent the world of commerce, of duties, of responsibilities. Several drunkards (one of the rare instances where Ritsos does not specify the number with obsessed precision) have fallen asleep. The man steps out into the garden (a contrary image to accounting), but as he walks he feels under his foot the round softness of a bud on which he has inadvertently tread, a detail typical of Ritsos and suggesting here the budding beauty of the garden crushed and all the various implications inherent in such an act taking place in a garden. Then comes a peroration to all man has forgotten, as though of a lost paradise, of unfenced limitless horizons, of distances in which he and his accounts and the drunkards and the crushed bud are but a few details of the absolutes of which man feels he is a part and yet apart: "O distant, you who are forgotten; O divination, / a drop from a secret moon-fountain on a single leaf." The man had turned off the light in the house when he went out, (the house which is the world), but suddenly all seven windows (and all that this magical number suggests) blaze up to reveal the drunkards standing on their beds, showing each other their erections, a vision perhaps of realities we usually keep hidden, whether for good or ill. There is no comment that accompanies this image. Some may interpret it as the vulgarity, the immorality, the absence of reverence in the modern world; others as the vitality, the erotic and fecund element in all of creation; some as the contrast between the far-off, distant, indefinite quality and place of man in this universe and the specific reality on this planet in which he lives out his brief existence. Thus, by presenting several clear, precise and vivid images in juxtaposition to one another, with but a hint of peroration, Ritsos forces the reader to interpret and reinterpret. Everything depends on the strength and quality of the initial vision that brought these images into being and arranged them in just this fashion. If genuine and true, the reader is himself moved to revelations that stir him profoundly; if, however, the original source was shallow, the reader will find himself, after the first initial shock of surprise, trying to put together the shards of an insignificant jigzaw puzzle, bits and pieces of which are missing, though enough may remain to suggest a vague design not worth the trouble of completing even in the imagination.

Ritsos has written two poems to celebrate the historically renowned town of his birth, Monemvasía in the Peloponnesos (Monovasiá is the demotic form). The first, a long poem entitled *Women of Monemvasía* (not included in this collection) was written during August 18–25, 1975, in Karlóvasi and published in 1978. It celebrates the women of his birthplace, young and old, housekeepers and warriors who conceal nothing, keep sleepless sentry before their homes, their hearths, their lamps, their kitchen utensils, and their gods, and embrace life with courage. It celebrates their gallantry, their suffering, their patience, their work, their creativity, women who with their milk and blood nourished the traditions of their town, of Greece, of humanity. Ritsos chose women to represent these Hellenic qualities because only they, he believes (or such young men as Neoptolemus, the hero of the long poem *Philoctetes*) can feel in harmony with their natures, are not ashamed of their sentiments, can express them with nuance, and can thus be used to confess the deeper secrets of the human soul. The sensitivity of a man can often go to such extremes that he attempts to hide it with austere expression.

The thirty-six sections of the second poem, *Monovasiá*, were written primarily in Monovasiá, Karlóvasi, and Athens from September 28, 1974 to October 19, 1976, and were published in 1982.

Monemvasía and its only village is a nine hundred foot rocky prom-
ontory (often called the Gilbraltar of Greece) once connected to the
eastern shore of the Peloponnesos by a narrow strip of land through
which the Byzantines dug a channel with removable bridges in order
to make entry all but impossible to besiegers. The Rock, as it is
known to the inhabitants, was at various times occupied by the Mino-
ans, the Papacy, the Venetians, the Byzantines and the Turks, all of
whom are present to this day in the walls, fortresses, citadels, houses
and churches in various stages of ruin or restoration. Right against the
central gate of the Venetian wall is the house where the poet was born
in 1909, as he informs us in "Items of Identification,"—or in 903
B.C. or 3909 A.D.—for he is also exploring the rebirth of the poetic
temperament at all ages, past, present or future, the courage and
endurance of his nation and the human race, for "The most common
history is dazzling in the eternity of its repetition" ("Deceptive Dis-
coveries") and "the frontiers of the ages . . . are abolished in the
clarity of the pellucid everlasting" ("The Dead"). This house is the
prototype of the old, delapidated grand homes which have haunted
many of his poems, particularly in his long poems "The Dead House"
and *Helen* where the seductress of Troy spent her last years and died.
It is not only the house of the Ritsos family, but also the house of
Atreus, the house of myth, where the poet lived the first twelve years
of his life with his German tutor, his piano lessons, carriages and
servants, all lost because of the gambling and economic incompe-
tence of his father, who died in an insane asylum in Athens. It is the
house haunted by the tubercular deaths of his elder brother and
mother, and by the mental imbalance of his beloved sister.

But the House is nevertheless overshadowed by the Rock, and by
two contrasting elements of this topography from which Ritsos has
derived the landscape and seascape of many of his poems, particularly
in "Romiosíni" and "Lady of the Vineyards." There is, on the one
hand, the hardness, stability, silence and nakedness of stone con-
trasted to the flowing, undulating, limitless luminosity and sonority
of the sea that laps or rages around the Rock from every side. The
antithesis of these two elements, their coexistence, their clash and
their mutual attraction to one another, are to be met in all of Ritsos'
poems. In "Geographic Origins" he describes his duality:

and you, with your back leaning against the rock, with your
   breast
bared to the sea—half fire, half coolness,

cut vertically, double, in a struggle only
to unite water with stone.

"Ah," the poet cries, "the voluptuousness/of two and of one, insuffi-
cient self-sufficiency." In these poems, amid rock and sea, amid Byz-
antine arcades and stoas, innumerable churches, foundations built
over foundations, we can follow the spiritual life of the modern
Greek poet rooted in a rich and varied heritage so assimilated as to
become synonymous with the universal poetic temperament, until
colors of personality and nationality are fused into the absolute white
light of Shelley's "Life like a dome of many-colored glass/Stains the
white radiance of eternity." Indeed, one of the poems in *Monovasiá* is
entitled "White," and it concludes:

Call it complicity—I too saw the seagull's egg. I know white.
I can shout it. I do not shout it. I shut my door early,
I can't shut my eyes. The luster of the huge open sea
disembowels the night like a fish and leaves me to the mercy
    of the mendacious stars.

As we have seen, the chief morphological characteristic of Ritsos'
short poems is their utter simplicity, for they are all written in com-
pound sentence structure with little complexity or subordination of
any importance. Even his long sentences are simple clauses strung
together and connected by semicolons. Indeed, his construction is
even simpler in Greek than it seems in English, for most of his
translators have tended to combine several compound sentences into
one in order to avoid the opening repetition of pronouns in verbal
conjugations which the inflected nature of the Greek language
avoids. Yet these simple sentences are laden with the names of
things, are heavily concrete and rarely abstract, and contain an end-
less variety of images juxtaposed in sequences which are often not at
all simple in their implications but border on the free-flowing associ-
ation of surrealism. It is this tension between simple sentence struc-
ture and ambiguous correlation of imagery that gives to Ritsos' poems
their concentrated, epigrammatic power and their wide range of
reverberations.

And yet, it must be emphasized that Ritsos is not a surrealist
poet, although, like most modern poets throughout the world, he
has made use of the manner in which surrealism has freed the imagi-
nation to make bolder and far-flung comparisons and associations

444

than traditional poets dared. In a surrealist poem there need not be any logical connection between one image and another, for each follows in the flow of dream or free association. Although the range of Ritsos' imagination is extremely wide, he tends to make associations more in the manner of the English metaphysical poets, for no matter how daring they may be or how wide the leaps between image and image, there is always, at least in the poet's mind, a distinct though complicated interrelationship between them, all related to a central theme or themes or vision. In these poems the poet is both concrete and metaphysical, specific and indefinite, clear and ambiguous, especially since his attempt, as he has often stated, is to catch the indivisible in the divisible, the invisible in the visible, perpetual motion in a moment of stasis. He wants to say something specific, but at the same time to permit his readers to pursue many implications. His poems have the hard, individual shape of those pebbles and rocks he gathers on the Aegean shore and inks with intricate designs: these, when cast into the reader's mind make a sharp impact and impression as they enter, but immediately after extend their implications ripple by ripple to the possible limits in the pond or the lake or the sea of each reader's mind. This is perhaps the most fundamental of the technical dualities of Ritsos' method.

As he has pointed out, Ritsos is fond of such words as "or" and "perhaps" which will not permit any one image or statement to stand integrally by itself but will force it always to face a contrast, an opposite, an antithesis, another point of view that breaks down the defenses between thing and thing, thing and person, idea and idea, and enriches the participants with each other's attributes until all partake of that interrelated ambiguity of which the very fabric of life itself is constituted. It will also be noted that the poet does not often speak in the first person, for that would involve him too deeply with things, ideas or images, and he would lose perspective and identity as his own voice and sensitivity suffocate among a multitude of contending forces. Instead, his poems are frequently stigmatized by the third person, "he said" (and all its varieties both singular and plural, masculine and feminine), which permits him thus to detach himself from what is happening or is said in the poem and to look upon them as a spectator and not a participant, as a dramatic poet. This is a technical device, of course, for in these poems Ritsos has expressed some of his most fundamental beliefs, some of his most searching speculations about the human condition, but such a remove permits him at once to be involved with an air of detachment in yet one more of those dualities basic to his general approach.

Although he belongs to a political party whose practical views are not at all dual but exact and mandatory, Ritsos has gone to the root of dialectical materialism in a conflict between thesis and antithesis that results in a new but dissolving synthesis that becomes in turn a new thesis which meets its inevitable negative in a constant evolutionary struggle to find an ultimate synthesis that does not exist. This attempt, at least in most of the poems in this collection, has brought Ritsos to a world view above petty prejudices where he sees all human struggle with a humane and participating compassion, and with an ultimately optimistic belief in man's destiny.

Kimon Friar
Villa Giornata
Ekali, Greece

THE LONG POEMS
OF
YANNIS RITSOS

Kostas Myrsiades

No selection of Yannis Ritsos' poetry in translation could completely represent this prolific poet. Since he began to write poetry in 1917 at the age of eight (his first published work appeared in 1934), he has composed some 181 individual "collections," sequences, or long poems included in more than 96 comprehensive volumes. This body of work covers thousands of poems whose lengths vary from less than a page to over one hundred pages. Now in excess of 5000 pages of print, Ritsos' productivity shows no signs of abating. Seven volumes of poetry were published in each of the three years 1972, 1974, and 1975 and eleven volumes in 1978. It is not unusual for the poet to write two or three poems a day; indeed, for his collection *Doorbell* (1976), he wrote 126 of 135 poems in a two to three week period, composing sixteen in one day. At any given moment, the poet has in his possession twenty to thirty manuscripts ready for publication.

Ritsos' latest work shows the poet's inspiration undiminished. He has honed his keen poetic eye to acute perceptions of that which the reader, in his daily experience, has left unnoticed. He comes across them in Ritsos' poetry infused with color, music, and wonder. The reader is thrust into a recognizable contemporary world in which a great variety of tasks and characters are endowed with a marvel and meaning once relegated to singular mythic acts and ancient heroes. Yet the poetic forms into which Ritsos casts his visions of contemporary life are surprisingly few. Like his themes and techniques, the forms the poet uses are not sharply distinguished, a fact he readily acknowledges in an interview conducted with Ritsos by this author on May 27, 1980:

> I never choose beforehand to write a dramatic monologue, a choral poem, a narrative poem, or a short poem. The ideas and feelings I happen to be expressing at any particular moment need a specific form through which they can be made known. Sometimes I need a short form to express a thought, a feeling.

447

At other times I need a longer form in order to satisfy my need to express something. In the choral poems, the poet speaks through many voices and looks at his theme from various points of view, from different angles, because the theme is such that it needs to be looked at in this way. In the dramatic monologue, the poet speaks through one voice with its various nuances, again because the subject matter needs to be seen in this way. The poet does not arbitrarily choose to write a choral poem or a dramatic monologue or any other type of poem, but rather he chooses the topic, and the way he sees it or wants to look at it dictates the form.

Ritsos' poetry, nevertheless, falls easily into two general categories. The first group, of a page or less, are referred to as "testimonies" (*Studies*, 1974)—a term that serves as the title of three collections of his short poems, *Testimonies* I, II, III (1957–1967). Vignettes, impressions, and unexpectedly juxtaposed images mesmerize the readers of the short poems and jolt them into a recognition of the surprises that await them in reality. The long poems, by contrast, are cast in a dramatic context and approach (their themes) through a variety of viewpoints and through a variety of masks or personas. They demonstrate flexibility in length and kind, appearing in three forms—the narrative poem, the choral poem, and the dramatic monologue—and ranging from two pages to over a hundred. The ten poems chosen for this selection—*Romiosini* (1945–1947) "Peace" (1953) *Moonlight Sonata* (1956), *The Bridge* (1959), *The Prison Tree and the Women* (1962), *Philoctetes* (1963–1965), *Orestes* (1962–1966), *Agamemnon* (1966–1970), *Helen* (1970), and *Belfry* (1972)—represent all three types of long poem from Ritsos' early period to the present.

Of the long poems, the choral poems constitute the smallest group. Similar to the dramatic monologue in their three-part form—prose prologue, poem proper, prose epilogue—they are arranged as a collection of separate speaking parts that function together as a tragic chorus commenting on events from different points of view. The speakers, however, are not identified beyond their sex, age, or occupation except in *Sponge Diver's Chorale* (1960), and *Sounder* (1973)—not included in this collection—where they constitute heterogeneous groups of characters of both sexes, different ages, and various occupations. The choral poem is thus in many ways a monologue in the first person plural. As in *The Prison Tree and the Women*, one voice may end in the middle of a line to be completed by a second voice. Thus the choral poem expresses a continuously developing thought progressively expressed by a number of voices and focuses on a given theme. In *The Prison Tree and the Woman*, the focus is on a tree that grows outside the prison yard. The tree, like the women in the prison, is itself imprisoned but escapes confinement by its upward growth, its form straight and unbending as it rises from the rubble toward the heavens; the women, too, rise above their misery to turn their thoughts to life.

The narrative poem represents the earliest of Ritsos' long compositions, dating from "War," composed between 1930 and 1935. It constitutes the largest group of long poems: eighty-three poems ranging from several pages to over one hundred pages each. As a group, the narrative poems do not share the prose prologue and epilogue structure of the dramatic monologue and choral poems. Rather, like the center section of the dramatic monologue, the narrative is simply a long poem in free verse, which in the instance of "war" is narrated in the third poem.

Early narrative poems (1930–1951) contain some of the poet's most widely-known and popularly received works, including *Epitaphios* (1946) and *Romiosini* (1945–1947), the latter now in its thirtieth edition. *Romiosini* clearly demonstrates the appeal of the early narrative. Its popularity derives form the national pride it evokes and Ritsos' ability to tie the hardships and sufferings of the common Greek to the harshness of the Greek landscape and Greek history. Divided into seven sections averaging forty-seven lines each, *Romiosini* calls on the indestructible spiritual force, "Romiosini," shared by man and the land he occupies:

Ah, who will barricade the passes, what sword will cleave through
    courage,
and what key will lock up the heart that with its door-leaves open
gazes on God's star-strewn gardens?

Necessary to the very being of the modern Greek, "Romiosini" is that without which, by definition, "Greek" may not exist. Thus the contemporary sailor "drinks bitter sea from the winecup of Odysseus" or the guerillas meet the legendary folk hero "Dighenís on those same threshing floors" of Byzantium on which for three days he fought death. The mother who will not "wring her hair over her seven slain sons" is all Greek mothers, ancient and modern, who, like the mythic

449

Niobe, have suffered the loss of seven sons. Past history is bound up with the spiritual force of *Romiosini*, becoming one with present reality as part of a larger continuous whole in which present-day resistance fighters interchange with Odysseus, Dighenís, and the Christian saints. Simple acts thus have national significance and mythical quality:

> A messenger arrives from the Great Valley every morning,
> the sweating sun glitters on his face,
> under his armpit he holds on tightly to Romiosini,
> as the worker grips his cap in church.

The imagery of "Peace," a later, more modest narrative work of sixty-three lines, is characteristic of the simplicity and directness of the early narratives. The poem's repetitions—each verse explores yet another meaning of peace—provokes a musical cadence like that of Ecclesiastes:

> When an automobile stopping in the street does not mean
>   fear,
> when a knock on the door means a friend,
> and the opening of a window every hour means sky.

As Ritsos' later narrative style developed, it approached more closely the dramatic mode. Increasingly in the poems from 1967–1974, as in *Belfry*, voices intrude into the third person narration until as many as a dozen may figure in a poem. The third person becomes a collective "we," or the narration is objectified by such phrases as "he said". In some places, the narration is more subjective, as in the conclusion of *Belfry* where the narrator speaks in the first person singular. Images are culled from the same sources as earlier poems but become disjointed and personal. In *Belfry* a montage of disparate images pictures a bleak, irrational contemporary world in which nothing is held sacred:

> Just think of it, chickens now laying eggs in beds! And
>   Captain Vangélis
> left with his pipe between his teeth
> for the 11:05 boat, clucking and clearing his throat
> so much that the elevator filled with eggshells and panes of
>   glass,

together with those colored pieces from St. Pelayía's West
window.

There the saints kept vigil one by one; in the morning
the leanest with the thick black mustache
waved the large white sheet, the shroud of Jesus,
beckoning to the cabin boy skimming by the sea's edge in his
small motorboat;
just as he rounded the pier, he pissed calmly into the sea.

Later narrative poems displace the literalness of some of Ritsos' earlier
verse to serve the poet's subject with greater economy. The role of the
poet has not, however, changed. He is still, in the poet's own words,
an "agent provocateur": "The true act is the just word, the just/and it
will be heard and it will be done. I no longer have anything to hide"
(Sounder, 1973).
    The dramatic monologues, at least thirty-three works to date,
were first introduced with the publication of Moonlight Sonata in
1956, for which Ritsos won that year's Greek State Prize in poetry. A
long poem in free verse set in the first person singular, the dramatic
monologue is framed by a short prose prologue which introduces the
main characters, action, and setting, and an epilogue which com-
pletes the action. The dramatic monologue is the expression of many
years of intense meditation. As a result, it deals with the contempla-
tion of action rather than with dramatic action itself. Ideas caught in
a labyrinth of images and memories are wrenched from inner depths,
while characters are purposefully kept ambiguous and their place in
time vague. Studied as a microcosm of Ritsos' work, the dramatic
monologue deals with themes essential to his poetry—the irresistible
force of life in the face of death, archetypal feminine tenderness, the
carnal bonds by means of which men are united to those objects
which express them, and the ravaged nightmarish home to which
men are umbilically tied. In Moonlight Sonata, a monologue of
decided beauty and power, the old house has become the past from
which its inhabitants cannot escape, a shell in which they live terror-
ized. Peopled by ghosts and memories that imprison the poet, the
house is itself a living organism:

This house, despite all its dead, does not intend to die.
It insists on living with its dead

451

on living off its dead
on living on the certainty of its own death
and even on accomodating its dead on dilapidated beds and
  shelves.

The isolation forced upon the poet in the house expresses a recognition of time lost and connections missed:

I know that every human being goes his way alone toward
  love,
alone toward glory and toward death.
I know this. I've tried it. It doesn't help.

In *The Bridge*, a figure identified as the poet explores the complement to that theme:

I believe that the first act of justice is the correct distribution
  of bread,
I believe that the first step to progress is the increase of the
  production of bread for all,
I believe that our first duty is peace,
I believe that our first freedom is not our loneliness
  but our comradeship . . .

It is such oneness, found ultimately in everyday occurrences, that bridges the chasm between heaven and earth.

The choral poems and dramatic monologues together constitute a third of Ritsos' published works. The full impact of the dramatic monologues, however, was not to make itself felt until the publication of ten mythic monologues beginning with *Orestes* in 1965 and ending with *Phaedra* in 1978.[1] In these most completely realized dramatic pieces, Ritsos produced some of his greatest poetry, a testament to the effects he was able to create through that form of poetry.

The ten mythic monologues make up a classical cycle in which ancient myths are presented as themes upon which the poet works contemporary variations. As the poet passes through time into timelessness, the myths flicker like shadows across the poem. Suspended in time, throwing the light of the past on the darkness of the present, the figures of these poems proclaim no truth, affirm no path. *Philoctetes* (1963–1965) places its figures in a world of seeming: a young man with "Achilles' features but slightly more spiritualized, as though he were his son Neoptólemos"; Philoctetes stranded on an island, "perhaps Lemnos." In a scene recalling Aeschylus' *The Libation Bearers*, Ritsos begins the monologue in *Orestes* with the return of Orestes and someone "like Pylades" to Argos.

> Two young men in their twenties stood before the gates. The expression on their faces made it seem as though they were trying to remember or recognize something and yet everything seemed so familiar, so moving to them, only somehow smaller—much smaller—than they remembered while they were in that strange land; as if they belonged to a different place, to a different time, —even the walls, the huge stones, the lion-gate and the palace beneath the shadow of the mountain, were all smaller. It is summer already. Night is falling. The cars and the big charter busses have gone. The place can breathe again in peace, —a deep sigh from the mouths of ancient graves and memories. A piece of newspaper, blown by an indefinite breath, fluttered on the burnt grass. The footsteps of the nightwatchman and then the large key that locks the inside gate of the tower are heard.

But the place looks different, smaller, since these two men were last here many years ago. The major landmarks are still in place—the lion gate, the palace—but into this supposedly Mycenaen world private cars and tourist buses intrude, and we are plunged back into the present. It is Ritsos, the modern Orestes, who stands before present-day Mycenae, wrestling with questions of love, death, and freedom which once plagued the ancient figure. On the same spot on which Orestes stood, stands modern man; time has stopped. The ancients are neither great models nor distant mysteries; they are ourselves. Neither Orestes nor Philoctetes is, however, permitted to escape his fated role:

> How does it happen that, with the smallest piece of thread
> from some of our moments, they weave
> our whole lifetime, harsh and dark, thrown
> over us like a veil from head to toe, covering
> our entire face and hands.

A man prepared to acknowledge past misdeeds and make amends, the hero of *Agamemnon* also finds that fate has a reality that reality itself lacks:

> A man, handsome, bare-headed, in battle dress, with a large, blood-stained sword in his hand, enters the empty hall. With his left hand, he takes the helmet from the console. He puts it on backwards. The horsetail in his face. Like a mask. He leaves. The voice of the raving woman: "Citizens of Argos, it's already too late, too late, citizens of Argos—"

In *Helen*, a poem for which the poet admits a special affection, the worthlessness of the past as a model for the present is brought home. Now an "old woman—one, two hundred years old!" whose servants fight over her possessions as they wait for her to die—she was once the most handsome woman in the world, over whose favors the strongest fought:

>   How pointless it all was,
> how purposeless, ephemeral, and insubstantial—riches, wars,
>   glories,
> jealousies, jewels, my own beauty.
>   What foolish legends,
> swans and Troys and loves and brave deeds.

Like her male counterparts of the other classical monologues, Helen is closed in the confines of her memories. She decays like the house she occupies, her past a void. The face that launched a thousand ships is overgrown with warts. Her body ravaged by death, her home is looted by greedy neighbors:

> "Ah, ah," they cried, as they hid things under their dresses
> Another phone call. Already the police were coming up.
> They sent the servants and women away, but the neighbors
> had time to grab the bird cages with the canaries, some
> flower pots with exotic plants, a transistor, and an electric
> heater. One of them grabbed a gold picture frame.

There are two aspects to Ritsos' long poems that require comment: his themes and his techniques. To understand those aspects, it is useful to refer to the poet's view of the role of poetry and the poet. Poetry, according to Ritsos in an interview in 1976,

> fulfills the poet's highest priority, which is to bring together fraternally human strengths and to organize them against tyranny, injustice, and vileness. Such a mission always leads the true poet. And the greatest honor for such a poet is to carry his social responsibility on his own shoulders to the end. It is in this way that the masses find worthy spokesmen and leaders.[2]

What Ritsos accepts without question is the poet's duty to serve the people as one of them and to purge egocentricity and personalism from his work. The poet, humbling his art, makes ours what is already ours, unhurriedly and simply. He expects no more recognition than the analogous mother who, like the poet with his poetry, gives birth to and nurtures her progeny. He subordinates himself to the people because, as Ritsos suggests in an essay on the Russian novelist and journalist Ilya Ehrenburg (*Studies*, 1974), the individual cannot be saved alone and for himself. Thus the poet must become more substantial for society, for the historical period in which he finds himself, for his nation, and for the problems that afflict that nation. In the end, the poet who has turned out of his private world into the social realm has, for Ritsos, achieved universality. Like Neruda, Ritsos suggests that to lay aside the private struggle and take on society's burdens is to speak not only with the voice of one's people (as he makes clear in "Thoughts on the Poetry of Paul Eluard" in *Studies*), but ultimately with the world's voice:

> The entire world begins to speak through the poet's mouth. That is why his voice deepens, widens, and strengthens. Isolated, specific, and private feelings are not served by a strong voice. They are only ridiculed by it.

Among Ritsos' themes, as a result, the socio-historic dominates. As Kimon Friar notes in *Modern Greek Poetry: From Cavafis to Elytis,* at the time Ritsos began to write few Greek poets other than Kostas Várnalis showed concern for the plight of the working man or the common peasant. Yet Ritsos' first collection of poetry, pragmatically titled *Tractor* (1930–1934), included such poems as "To Marx," "To the Soviet Union," "The Individualist," and "Revolutionaries." Again in such poetry as "Letter to Joliet-Curie" (1950) and "The

World's Neighborhoods" (1949–1951) the collective or "we" point of view dominates. In more recent poetry, those who people his poems are once more peasants—from the old village women of *The Women of Monemvasía* (1975), to the forty-eight speaking voices representing a cross-section of the working class in *Sounder* (1973).

Ritsos' characters are either of the masses, or national laic heroes—the young worker of the May 1936 demonstration in Thessaloniki in *Epitaphios*; the resistance fighters in *Romiosini*; Aris Veloukhiótis, leader of ELAS (The National Popular Liberation Army) in *Postscript to Praise* (1945); Nikos Veloyánnis, the assassinated Marxist is *The Man with the Carnation* (1952); Grigoris Lambrákis, the socialist deputy assassinated in Thessaloniki in 1963, in *May Lament* (1963); or Nikos Zahariádhis, Secretary General of KKE (the Greek Communist Party) in *Our Comrade* (1945). International popular heroes also figure in his poetry—Patrice Lumumba, the African revolutionary leader, in *The Black Saint* (1961), Marx and Christ in *Great Hour* (1930–1934). On the whole, however, the events he focuses on are those that shaped recent Greek history—the Polytechnic University student unrest in 1973 in *A Week's Diary* (1973) and in *Body and Blood* (1976); American involvement in Greece and Vietnam in *Belfry*. Even such contemplative verse as *Philoctetes, Orestes, Agamemnon,* and *Helen* interpret contemporary events. Indeed, the dates of composition, included at the end of each poem, themselves remind the reader to remain aware of events of the times. To read Ritsos' poetry is thus to follow the most important stages of modern Greek political history and to witness its effects on the lives of the people. Not only an early poem like "Germany" (1930–1934), which documents the brutality of pre-World War II German ideology, but also such later poems as the classical monologue cycle, which speak of events surrounding the Papadhópoulos regime of 1967–1974, are of socio-historical interest.

Ritsos' social and historical themes do not, however, completely describe Ritsos' poetry. Particularly in the dramatic monologues and in many of the choral poems, the classical past provides an equally compelling source of themes, as well as a vehicle by means of which Ritsos could treat contemporary problems with historical detachment. Moreover, Ritsos uses the past to tie together various aspects of the Greek experience into one coherent whole. *The Annihilation of Milos* (1969), loosely based on the massacre of the inhabitants of Milos by their Athenian allies (described in Thucydides' *Peloponnesian Wars*, V), presents three old women who have lost their sense of time and live in their memories on a lonely and isolated present-day Milos. "Yes," we are told, "they are women of Milos, but on another island now . . ." In *The Dead House* (1959), vague references to a bath, a mistress as a murderess, such terms as "slaughtered," and the dead house of the title evoke the Mycenaen past and the myth of the House of Atreus. But such allusions refer equally to Medea and to the present as well as to past horrors. The psychology and suffering of the figures is thus extended across time.

In *Phaedra* (1974–1975), Ritsos' most recently published dramatic monologue, familiarity with the myth is again freely exploited. Only essential information is given. The prose sections suggest the Hippolytus-Phaedra story, the figures being nowhere mentioned by name but, rather, implied by their actions and the actions of others. Complete identification of the myth, however, requires the epilogue, as if the poet wishes his audience to hang suspended in uncertainty until he closes off his action. Only then is the poet willing to display the unmistakable signs of the myth—the hanged Phaedra, the note, the curse, the nurse, Antiope, the statues of Aphrodite and Artemis.

The initial setting, too, is typically vague and undetermined. The action occurs in a large room of a great old house, a common setting for the monologues. A rapid montage of images—the chair, the couch, the room, the silence—is displayed by the omniscient writer, creating a concrete and definite appearance that is really no more than a Spring afternoon in some large old room where a woman "perhaps over 40" rhythmically sways in a rocking chair. While immediacy is suggested by "the young man who comes out of the shower, naked, dripping wet, with a towel around his waist," the reality of present time is ultimately compromised by interjected references to a supposed past of slaves and classical gods, among other general references to the Hippolytus-Phaedra story itself. In his spare and taut style, Ritsos sketches a picture in his prologues and epilogues that seems far more substantial and rooted than that which the reader is actually provided. Focusing on minute details of little immediate interest to the drama, Ritsos creates a mood of concrete intangibility. This is the "poetic vapor" that is not only to envelop the imaginary stage of the prologue and epilogue, but which, by inverting its function, will later give expression to the inexpressibly abstract, that which weighs so heavily on the speakers of the poet's central monologues.

Social, historical, and mythic themes in Ritsos' poetry are irretrievably bound to personal themes deriving as much from the poet's own life as from his identification with the common Greek, his love of the land, or his sense of his heritage. Certainly Ritsos' personal history has been a rich and deeply felt resource for his poetry. At the age of twelve he lost his older brother, Dhimítris, to tuberculosis. Within three months, his forty-two year old mother died of the same disease; five years later Ritsos himself became a victim of tuberculosis. His father, mentally unstable, was interned in the asylum of Daphni near Athens in 1932. His sister, Loúla, suffered mental problems and was institutionalized in 1936. From 1927 to 1938, Ritsos found himself in and out of sanitoriums, working in the interim as a professional actor and dancer with a variety of theatrical groups. In early January, 1945, he joined EAM (The National Liberation Front) forces in Northern Greece and wrote the theatrical work *Athens in Arms* for the Peoples' Theatre of Macedonia. Exiled on the island of Lémnos and interned in a number of camps (Kondopoúli, Makróni-sos, Áyios Efstrátios) from 1948 to 1952, he was at last provided fifteen years of respite during which he produced half of his poetic output. The Papadhópoulos coup on April 21, 1967 led to further arrests and imprisonment on the Greek islands of Yáros and Léros. In August 1968, he was hospitalized at the cancer center in Athens for forty-four days and then exiled to Samos under house arrest at his wife's home.

Autobiographical sections of Ritsos' poetry deal with the poet's tragic family experiences, his personal involvement in Greece's recent political history, and his vision of his poetic mission. Autobiographical references interpenetrate social and mythic themes throughout his poetry, as we find in *The Dead House* in which the poet introduces details of his own family life. Here an aged Electra in Argos speaks of her two brothers and two sisters, a deviation from the myth which tells of one brother and three sisters:

And the house—not Agamemnon's. And the younger
    brother
with the artistic tendencies? Who was he? There was
no second brother. So then? What did he need the house
    for?[3]

The house is the poet's own, the family his own two brothers and two sisters. Taking on the persona of Electra and acting in the space which she occupies, the poet can speak through her of his personal life, remaining at the same time alienated from it. As we see in his description of the rooms in *The Dead House*, the poet's objectivity allows him to look at "things from up high/from some distance, so we can have the feeling/we're overseeing and ruling over our fate."[4] Only at a distance can he come out of himself, rendered whole enough to look at himself, in himself, to manipulate this experience, to command it, and thus to draw from it the lessons it offers. At dusk, as "everything bends down low to the warm earth,"[5] the poet is shed of his desires and, shivering with the sharp, clean, healthy coldness of his objectivity, he is able to see all experience as one. From this distance one can see that things are as they always were, today's experiences the same as yesterday's. Distance and meaning, "only lightning lights them and puts them out for a moment/pierces them and nails them, transparent in the void, void themselves."[6] In *The Dead House* the poet recalls the mythic past through associations with events and objects whose place in time is not itself certain, keeping the reader suspended in time:

> The lady forgot to dress-up her children. She entered the
>   bath.
> She filled it with warm water and didn't wash herself. After a
>   while
> she locked herself in her room and put on her make-up in
>   front of the mirror
> red, red, deep red, like a mask, like a dead woman, like a
>   statue,
> like a murderess or even like someone murdered already.
> And beyond, the sun was setting[7]

Vague references to the bath, to the lady as a murderess, to the word "murdered," to the dead house of the title, evoke the Mycenean past and the myth of the House of Atreus. But the references are not specifically of one period or one myth. The lady, the children, the bath could refer to Medea as well as to Clytemnestra, to present as well as past horrors. Time and space are here dissolved so that the poet may extend through time the psychology and suffering of these figures. Ritsos can see himself in Clytemnestra or Medea because he *is* Clytemnestra, he *is* Medea; all Greeks participating in Greek history have experienced their agony. By extension, in the poem "The Actual Cause" (1969), Agamemnon becomes all men who give no credence to their Cassandras:

No, it is not that Apollo withdrew his pledge
and that spitting on Cassandra's mouth removed
all persuasion from her speech, thus rendering for her
and others ineffective her prophetic words—no. Only
that no one wants to believe the truth. And when you gaze
    at
the net inside the bath, you believe it readied
for tomorrow's fishing trip and heed not all within you
and without, ascending, on the castle's marble stairs,
the vague augery in ill-fated Cassandra's pleas.

This uninterrupted thread of history is lent eloquence by the poet in "Ancient Amphitheatre (as translated by Kimon Friar in *Modern Greek Poetry*.)" Here, a Greek youth in the center of an ancient amphitheatre cries out:

                            opposite,
from the precipitous mountain, the echo answered—
the Greek echo, which does not imitate or repeat
but simply continues to a height immeasurable
the eternal cry of the dithyramb.

Far from imitating or repeating the splendor of the original (the past), the echo (the present) intensifies it, illuminating and extending the eternal cry of the human condition.

Thus, in Ritsos' poetry the focus is on ingesting the past; anachronism gives way to synchronism as all Greek history is understood to exist at the same moment. The ten-year-long Trojan struggle from which Ritsos draws most of his masks becomes the decade of war from 1912 to 1922 in which the Greeks fought the Turks; it becomes as well the decade of Greek resistance and the Greek Civil War between 1940 and 1950. In each era, the squabbling between comrades and factions is common; in each era the greed, self-interest, and self-aggrandizement of others cause the pain and suffering of an Ajax, of a Ritsos, of any man fighting for his ideals. That is why it is possible for Ritsos' Ajax (in *Ajax*, 1967–1969) to describe the darkness in which he lives by comparing it to being

inside a big sombre church in the burning sun, the ikons,
pale, lofty, whispering among themselves about you—
a colossal snake, a lion with a thorn in its paw,

460

a severed head on a tray two darkened eyes,
a large solitary one . . . .

Christian myth becomes interchangeable with pagan myth. The two
are woven into one uninterrupted thread, for both are part of the
modern Greek experience. Alongside a St. Demetrios or a St. George
(indicated by the large snake used to depict these saints in Byzantine
iconography), alongside the severed head of St. John the Baptist, are
placed Oedipus' gouged-out eyes and the Cyclops' single large one.
In *Romiosini*, the Minoan sunset still fades in the distance where
ancient Greece still exists. The old women spinning the sea, like the
three ancient fates who might have sat on the same spot, descend on
the city of Misolóngi, the site of a famous siege in the years of the
War of Independence.

The eternal nature of time for Ritsos has a spare and essential
aspect. As in *Ajax*, the number of characters are reduced. Only a
voiceless and nameless figure (Ajax's wife Técmessa) appears briefly
as an audience for Ajax in the prose prologue and epilogue of the
poem. The reader is informed in the prologue that,

A large-bodied, very powerful man lies on the floor, among
broken dishes, pots, butchered animals, cats, dogs, chickens,
sheep, goats, a white ram tied erect on a pole, a donkey, two
horses. He wears a white nightgown, torn, full of blood —
somewhat like an ancient robe — which practically leaves his
robust body bare.

The setting, once again, is anywhere in time. The butchered animals,
the nightgown full of blood, "somewhat like an ancient robe," are
suggestive of Sophocles' *Ajax*, while the "broken dishes, pots" place
the figure in a contemporary situation. Synchronic and imprecise,
such a scene establishes the poet's treatment of the past as continuously
present history and not as isolated phenomena, at the same time that
it feeds the personal meaning of Ritsos' heroes, for the emotions
which condition the inner man are basically the same in all ages. *Ajax*
indicates how this process operates. Here action is suspended and the
poet focuses on the outcry of a wronged Ajax, based on the famous
speech in Sophocles' play which occurs some 400 lines into that
work:

                                    My name is Ajax:
            Agony is its meaning. And my fortunes
            Are cause indeed for an agony of wailing. . .
                          . . . yet am I left an outcast
            Shamed by the Greeks, to perish as I do![8]

From Ritsos' opening refrain (which also closes the poem) — "Woman,
what are you looking at? Close the door, latch the windows, bolt the
pen" — the focus of the poem is a man who, having served his country
selflessly in his best years, now finds himself rejected by man and
god:

    I yearn nothing — what is the worth? — I would rather want.
    My old feats seem like lies. All the prizes meant for me,
        others usurped
    through crafty lots and briberies; when I, during the hour of
        judgment in the life of the Greeks,
    cast into the helmet not fresh lumps of earth
    but my big, clear, nuptial ring and came forth first
    against the enemy body to body. And again,
    when the ships were burning and smoke and flames filled the
        sky
    as if the sea ignited, when Hector
    leapt unrestrained into the trenches, I again
    stood first before him. The Atridae seem not to remember;
    they care only for pillage and rewards. Let them apportion
        these
    with fraud, deceit, and fear — til when? One day
    they too will stand naked before the night and its lengthy
        road;
    then in nothing will the stolen shield be of use, no matter
        how beautiful and big.

Ostensibly the passage concerns Ajax's condemnation of his comrades
for denying him the armor of Achilles which, through deceit, went to
Odysseus. A closer view, however, reveals that Ajax is but a mirror of
Ritsos himself who rails at his own comrades for not recognizing his
long struggle for the freedom of his country (a struggle which for Ritsos
meant seven years of prison and torture and seven more of broken
health in sanatoriums). *Ajax* is a cry of anguish against those friends
who forsook him in a moment of need (his detention in Léros in 1967

by the Papadopoulos' regime in a camp for left-wing activists). Perhaps most importantly, Ajax serves as a mask behind which, protected from prying eyes, the poet is free to confess himself. Distanced from his own emotions, Ritsos objectifies them. He is lucid, revealing, and yet safe from the government censors who sought him out. On Léros and later on Samos, to which Ritsos was removed in 1968 in response to a recurring tubercular condition, the poet wrote his *Ajax*, punished by the very nation he had fought to protect it against the Nazis. Thus when Ajax says, "I cast into the helmet not fresh lumps of earth/but my big, clear, nuptial ring and came forth first/against the enemy body to body," it is Ritsos speaking to fellow Greeks who fled the Nazi occupation, reminding them that while they fled into hiding and exile to await the war's end, he remained behind, offering his most valuable possession, his life. It was he who stood before Hector, the enemy's best, while others amassed what wealth could be made from the destruction of their fellow humans. With all his suffering, the poet learns, "in nothing will the stolen shield be of use, no matter how/beautiful and big." It is a lesson learned by standing "naked before the night and its lengthy road," divesting oneself of all hates, prejudices, and material wants and accepting forthrightly life's true meaning, the realization and presence of death. Ritsos' hero comes to this conclusion much in the manner of another contemporary traveller, Nikos Kazantzakis' Odysseus, who, in the final verses of *The Odyssey*, moves his hand momentarily to pluck off his bare body a piece of down fallen from a passing bird as he sails naked and motionless on an iceberg toward the South Pole. Even a piece of down is excessive material weight for the modern Odysseus who has come face to face with life's inner meaning.

In this quest for meaning, it is Ritsos' highly visual style that confers upon his poetry the immediacy and concreteness of present reality. In "Peace," he creates that effect through images of daily life — a worker emerging freshly-shaven from a neighborhood barbershop, the odor of "warm bread on the world's table." Ritsos' personifications ("the Cretan moon rolls through its pulleys,/creak, crack with twenty rows of cleats on its bootsoles," *Romiosini*), and similies ("My good ladies with your white thighs, your white buttocks like boiled cauliflower," *Sounder*) result in striking images that give unexpected life to banal objects.

Early sensitivity to domestic detail is transformed in later poems into a preoccupation with hard material reality, as in the opening verse of *Belfry*:

The mute days came sprawled on the sidewalks
above hidden sewers with warped shoes;
in a corner of the room, stilts covered with a bedsheet —
these were what the nightmare wore at night up to the
    curtain frame,
and hunger strikers with a cut lemon in their fists,
waiting, waiting, shutting their eyes more and more tightly.

Moreover, as his style changes, the added meaning created by juxtaposition of objects increasingly determines the mood of his poems. Where striking images characterize earlier poems, they dominate later ones. The growing body of Ritsos' poetry capitalizes more and more completely on its wealth of images, just as it grows more and more to rely on the interweaving of themes. In *Romiosini, Philoctetes, Orestes, Agamemnon,* and *Helen,* memories pass before the reader as a series of ancient and contemporary masks displayed in tableaux that come to life at the touch of some unknown stimulae. In *Belfry,* lucid images race before the reader who finds himself invited to a feast of disembodied thoughts. In *The Net* (1970), disturbed, fragmented thoughts are heaped in nightmarish confusion interspersed with periodic moments of sober clear-headedness. In *Ismene* (1966–1971), a comparable process results in a Dionysian frenzy of sensuality and violence.

In the midst of such profusion, the highly personal tone of Ritsos' poetry is carefully muted. The poet's insistence upon distancing himself from the private themes he explores is indicated by the number and variety of voices he uses to speak to his readers. Such objectivity creates, nevertheless, its own effects, for it lends Ritsos' art a sense of the dramatic. The third person point of view in the narrative poems implies not only the voice of the poet, but that of the originator of the comment and the receiver. The dramatic confrontation is thus between the poet and reader, the poet and the speaking figure of the poem, or between different aspects of the poet himself. In the monologues, the dramatic element is created by the poet setting his characters upon a stage. In *Agamemnon,* for example, the prologue "sets" a "stage" upon which appear a warlord and his wife:

He places his left hand on her hair, careful lest he spoil her beautiful coiffure. She pulls away. She stands upright, a little further away. His smile appears distant, weary. He speaks to her. You don't know if she is listening.

Knowledge of the myth of the house of Atreus specifies the reader's expectation, suggesting a drama the image of which will remain with the reader throughout the monologue that follows. In *Philoctetes*, too, the poem is set like an opening scene revealed by a rising theatre curtain:

> Summertime on the deserted shore of an island — perhaps Lemnos. Early evening, colors beginning to fade. A boat anchored in the rocky cove. The crew, a little way below, washing, exercising, wrestling, their shouts and laughter audible. Here above, two men are seated before a stony cavern fitted out as a dwelling place.

A dialogue is implied, a dramatic interaction is anticipated.

The implied presence of a stage in the dramatic monologues reinforces this created sense of the dramatic, while in the choral poems the staccato and rapid movement of the voices creating the ritualistic effect of a classical chorus suggest a chorus' movements as well. In such a choral poem as *News Bearers* (1967–1969), progressive shortening of the long lines with which the poem begins enhances both the sense of movement and the reader's sense of participation in a performance. Refrain-like repetition — "Bone, rock, iron — iron, rock" — suggests the cadence of some ancient performed ritual.

In itself, repetition is a characteristic technique of Ritsos' poetry. Earlier, its use is incantational or improvisatory, somewhat like oral poetry, so that when the poet experiences a rush of emotion in "The World's Neighborhoods," it is replicated by the breathless haste of the spoken word:

> Freedom or death
> freedom or death — the people
> in the open cars shouting — and the leaflets
> and the people chasing the leaflets and shouting hurrah
> stumbling over the tanks and shouting hurrah
> hurrah, hurrah, hurrah,
> freedom or death, freedom or death — the people
> in the open cars shouting
> freedom or death, freedom or death

the people who fought and fell
who fell and smiled
who kissed the people and smiled
who pulled the wedged bullets out of their chests with their
    fingers
and came back among us and fought
and fought and smiled.

In later poems, the repetition is controlled, balanced, and musical. The repetition of "house" at the beginning of each of four lines in *Belfry*, for example, has such balance and tone:

House with a garden, with red shirts on the washline,
house with a balcony, with plaster statues,
house without a balcony, itinerant knife-grinders piss in the
    corner,
house with a lank Crucifixion outside the door, with the
    paralyzed woman on the bed . . .

Here, as Kimon Friar has pointed out in *Modern Greek Poetry*, the poet capitalized on his fondness for music, an affection that carries over to the titles as well as to the structuring of many poems, including *My Sister's Song* (1936–1937), *Spring Symphony* (1937–1938), *Rhapsody of Naked Light* (1939), *An Old Mazurka to the Rhythm of Rain* (1942), *The Ocean's March* (1939–1940), *Moonlight Sonata* (1956), *Exercises* (1950–1960), *May Lament* (1963), *Eighteen Short Songs of the Bitter Motherland* (1968), and *A Hymn and Lamentation for Cyprus* (1974).

Yannis Ritsos' poetry is one built upon suffering that metamorphoses its most immediate meaning into universal statement. Using for its material the inescapably mundane, it penetrates the most intimate feelings of sentient man. While his appeal as a poet may lie in his ability to integrate his roles as poet of the socio-historic, the mythic, and the autobiographical, his genius is his ability to achieve a poetry of instinct and inspiration, a poetry detected, as expressed in his short poem "There" (*Scripture of the Blind*), "in an intangible position of studied silence—there/where poetry always waits to be discovered." Out of Ritsos' early verse of politics and pain comes a poetry that refuses to be confined. In this, as Ritsos claims in "The Poem and the Poet" (*Scripture of the Blind*), it is like

the tigress' tongue
in the cage — a red tongue, venomous, between
her pointed gleaming teeth . . . .

Kostas Myrsiades
West Chester University

* * *

NOTES

1. *Orestes* (1962–1966), *Philoctetes* (1963–1965), *Persefone* (1965–1970)
    Agamemnon (1966–1970), *Ismene* (1966–1971), *Ajax* (1967–1969),
    Chrysothemis (1967–1970), *Helen* (1970), *The Return of Iphigenia*
    (1971–1972), *Phaedra* (1974–1975).
2. Yannis Ritsos, as quoted by Stelios Yeranis, *Ta mikra mou thavmata*
    (Athens: Kedhros, 1974), inside front cover.
3–7. Yannis Ritsos, "The Dead House," in *The New Oresteia of Yannis
    Ritsos*, translated by George Pilitsis and Philip Pastras (unpublished
    manuscript).
8. Sophocles, *Ajax*, translated by John Moore, in *Sophocles II: Complete
    Greek Tragedies*, Edited by David Greene and Richmond Lattimore
    (New York: Modern Library, 1957), p. 27.

لی

YANNIS RITSOS:
A CHRONOLOGICAL INDEX
OF PUBLISHED AND SELECTED
UNPUBLISHED WORK
1938–1988

Compiled by Kostas Myrsiades

Key: Indented titles represent individual "collections," sequences, or long poems included in more comprehensive volumes.

TITLE	DATE(S) OF COMPOSITION	DATE OF PUBLICATION
TRACTOR		1934
Tractor	1930–1934	
Portraits	1930–1934	
Great Hour	1930–1934	
PYRAMIDS		1936
Pyramids	1930–1935	
Odes	1930–1935	
War	1930–1935	
EPITAPHIOS	1936	1936
MY SISTER'S SONG	1936–1937	1937
SPRING SYMPHONY	1937 1938	1938
THE OCEAN'S MARCH	1939–1940	1940
AN OLD MAZURKA TO THE RHYTHM OF RAIN	1942	1943
TRIAL		1943
The Stranger	1935	

TITLE	DATE(S) OF COMPOSITION	DATE OF PUBLICATION
Lamp of the Poor and Humble	1936	
A Firefly Lights the Night	1937	
Midday Summer Dream	1938	
Earth and Light	1939	
The Seagull's Young Brother	1939	
Rhapsody of Naked Light	1939	
Sea Rain	1941	
Saturday Night in Autumn's Quarter	1941	
Midday Windows	1941	
Winds in the Western Suburbs	1941	
Behind the Last Cloud	1942	
OUR COMRADE	1945	1945
THE MAN WITH THE CARNATION	1952	1952
VIGILANCE		1954
Silent Season	1941–1942	
Shift of the Evening Star	1941–1942	
Sojourn of the Sun	1943	
Three Chorals	1944–1947	
Romiosini	1945–1947	
Letter to Joliet Curie	1950	
We and the River	1951	
Skirmish	1952	
Good-Bye Vladimir Mayakovsky	1953	
Peace	1953	
MORNING STAR	1955	1955
MOONLIGHT SONATA	1956	1956
THE WORLD'S NEIGHBORHOOD	1949–1951	1957
ALEXANDER BLOK: THE TWELVE [Translation]	n. d.	1957
CHRONICLE	1957	1957

TITLE	DATE(S) OF COMPOSITION	DATE OF PUBLICATION
FAREWELL	1957	1957
PITCHER		1957
Sob	1957	
All Soul's Day	1957	
Long Island	1957	
Year's Spirit	1957	
The Mountain with the Plan		
Trees	1957	
WINTER CLEARNESS	1957	1957
WHEN THE STRANGER COMES	1948	1958
UNSUBJUGATED CITY	1952–1953	1958
THE ARCHITECTURE OF TREES	1958	1958
BEYOND THE SHADOW OF THE CYPRESS TREES [Drama]	1958	1958
THE OLD WOMEN AND THE SEA [Drama]	1958	1959
A WOMAN BESIDE THE SEA [Drama]	1959	1959
THE WINDOW	1959	1960
THE BRIDGE	1959	1960
ANTHOLOGY OF RUMANIAN POETRY [Translation]	n. d.	1961
THE BLACK SAINT	1961	1961
POEMS, VOLUME I		1961
Tractor	1930–1934	
Pyramids	1930–1935	
Trial	1935–1943	
The Stranger	1935	

TITLE	DATE(S) OF COMPOSITION	DATE OF PUBLICATION
Lamp of the Poor and Humble	1936	
A Firefly Lights the Night	1937	
Midday Summer Dream	1938	
Earth and Light	1939	
The Seagull's Young Brother	1939	
Rhapsody of Naked Light	1939	
Sea Rain	1941	
Saturday Night in Autumn's Quarter	1941	
Midday Windows	1942	
Winds in the Western Suburbs	1941	
Behind the Last Cloud	1942	
Sojourn of the Sun	1943	
Epitaphios	1936	
My Sister's Song	1936–1937	
Spring Symphony	1937–1938	
The Ocean's March	1939–1940	
Notes on the Margins of Time	1938–1941	
An Old Mazurka to the Rhythm of the Rain	1942	
The Final Century Before Man	1942	
POEMS, VOLUME II		1961
Vigilance	1941–1953	
Shift of the Evening Star	1941–1942	
Silent Season	1941–1942	
Three Chorals	1944–1947	
Romiosini	1945–1947	
The Lady of the Vineyards	1945–1947	
Letter to Joliet Curie	1950	
We and the River	1951	
Skirmish	1952	
Good-Bye Vladimir Mayakovsky	1953	
Peace	1953	
Displacements	1942–1948	
The Graves of Orgaz	1942	
The Wavering Scales	1943	
My Son, My Moon	1948	
The Old Men and Tranquility	1948	
Parentheses I	1946–1947	
Smoked Earthen Pot	1949	
Unsubjugated City	1952–1953	
Morning Star	1955	

TITLE	DATE(S) OF COMPOSITION	DATE OF PUBLICATION
Pitcher	1957–1958	
Sob	1957	
All Souls' Day	1957	
Long Island	1957	
Year's Spirit	1957	
The Mountain with the Plan Trees	1957	
The Absent Form	1958	
THE DEAD HOUSE	1959	1962
UNDER THE MOUNTAIN'S SHADOW	1960	1962
THE PRISON TREE AND THE WOMEN	1962	1963
TESTIMONIES I	1957–1963	1963
ATTILA JOZSEF: POEMS [Translation]	n. d.	1963
TWELVE POEMS FOR CAVAFIS	1963	1963
GAMES OF SKY AND WATER	1960	1964
POEMS, VOLUME III		1964
Train Whistles	1939–1954	
Sketches	1954–1960	
Circular Glory	1954	
White and Black	1954	
Two Accounts	1958	
A Dog in the Night	1958	
Afternoon Landscape	1959	
Public Garden	1959	
The Last Confronter	1959	
Discourse of a Sick Man	1960	
Dead Summer	1960	
General Test	1956–1959	
The Man with the White Raincoat	1956–1957	
Holiday of Flowers	1957	

TITLE	DATE(S) OF COMPOSITION	DATE OF PUBLICATION
The Scene Before the Last	1957	
The Earth Below the Rain	1958	
Helen at the Cemetery	1958	
The Proxy	1958	
This Was the Song	1959	
The Tenant	1959	
Itinerant Musicians	1959	
Farewell	1957	
The Bridge	1959	
Supplement	1959–1960	
Spring	1959	
The Beds	1959	
Duration	1960	
Games of Sky and Water	1960	
Exercises	1950–1960	
The Last and First Man of Lidici	1960	
Testimonies I	1957–1963	
VLADIMIR MAYAKOVSKY: POEMS [Translation]	n. d.	1964
PHILOCTETES	1963–1965	1965
DORA GABE: I, MY MOTHER AND THE WORLD [Translation]	n. d.	1965
ROMIOSINI	1945–1947	1966
TESTIMONIES II	1964–1965	1966
ORESTES	1962–1966	1966
NAZIM HIKMET: POEMS [Translation]	n. d.	1966
ILYA ERENBURG: THE TREE [Translation]	n. d.	1966
NIKOLAS GUILLEN: THE BIG ZOO [Translation]	n. d.	1966

TITLE	DATE(S) OF COMPOSITION	DATE OF PUBLICATION
ANTHOLOGY OF CZECH AND SLOVAK POETS [Translation]	n. d.	1966
OSTRAVA	1962	1967
CHRYSOTHEMIS	1967–1970	1972
HELEN	1970	1972
ISMENE	1966–1971	1972
THE RETURN OF IPHIGENIA	1971–1972	1972
FOURTH DIMENSION		1972
When the Stranger Comes	1948	
Moonlight Sonata	1956	
Chronicle	1957	
Winter Clearness	1957	
The Window	1959	
The Dead House	1959	
Under the Mountain's Shadow	1960	
Philoctetes	1963–1965	
Orestes	1962–1966	
Ajax	1967–1969	
Persephone	1965–1970	
Agamemnon	1966–1970	
Chrysothemis	1967–1970	
Helen	1970	
Ismene	1966–1971	
The Return of Iphigenia	1971–1972	
STONES, REPETITIONS, BARRIERS		1972
Stones	1968	
Repetions	1968–1969	
Barriers	1968–1969	
GESTURES	1969–1970	1972
EIGHTEEN SHORT SONGS OF THE BITTER MOTHERLAND	1968	1973

475

TITLE	DATE(S) OF COMPOSITION	DATE OF PUBLICATION
FESTIVAL AND LAURELS		1973
"Festival and Laurels," from REPETITIONS	1968	
CORRIDOR AND STAIRS	1970	1973
NGRAGANTA	1972	1973
PETRIFIED TIME	1949	1974
SMOKED EARTHEN POT	1949	1974
STUDIES [Criticism]		1974
The Poetry of Erenburg	1961	
By Way of an Introduction to Testimonies	1962	
About Mayakovsky	1963	
Observations on the Work of Nazim Hikmet	1963	
Thoughts on the Poetry of Paul Eluard	n. d.	
The Wall in the Mirror and The Caretaker's Desk	n. d.	
THE ANNIHILATION OF MILOS	1969	1974
THE WALL IN THE MIRROR	1967–1971	1974
BELFRY	1972	1974
PAPER POEMS	1973–1974	1974
A HYMN AND LAMENTATION FOR CYPRUS	1974	1974
THE FINAL CENTURY BEFORE MAN	1942	1975
POSTSCRIPT TO PRAISE	1945	1975

TITLE	DATE(S) OF COMPOSITION	DATE OF PUBLICATION
EXILE'S JOURNALS		1973
Exile's Journals I	1948	
Exile's Journals II	1948–1949	
Exile's Journals III	1950	
NEWS BEARERS	1967–1969	1975
THE TIMELY		1975
Postscript to Praise	1945	
Petrified Time	1949	
Exile's Journals	1948–1950	
The World's Neighborhoods	1949–1951	
The Man with the Carnation	1952	
The Architecture of Trees	1958	
Men and Places	1958–1959	
The Black Saint	1961	
May Lament	1963	
News Bearers	1967–1969	
THE LADY OF THE VINEYARDS	1945–1947	1975
POEMS, VOLUME IV		1975
Verses from Torn Poems	1938–1952	
Elevator Operator	1958	
Light-Keeper	1958	
Summer Preparatory School	1953–1964	
Sponge Divers' Chorale	1960	
Delphi	1961–1962	
Small Dedication	1960–1965	
The Annihilation of Milos	1969	
Hints	1970–1971	
The Hour of the Shepherds	1962	
Tiresias	1964–1971	
Sectional Plan	1971	
THE CARETAKER'S DESK	1971	1976
LEO TOLSTOY: THE QUARRELSOME GOAT [Translation]	n. d.	1976

TITLE	DATE(S) OF COMPOSITION	DATE OF PUBLICATION
BECOMING		1977
The Net	1970	
Ngraganta	1972	
Belfry	1972	
Sounder	1973	
A Week's Diary	1973	
Doorway	1973–1974	
Traffic Cop	1974–1975	
Billposter	1974–1975	
Women of Monemvasia	1975	
Lamppost	1976	
Body and Blood	1976	
The Monstrous Masterpiece	1977	
THE DISTANT	1975	1977
SOUNDER	1973	1978
DOORWAY	1973–1974	1978
TRAFFIC COP	1974–1975	1978
BILLPOSTER	1974–1975	1978
WOMEN OF MONOMVASIA	1975	1978
BODY AND BLOOD	1976	1978
THE MONSTROUS MASTERPIECE	1977	1978
A FIREFLY LIGHTS THE NIGHT	1937	1978
PHAEDRA	1974–1975	1978
SO?	1976	1978
DOORBELL	1976	1978
SCRIPTURE OF THE BLIND	1972–1973	1979
MIDDAY SUMMER DREAM	1938	1980

TITLE	DATE(S) OF COMPOSITION	DATE OF PUBLICATION
SIDESTREET	1971–1972	1980
TRANSPARENCY	1977–1978	1980
MONOCHORDS	1979	1980
EROTICA		1981
A Small Suite in Red Major	1980	
Naked Body	1980	
Carnal World	1981	
COMMON SONGS	1931–1981	1981
SERGEY YESENIN: POEMS [Translation]	n.d.	1981
ARIOSTOS THE MINDFUL NARRATES MOMENTS OF HIS LIFE AND SLEEP [Fiction]	1942	1982
MUFFLED	1972	1982
MONOVASIA	1974–1976	1982
ITALIAN TRIPTYCH		1982
Decanting	1976	
The World Is One	1978–1980	
Statue in the Rain	1980	
SPONGE DIVERS' CHORALE	1960	1983
TIRESIAS	1964–1971	1983
WHAT STRANGE THINGS [Fiction]	1983	1983
TANAGRA FIGURINES	1967	1984

TITLE	DATE(S) OF COMPOSITION	DATE OF PUBLICATION
VICTORY SONGS		1984
Transparency	1977–1978	
Conflagration	1978–1979	
Parlour	1979–1981	
Eudiometer	1980–1981	
The Director and the Moon	1982	
Blessed	1983	
WITH A NUDGE OF THE ELBOW [Fiction]	1983	1984
PERHAPS IT'S ALSO THAT WAY [Fiction]	1984	1985
THE OLD MAN WITH THE KITES [Fiction]	1984	1985
NOT ONLY FOR YOU [Fiction]	1984	1985
SEALED WITH A SMILE [Fiction]	1984	1986
DIMINISHING QUESTIONS [Fiction]	1984	1986
ARIOSTOS REFUSES SAINTHOOD [Fiction]	1985	1986
3 × 111 TRISTYCHS	1982	1987
CORRESPONDENCES	1985	1987
PARENTHESES II	1950–1961	n. p.
TESTIMONIES III	1966–1967	n. p.
SLOWLY, VERY SLOWLY IN THE NIGHT	1988	n. p.

∾

ACKNOWLEDGMENTS

Yannis Ritsos

All translations in this volume, *Yannis Ritsos: Selected Poems 1938–1988*, are published with the permission of Yannis Ritsos and/or of Kedros Publishers (Athens, Greece), the publishers of the work of Yannis Ritsos in the original modern Greek.

Journals

Grateful acknowledgment is made to the editors of the following journals in which many of the translations in this book (or earlier versions of them) originally appeared: *The American Poetry Review, Antaeus, The Antioch Review, Arizona Quarterly, Baltic Avenue Poetry Journal, The Beloit Poetry Journal, Boundary 2, Chelsea, Chicago Review, College Literature, Denver Quarterly, Durak: An International Magazine of Poetry, Epoch, Exile: A Literary Quarterly, The Falcon, Field, Footprint Magazine, Grove: Contemporary Poetry in Translation, The Hudson Review, Journal of the Hellenic Diaspora, The Literary Review, Mundus Artium, The New Orleans Review, The Ohio Review, Ploughshares, Poet Lore, Poetry Now, Poetry Wales, Portland Review, Seneca Review, Shenandoah* and *Translation*.

The Translators

Athan Anagnostopoulos. From *Petrified Time*: "Recognition" and "The Roots of the World"; from *Train Whistles*: "Midnight" and "Postponed Decision"; from *Summer Preparatory School*: "Bodies," "Sunflowers," "Absence," "Probabilities," "Adolescent," and "Accented Colors"; and from *Small Dedication*: "Calm" and "Lyric Poem" copyright © 1989 by and reprinted with the permission of Athan Anagnostopoulos.

Peter Bien. *Philoctetes* copyright © 1989 by and reprinted with the permission of Peter Bien. An earlier version of this translation of *Philoctetes* originally appeared in *Shenandoah*.

Andonis Decavalles. From *The Wall in The Mirror*: "Exultation," "Mutual Concessions," "Unfamiliar Instrument," "Moderation," "Our Land," "Need to Express," "Wax Dummies," "Dangers," "The Yard," "Invention of the

From *Erotica*: "The Carnal Word" copyright © 1982 by Kimon Friar and reprinted from *Erotica: New Poems by Yannis Ritsos* with the permission of The Sachem Press.

"Peace" and *The Prison Tree and The Women* originally appeared in *The Falcon*. Portions of *Romiosini* and *Moonlight Sonata* were originally collected in *Modern Greek Poetry: From Cavafis to Elytis* (New York: Simon and Schuster, 1973), translated and edited by Kimon Friar. *Twelve Poems for Cavafis* originally appeared in *The American Poetry Review*.

N. C. Germanacos. From *Stones*: "Double Condemnation" and "Silence"; from *Repetitions*: "Alcmene," "Philomel," "Talos," "Achilles after Death," "Marpessa's Selection" and "Memorial Service at Poros"; from *Barriers*: "Tricks," "Roughly Square," "Last Will and Testament," and "One Word"; from *Gestures*: "Spinelessly," "Generalization of Distrust," "Departures I," "Departures II," "Departures III" and "The Fate of the Observer"; from *The Wall in the Mirror*: "Evening Procession," "Return" and "Presence"; from *Paper Poems I* "Put the flower pots . . .,' " "He whitewashed the house . . .," "White on white . . .," "You can't count. . . .," "Glory . . .," "Better this way . . .," and "Words have another shell . . ."; and from *Paper Poems II*: "The word had me . . ." copyright © 1989 by and reprinted with the permission of N. C. Germanacos.

From *Corridor and Stairs*: "Only," "The Unhidden," "What's the Use?," "Inevitably," "Compromises," "Why the Question?," "Charioteer 1970," "Indiscriminately," "The Same Meaning," "The Unacceptable," "The Biased Man," "The Fundamentals," "Perforation," "Memorial Services," "In the Old Garden," "Shelters," "Corridor," "Normal Occurence," "Provincial Spring," "Whitewash," "Experiences" and "The Stairs" copyright © 1976 by N. C. Germanacos and reprinted from *Corridor and Stairs* (Dublin: Goldsmith Press) with the permission of N. C. Germanacos.

George Giannaris. *The Bridge* copyright © 1989 by and reprinted with the permission of George Giannaris.

Karelisa Hartigan. From *Repetitions*: "The Graves of Our Ancestors," "After the Defeat," "After the Breakdown of the Treaty Between the Lacedaemonians and the Athenians," "The New Dance," "Niobe" and "The Golden Fleece" copyright © 1989 by and reprinted with the permission of Karelisa Hartigan and Kimon Friar.

Edmund Keeley. From *Parentheses I*: "Maybe, Someday" and "The Same Star"; from *Parentheses II*: "Hands," "Nocturnal," "Incense," "A Wreath" and "Message"; and from *The Distant*: "Striding Over," "The More Sufficient," "The Statues in the Cemeteries" and "The Distant" copyright © 1979 by Edmund Keeley and reprinted from *Ritsos in Parentheses* with the permission of Princeton University Press.

punched a hole. . .,' " "12. 'The oranges fell. . .,' " "17. 'The small moon. . .,' " "26. 'Long summer nights. . .,' " "37. 'Parades, heroes. . .,' " "64. 'A dark rainy night. . .,' " "80. 'Barefoot. . .,' " "04. 'From a beautiful mouth. . .' " and "92. 'Kisses and poetry. . .' "; From *Second Series*: "14. 'In the white egg. . .,' " "26. 'The new moon. . .,' " "52. 'Naked, astride an elephant. . .,' " "61. 'Gautemala, Nicaragua, Salvador. . .,' " "63. 'Where is time. . .,' " "80. 'Seek not, want not, be not. . .' " and "104. 'They tag you an illiterate. . .' "; From *Third Series*: "101. 'Corpses below wooden crosses. . .' "; from *Correspondences*: "Those Years," "Hearing", "It Exists", "An Acrobat", "They" and "Bitter Knowledge"; from *Slowly, Very Slowly in the Night*: "Inertia", "Same as Always", "Cardplayers", "Snowy Weather", " 'Perhaps' ", "The Nails", "Unjustly", "Distinct Motion", "The Black Boat" and "Alterations"; "The Long Poems of Yannis Ritsos" and "Yannis Ritsos: A Chronological Index of Published and Selected Unpublished Work" copyright © 1989 by Kostas Myrsiades.

Philip Pastras and George Pilitsis. *Orestes* and *Agamemnon* copyright © 1989 by and reprinted with the permission of Philip Pastras and George Pilitsis. Earlier versions of *Orestes* and *Agamemnon* originally appeared in the *Journal of the Hellenic Diaspora*.

Minas Savvas. From *Exile's Journals I*: "6 November 1948: 'Night. The little bell. . .,' " "12 November 1948: 'In the afternoon. . .,' " "17 November 1948: 'We lit a fire. . .' " and "21 November 1948: 'Sunday is a large closet. . .' "; from *Exile's Journals III*: "1 May 1950: 'The soldier stepped on his cigarette. . .,' " "6 May 1950: 'One vessel leaves, another comes. . .,' " "7 May 1950: 'Black, black island. . .,' " "19 May 1950: 'The insane and the invalids increase. . .,' " "24 May 1950: 'We've written our wills so beautifully. . .' " and "30 May 1950: 'The soldiers, unshaven. . .' "; copyright © 1977 by Minas Savvas and reprinted from *Chronicles of Exile* (Los Angeles: The Wire Press) with the permission of Minas Savvas.

From *Exercises*: "The Statues," "Deadly Victory," "After the Fire," "The Unjust," "A Proletarian Speaker," "Episode," "To an Unknown Direction," "Always So," "Noon," "Wonder" and "Question" copyright © 1989 by and reprinted with the permission of Minas Savvas.

From *Exercises*: "Beauty" and "Harvest of the Void," translated by Minas Savvas, copyright © 1980 by and reprinted from *Subterranean Horses* with the permission of Carnegie Library of Pittsburgh-International Poetry Forum.

From *Gestures*: "New Pretexts" and "Slight Ailment"; from *Corridor and Stair*: "Calculated Behavior" copyright © 1989 by and reprinted with the permission of Minas Savvas.

John Stathatos. From *Exercises*: "A Life," "Return of a Deserter," "Hunters," and "Coincidentally" copyright © 1975 by John Stathatos and reprinted

﮾

BOA EDITIONS, LTD.

NEW AMERICAN TRANSLATIONS SERIES

∾